ESSAYS ON PEACE THEOLOGY AND WITNESS

Willard M. Swartley, Editor

Occasional Papers No. 12

Institute of Mennonite Studies
3003 Benham Avenue
Elkhart, Indiana 46517

1988

POLICY STATEMENT FOR THE *OCCASIONAL PAPERS*

Occasional Papers is a publication of the Institute of Mennonite Studies and authorized by the Council of Mennonite Seminaries. The four sponsoring seminaries are Eastern Mennonite Seminary (Harrisonburg, VA), Goshen Biblical Seminary and Mennonite Biblical Seminary (Elkhart, IN), and the Mennonite Brethren Biblical Seminary (Fresno, CA). The Institute of Mennonite Studies is the research agency of the Associated Mennonite Biblical Seminaries.

Occasional Papers is released several times yearly without any pre-scribed calendar schedule. The purpose of the *Papers* is to make various types of essays available to foster dialogue in biblical, theological and practical ministry areas and to invite critical counsel from within the Mennonite theological community. While most essays will be in finished form, some may also be in a more germinal stage-- released especially for purposes of testing and receiving critical feedback. In accepting papers for publication, priority will be given to authors from the CMS institutions, the College Bible faculties in the Council of Mennonite Colleges, the Associate membership of the Institute of Mennonite Studies, and students and degree alumni of the four seminaries.

Because of the limited circulation of the *Occasional Papers*, authors are free to use their material in other scholarly settings, either for oral presentation at scholarly meetings or for publication in journals with broader circulation and more official publication policies.

Orders for *Occasional Papers* should be sent to the Institute of Mennonite Studies, 3003 Benham Avenue, Elkhart, IN 46517.

Editor: Willard M. Swartley, Director
          Institute of Mennonite Studies
Associate Editor:
          Elizabeth G. Yoder, Assistant Director
          Institute of Mennonite Studies

CONTENTS

Jratis

120419

PREFACE

John K. Stoner

The essays in this volume of *Occasional Papers* were originally presented at Peace Theology Colloquium IV, June 20-23, 1985, an event which had a ten-year history. The Colloquium was held on the campus of the Associated Mennonite Biblical Seminaries and was co-sponsored by the Institute of Mennonite Studies. The reader will find it helpful to know something of the purpose and history of the Mennonite Peace Theology Colloquia in order to place these papers in context. The objectives of the Peace Theology Colloquia were stated as follows in 1975:

a. To provide a forum where issues in peace theology can be seriously discussed, a forum where views can be clarified and more effective ways of communicating concerns can be developed in order to strengthen peace concerns within the Mennonite constituency and to more effectively witness to peace as a part of the Christian gospel to other Christian groups.

b. To facilitate the development of stronger peace studies programs at Mennonite schools by providing opportunities for sharing information and perspectives from different peace studies programs.

These objectives were approved by the Peace Section of the Mennonite Central Committee, which in 1975 initiated the first peace theology colloquium in response to expressions of interest from Mennonite teachers and MCC administrators.

A May 1976 letter written by Ted Koontz, then Executive Secretary of Peace Section (U.S.) said of the first colloquium, then inn planning: "It is our strong desire to create an ongoing forum, modeled somewhat after the Mennonite Mission Study Fellowship, to which a core of scholars and others will commit themselves over a period of years."

The objectives of the colloquium movement were further defined in a 1978 memo written by Marlin E. Miller to Urbane Peachey, in planning for Peace Theology Colloquium II:

1. To provide a platform for interdisciplinary conversation and debate between Mennonites teaching in college and seminary peace studies programs;

2. To provide a forum for theological and ethical discernment on peace and peace-related issues and directions, bringing together Mennonites from church agencies and academia;

5

3. To facilitate personal acquaintance, fellowship, and continuing dialogue between peace educators, ministers, and activists from the various Mennonite groups.

Conversation, debate, discernment and fellowship emerge as ongoing purposes of the Colloquia. Individuals who are not Mennonites may be struck by the strong internal Mennonite focus of the stated objectives. They might hope to see more accent on ecumenical dialogue, and that is an understandable interest. But the fact is that Mennonite scholars and church agency people have fewer opportunities to meet for serious peace theology dialogue than might be supposed, and so they (we) are poignantly aware of the need for this primarily internal forum. So much by way of explaining why the colloquium tradition is not more interchurch in character. That too needs to be done, but as someone has said, "You do what you can."

The history of the four Colloquia held to date is this:

I. An Examination of John H. Yoder's *The Politics of Jesus*. October, 1976, St. Paul's School of Theology, Kansas City, Missouri.

II. A Theology of Justice. November, 1978, Bethel College Mennonite Church, North Newton, Kansas

III. Toward a Theology of Justice and Human Rights. October, 1981, Bluffton College, Bluffton, Ohio.

IV. Four topics: How Do We Do Peace Theology? Power and Justice in Peace Theology. Rethinking Christian Witness to Society and State. Biblical Concepts of God. June, 1985, Associated Mennonite Biblical Seminaries, Elkhart, Indiana.

The fifth colloquium is scheduled as follows:

V. Anabaptist Dialogue with Liberation Theology. June 10-12, 1988, Canadian Mennonite Bible College, Winnipeg, Manitoba.

The topics for colloquia are selected by a process including input from the previous colloquium body, suggestions from individuals and final decision by a colloquium planning committee. The planning committee is made up of five or six individuals representing Mennonite colleges and seminaries in the U.S. and Canada, an activist/practitioner and a staff person in the MCC U.S. Peace Section (Akron, PA) or in the MCC Canada Peace and Social Concerns Committee (Winnipeg, Manitoba).

John K. Stoner, Executive Secretary
MCC U.S. Peace Section, Akron, PA.

PREFACE SUPPLEMENT

The objectives for the Consultation from the Institute's side arose from the Institute's present goals of encouraging discussion, research and writing on both our peace understandings of the biblical text and on our understanding of the biblical view of peace, both in the Old Testament (*shalom*) and in the New Testament (*eirene*). The papers prepared under topic 4 of the consultation are related specifically to this agenda.

These two essays by Ben Ollenburger and Gayle Gerber Koontz, as well as the shorter essay by Ted Grimsrud, are directed to specific biblical topics that are frequently construed as putting the biblical testimony in tension with, or even in opposition to, the peace theology and witness of the Mennonite church. These three essays contribute perspectives that help us better understand the relationship between ourselves and the Bible on these "problematic" topics: God as Warrior, God and patriarchy, and God as Avenger in the cause of justice.

The format of this consultation was highly participatory. Each participant contributed a short written statement directed to one of the major papers or submitted a contribution on one of the general themes of the conference. Grimsrud's paper falls into the latter category. In addition to these published papers, the Institute has in its file several dozen one to four page responses in the form of questions, affirmations and critique of these papers. At first it was our intention to publish the responses also, but further reflection and the length of the volume led us to decide against this. For readers of this volume who would like a copy of the shorter statements, the Institute will provide such for $1 upon request.

The papers in this collection raise many issues, and at times chart new directions. The introductory essay by Edgar Metzler puts some of the basic issues in stark form, calling us to both rigorous thought and new levels of commitment in our Christian discipleship. Stanley Hauerwas's response to Harry Huebner's paper was written upon request to be printed in this collection. It too focuses well some ongoing crucial issues for discernment and discussion. In making these papers available in this form, the intention of the co-sponsoring agencies of the consultation hope that these papers will contribute to and invigorate the ongoing dialogue on peace theology and witness, for all those who want to join the conversation and walk on this way.

Willard M. Swartley, Director
Institute of Mennonite Studies
and Editor, *Occasional Papers*

INTRODUCTION

RESPONSE TO THE IDEA OF A
"PEACE THEOLOGY COLLOQUIUM"
or
An urgent plea to Mennonite theologians to provide
undergirding and critique for our growing activism

Edgar Metzler

Have we ever had a peace theology? We've had a theology of:

1. Nonresistance, which helped us stand up to the state's demand to kill.

2. Nonconformity, which reinforced our conviction to withdraw from worldly activities such as fighting.

3. Discipleship, whereby it was impossible to imagine following our leader, Jesus, into war.

4. Service, more recently developed, which motivated us to constructive amelioration of the disastrous consequences of developments we had not tried to prevent or modify as they were from realms, such as politics, in which we did not participate.

5. Servanthood, a potentially powerful image, but thus far mainly a way for white male leadership to talk piously about our roles while retaining all the positions of power.

6. Two kingdoms, used more to define limitations than suggest creative possibilities.

Have we had a theology of peace? Not really. Do we need one? Definitely.

Mennonite critics, such as those who write in *Guidelines* and *Sword and Trumpet* are right. We are moving beyond non-resistance. (But not "forsaking" it as some charge. I am willing to bet my extra copy of *The Politics of Jesus* that the highest percentage of conscientious objectors--the traditional test of nonresistance--in any future military conscription will be among those activists now charged by the critics as no longer nonresistant.)

The language of nonresistance seems too narrow a biblical base to ground the involvement of a growing number of Mennonites in public witness and action for peace. Their involvement is for reasons we should applaud. It is not ideological or shaped by some revised theoretical abstractions about church and state.

9

It is the same motivation that caused Dirk Willems to
rescue from an icy grave his would-be captor, that moved
hundreds of Mennonites to help Europe rebuild after World
War II and that today motivates their latter-day colleagues
in trouble spots around the world. That motivation is the
love of God which always moves us to share and serve.

If we care about our neighbors, we will be moved by the
Holy Spirit to care about what happens to them if there is
nuclear war, if the United States invades Nicaragua or the
Soviet Union continues to overrun Afghanistan, or if ter-
rorism continues in the Middle East because justice is denied
and postponed.

The sense of justice which moves persons to act on these
concerns is more the visceral compassion of biblical, Holy
Spirit-filled persons than the application of philosophical
concepts of what is just. But precisely because this new
surge of peace witness arises out of such good motives, it
needs the service of theology to maintain its integrity.

Twelve years ago, Kosuke Koyama, from an Asian perspective asked a question similar to those being raised on the
other side of the world by the emerging theology of liberation, "Is not involvement the only soil from which theology
germinates?" A necessary question, but it is the other side
of the equation--reflection--which we are tempted to slight.

If the new activists are too busy lobbying and protesting
to reflect theologically, they are acting in a traditional
Mennonite way. Harold Bender's article on theology in the
Mennonite Encyclopedia begins, "An old and almost universal
tradition among Mennonites views theology with much dis-
trust." Robert Friedmann once asked whether "one can
properly speak of an Anabaptist theology."

I believe many of the emerging activists would welcome
help in reflecting upon their witness. Fortunately, some of
the activists are also theologians!

Motivations are always mixed. In the heat of the struggle, preoccupation with either goals or means can lead to
unintended consequences. Activism needs theology to provide:

-Perspective on the rich diversity of biblical faith and
the diabolic ambiguity of power

-Balance in terms of the church's multifaceted callings
to worship, nuture, heal, evangelize, serve, etc.

-Communication of gospel categories to secular concerns

-Vision that is larger and longer term than public policy
debates.

In recent years Mennonite scholars have begun to think
and write about peace in a more biblically comprehensive and
holistic manner. The IMS Shalom project promises more in

that direction. Some needs especially for the constructive critique and more solid grounding of our peace witness in the world include:

1. The meaning of salvation, including what it is we are saved "for" and how the "world" is being saved and the relation of salvation to our "enemies"

2. Recognition and celebration of God's creative activity before the Fall and the meaning of the emerging "new creation"

3. Expanding the recently discovered biblical emphasis on justice

4. The two kingdom doctrine(s) and our view of history

5. The recovery of grace and pleasure for ethics

6. The concept of sin in transpersonal dimensions

7. Kingdom realities beyond the church

8. The significance of neglected biblical images, such as salt, light, leaven

9. Church and state in a pluralistic, liberal, democratic society.

Glen Stassen has suggested that much of the writing about peace assumes the calling of the Christian is to be a judge. Whether from a pacifist or just war perspective, the Christian is asked to make a judgment after the fact. Action for war has already been taken by others. Do we participate at all or in what degree?

More Mennonites are asking a further question: How can I be a peace*maker*, that activity which Jesus blesses?

Can we change the name of what we are about to do to *Peacemaking Theology Colloquium?*

HOW DO WE DO PEACE THEOLOGY?

J. Lawrence Burkholder

If the term "peace theology" were used deliberately in preference to "theology of peace" it could be said to be a propitious choice. Doing peace theology is not participating in an idiosyncratic exercise in which a mere facet of theology is addressed or where systematic theology, independently conceived, is simply balanced or completed. Furthermore, peace theology is not simply a response to a particular historical situation--even to the threat of an atomic holocaust. Peace is not a neglected doctrine whose time has come, and certainly not an appendix to orthodoxy.

Peace theology is church theology concerned with all traditional doctrines within which peace is a controlling and pervasive idea. Peace is of the essence of theology. Peace is what theology is about because the Gospel is about peace. As a central idea, peace shapes all doctrines. It is not limited to ethics. Peace theology impacts such traditional doctrines as God, creation, sin, Christ, redemption, Holy Spirit, church, ethics and eschatology--whatever the order and however they may be framed. Peace theology is orthodox theology with peace at the center.

The ideal way to do peace theology is to do a systematic theology from a peace point of view. To my knowledge this is seldom done. Possibly *Systematic Theology* by Gordon Kaufman is an exception. In *Systematic Theology* Kaufman speaks about the "nonresistance of God." Most so-called peace theologies are really theologies of peace in monograph or tractarian forms. These may have the advantages of accessibility and contemporaneity. But they fail to come to terms with reality as a whole. They may focus on the person and teachings of Jesus and the kingdom of God but fail to relate these doctrines to the structure of reality as represented by creation, the complexities of universal history and of culture. In a systematic theology, one is forced to come to terms with the total range of doctrines and their relation to one another as they reflect a comprehensive view of the world. It may be pointed out parenthetically that Mennonites have made few attempts at systematic theology *per se*. Hence some of the broader implications of peace have yet to be explored in depth.[1]

I would propose that a peace theology would follow the traditional order of classical orthodoxy.[2] Orthodox solutions may not come off entirely successfully in the modern world since they may reflect philosophical presuppositions

and cultural attitudes that are neither understood nor
appreciated by modernity. However orthodoxy may be defended
in so far as it represents issues that one may avoid at the
peril of reductionism and superficiality. Orthodoxy seeks to
answer perennial issues grounded in human experience and
tested by time. Essentialist views of Christ and the Trinity,
ontological views of the fall and creation, and idealistic
views of the human spirit may seem ridiculous to empirically
oriented people of our time, but the questions that they seek
to answer cannot be avoided.

Certainly a peace theology modeled along traditional
orthodox lines would be ambitious--some would say
impossible. In addition to the fact that systematic
theologies are seldom written these days and that each
orthodox doctrine harbors at its center a logical contradiction, a peace theology would be burdened by the need to
acknowledge, if not reconcile, doctrines which are generally
correlated dialectically.

A peace theology would be worked out within the broad
parameters of biblical faith. After all, violence in its many
forms cannot be isolated from fallenness of humankind, the
corruption of the earth, the cruelty of nature and the
tragedies of history. Likewise, peace cannot be isolated
from the redemption of the world including the transformation
of nature and the renewal of the cosmos. Placed within such
universal parameters we are speaking about paradise lost and
paradise regained. The fall and restoration of humankind is
the context of a peace theology.

It is obvious that this occasion does not even allow one
to outline a systematic theology with peace as its organizing
center. All that can be done is to indicate some basic considerations and some critical decisions that would have to be
made. I cannot claim to have solved in my own mind all of
the issues that are bound to arise. Certainly I cannot suggest solutions that would result in reducing the inherent
mystery of theology by demonstrating an extraordinary degree
of coherence. Christian theology, reflecting faith, is
coherent yet incoherent. But at least I will suggest some
cases in which propositions of a paradox or horns of a
dilemma may be preferable in the face of the practical necessity for decision. The body of this paper will consist of
suggestions for the construction of a hypothetical peace
theology.

I. A Profound View of the Fall
of Human Beings and Creation

The doctrine of original sin was once declared by the
London Times as the "only empirically verifiable doctrine of
the Christian faith." Its verifiability should not, however,
lead us to assume that sin is easily understood. If sin were
simple willfulness, then it would not only be known but
spared the mystery and fascination with which it is associated. But sin is complex and brings with its consideration
a host of ideas of the most inexplicable kind. I refer to
ideas such as innocence, depravity, the cosmic fall, natural
evil, temptation, suffering, futility and death. In the Old
Testament these ideas are set forth most poignantly through
myth. They are related to sin even though the relationships
cannot be understood as casual connections. What is the connection between sin and natural evil? What has sin to do
with death? How is the earth corrupted and animals made
carnivorous through acts of human will? What is the relationship of sin to a cosmic fall? We simply do not know.
However, in the depths of human experience, guilt and
finitude, egoism and creativity, sin and suffering, guilt and
moral awareness are inseparable even though distinguishable.

At any rate, peace theology would do well not to play
down the implications of sin, its universality, its ontological reality, its consequences for nature and its cultural
embodiment. For in order to know what redemption of the
world is, one must know what is being redeemed. Furthermore,
as a matter of practical decision making, it is essential to
recognize the cultural entanglements of sin. It is incumbent
to recognize that evil is seldom found in pure form. Rather
it is entwined, seemingly inseparably, with such realities as
family, community, nation and religious faith. Faith in "holy
war" for which men and women, young and old give their lives
in suicidal raids suggests that sin is not understood, let
alone overcome, by simple moral analysis.

Since sin is original it follows that redemption would be
possible only if human nature were radically changed and the
world were restored to its original goodness. A theology of
peace therefore would contend that peace is contingent upon
transformation of reality as it is represented by a "new
creation"--a "new heaven and a new earth" and cosmic
restoration when the "lamb will lie down with the lion." In
other words, sin is so pernicious and so entangled with culture and with natural evil that redemption can be
accomplished only by total transformation.

Anything less than a profound view of sin would result in what has been a general characteristic of "liberal" pacifism, namely an excessively optimistic view of humanity and of human possibilities. Classical doctrines of sin which recognize connections with creatureliness, structural and cultural disorders would at least prevent easy solutions to the problem of human conflict. The tendency of pacifists to expect permanent results from partial solutions needs to be tempered by sober views of reality. To suggest that "if only" this or that were done peace would come, all too frequently signals oversimplified estimates of the human situation. Traditional orthodox views of sin and depravity should be seen as a corrective to rational optimism of the Enlightenment, utopian views of Marxism, naturalistic views of behaviorism, optimistic views of liberalism and simple volitional views of sectarianism. At the same time, it must be acknowledged that classical conceptions of depravity have been used historically as an excuse to justify conservative social structures, not to speak of entrenched power and war.

II. Messianic Hope for Restoration

After setting forth a realistic view of the fall through an interpretation of Genesis 1-11 in which the moral and metaphysical consequences of sin were taken very seriously, attention would be placed upon the hope for restoration as it developed within the history of Israel. It is common knowledge that Israel represents a vision of peace, justice and tranquillity which accompanied its national experience. The hope for restoration took many contrasting forms including return to the simplicities of the wilderness, national triumph, ethical reform, and transformation. These views coincided with the fortunes and misfortunes of Israel. Election and suffering in the life of God's own people presented an acute problem which remained with Israel and finally led some to conclude that Israel was called to suffer rather than triumph. Hence the idea of the suffering servant.

Messianism was of course not limited to Israel. Even the symbol of a "shepherd king" was found in Egypt. What is unique in Hebrew messianism is its tendency to move from national to universal images and from egoistic to ethical solutions.

Messianism provided a vision of the ultimate goal of history--a king who would combine *goodness* and *power.* Israel's kings were sometimes powerful, but few of them were righteous. Images were predominantly royal. However some

prophets despaired of the historical possibility of a con-
junction of power and goodness in a human monarch.   The
frustrations of Israel lead therefore to images of divine
intervention through a *heavenly* being (Son of Man) who would
do what only God is presumed to do--to combine sovereignty
and holiness. Messianism represents the ultimate issue of
ethics--namely, the relation of power and goodness. Power is
essential for order, but power has always either corrupted
the mighty or placed them within situations in which they
could not do right even when they wanted to.   Apocalypticism
is the product of desperation in the face of the ultimate
ethical problems of historical existence.

It is quite impossible to set forth here the Hebrew ideas
of justice, love and peace as one would in a theology of
peace.   Biblical literature is full of studies of these terms
as they developed in Israel.   Let us say that for the most
part they are imprecise and are not easily turned into Greek
or Western equivalents.   The interchangeability of concepts
such as justice, righteousness, mercy, love and kindness
leads to the general observation that such language is
redemptive rather than technical.   They are of the language
of hope for a new order within which all that is wrong will
be made right.

Central to the vision of the rule of God is the concept
of peace.   *Shalom* is a term with many applications.   It is
used to describe not only a process of conflict resolution in
all areas of life, but an ultimate state of harmony and well-
being within which the Spirit of God is in effective control
of human relations.

It is impossible to describe what *shalom* represents concretely since its final and complete expression lies beyond
human experience.   It represents paradise, a perfect world in
which God's intention for creation is restored.   To
understand what *shalom* may mean we must speak in negative
terms.   It is a world within which sin and its "consequences"
are removed. In the new world of perfect community, strife,
hatred, jealousy, injustice, abuse of power, inordinate ambition, sexism, international wars, sickness, privation, depression, generational conflict, poverty, slavery, oppression and
death--indeed, all the ills of human existence will be
removed.   Obviously we are dealing here with a utopian
vision which serves on the one hand to judge all that is
wrong with the world as we know it, and on the other hand to
inspire faith in God through whose intervening grace and
power the goal of history will be realized.

The utopian hope of *shalom* has many features in common with utopianism outside Israel. A distinctive feature of Hebrew utopian thought, however, is the degree to which it rests upon the sovereign grace of God. The prophetic call was primarily to remove the roadblocks, so to speak, rather than to bring the Kingdom by human instrumentality. How to "prepare" for the coming of the Lord was a matter of frequent discussion and differences of opinion. This was the major concern of the Jews during the time of Jesus. It was, indeed, an issue upon which Jesus appeared to take a deliberate stand.

III. Jesus Christ Prophet and "King"

A peace theology would find much common ground with most orthodox theologies when it comes to Old Testament interpretations. Albeit, it could be said that peace issues are more likely to appear in connection with the interpretations of Jesus and the New Testament in general than with Old Testament backgrounds. A peace theology would be strongly *christological.* After all, Christianity is a religion about what God has done and will do through Jesus Christ. It would be christological in the sense that Jesus' person, life and teachings would be accepted as authoritative for his followers and indicative of his position among the powers of the world and in the cosmos. It if were impossible today to ground Jesus' authority in "essentialist" terms (Nicea), his authority could be grounded in the resurrection as a sign of God's unique approval of Jesus.

Furthermore, a peace theology would undertake an interpretation of Jesus' life and ministry in the Jewish context. Here Jesus could be portrayed as essentially a prophet who spoke to issues concerning the coming of the kingdom of God in relation to contemporary Jewish problems. Attendant to his preaching, were miracles, healings and mighty works. Furthermore, to be in the presence of the historical Jesus was for many of his followers to be in the presence of God-- that Jesus spoke with the authority of God was one of the problems which he posed for the leaders of the Jewish theocracy.

As a prophet, Jesus spoke out against oppression of the poor and in general sympathized with the underprivileged. He announced the coming of the kingdom of God and promised *shalom.* He called some to follow him in his ministry and learn from him. He was considered by them and others to be a rabbi.

For our purposes, one need not elaborate on his earthly life except to say that the *form* of his life was deliberate. Most significantly, he chose not to identify with zealotry in the use of violence. Rather, he chose to bring about social and political change through preaching and demonstration of the power of God by miraculous works. His works should be interpreted as signs of the coming of the Kingdom. Indeed, the extent to which his miracles of healing and his works of love become a reality is the extent to which the restoration of the world is becoming a reality. Also, his sayings, as collected in the Sermon on the Mount and elsewhere indicate how his followers should live in anticipation of the coming of the kingdom. They should love their enemies, live without anxiety, forgive without limits, give with abandon, share indiscriminately, lend without insisting upon return. Their lives should be based upon absolute trust in God. They should not murder; indeed, they shall not hate. They should be absolutely honest and as a matter of rule, they should live on a higher level than do the Pharisees and the Scribes—the most scrupulous keepers of the law in Israel. Whether the command to be "perfect" refers to "moral" perfection or "wholeness" may be of interest to those who would consider whether Jesus' ethic is to be measured by a philosophical moral calculus or with Hebrew ideas of redemption. At any rate, the ethic is so radical and uncompromising that it cannot have been based upon an estimate of human possibilities and institutional necessities. No concessions are given to "natural self-regarding impulses," as Reinhold Niebuhr used to say, and no concessions are made to existing social structures. His ethic is a kingdom ethic for those to whom the kingdom is already becoming a reality.

The key concept of Jesus' ethic is love. *Agape* love is noncalculating and indiscriminate. It extends even to the enemy. Love of friends is normal—even sinners love one another. The command to love enemies stood in opposition to dominant national strategies for the coming of the kingdom of God of Jesus' day. Although Jesus did not offer policies of national restoration based upon meticulous political calculations, his teachings and his own vocational styles lead to the conclusion that he taught *shalom* as a national goal and nonviolence as a means for his disciples.

To characterize Jesus as a "prophet, priest, and king" belongs to the traditional theological stereotype. That he was, in fact, a prophet is uncontested. Likewise, in a sense, he was a priest, though it is hard to place him in that role as the office was defined during his time. Critical to our

discussion is whether Jesus really presented himself as the
legitimate heir to the throne of Israel. Did Jesus consider
himself called to become the ruler of Israel around 30 A.D.
or was the Triumphal Entry only a demonstration? Was Jesus
simply acting out as he rode the colt into Jerusalem, or was
he seriously offering himself as the legitimate ruler of
Israel? When Jesus entered Jerusalem, was he engaging in
politics in the sense of seeking power to rule, or was he
preaching a religious and political sermon? Did Jesus plan
to become an earthly king and do what political leaders do,
such as devise and implement policies, tax its citizens,
administer justice, judge and defend using power as needed?
Did the "politics of Jesus" include the will to exercise real
political power? If so, how would he have carried out his
program?

Such questions may seem idle to those who feel that the
outcome of the conflict is all that should concern those who
name the name of Jesus. To be sure, the Triumphal Entry was
a crisis, a turning point, leading to the cross and there fol-
lowed theologies of the cross that dominated New Testament
interpretations of his life and ministry. But a theology of
peace cannot avoid the questions of political responsibility
if, indeed, Jesus was a real political contender. To put it
bluntly, if Jesus sought political power, what is to prevent
his followers from doing the same?

Furthermore, if Jesus did seek political power, how would
he have exercised power were he to have been accepted by the
nation? Would he have administered power in the spirit of
the Sermon on the Mount? Would he have ruled without
resisting evil? Would he have ruled without an army and
police force? Would the principle of his judgment have been
agape love or would his judgment include elements of punitive justice as well? Would he simply have forgiven the
enemies of the nation seventy times seven? What would he
have done with those who oppressed the poor (or would there
have been no poor?)

That Jesus was concerned about politics can no longer be
doubted. Certainly, he was involved as a provocative critic
and agitator. Clearly, he was considered a threat to the
existing order. But since he was rejected, humiliated and
crucified, we simply cannot know on the basis of Jesus'
example how love and power could be combined unambiguously
in the political realm, if, indeed, they can be.

This, however, is clear. When Jesus was confronted by
hostile authorities, his response was nonviolent. Were his
crucifixion seen in isolation from his life and ministry, one

would be inclined to attribute his nonviolent responses to
the hapless weakness of an individual in trouble with an
autocratic power. But his response was interpreted by his
disciples and, most certainly by the first century church, as
a logical extension of his teachings. Hence, the cross
should be seen not simply as an accident but as an expression of love for the enemy.

Throughout history the central image of Christianity has
been the cross. No event has caught the imagination of the
West with greater poignancy than the crucifixion. It has
been termed the event that beyond all others expresses the
character and the purposes of God for history. Through the
cross universal salvation is made possible, reversing the
Fall (Rom 5:18). From the crucifixion, soteriology becomes a
dominant theme in Christianity, expressing itself in a thousand ways from the cathedral mass to the sawdust trail. What
to make of the cross has been the predominant concern of
theologians and the inspiration of crusaders.

The meaning of the cross has been more ambiguous for
ethics than for soteriology. There is virtually unanimous
agreement that the cross is the perfect expression of love.
All that Jesus said and did was gathered together in Christ
at the crucifixion. Following the resurrection it was deemed
by the Apostles to be an expression not only of the love of
God but also of the power of God through which the world
will be restored to its original goodness. The cross, which
literally meant absolute weakness and death, was ironically
set in contrast to the ways of conquering kings and mighty
emperors. The cross was regarded not only as a concrete
event but also as a spirit of sacrifice and submission that
would characterize the attitudes of Christ's followers.

A theology of peace would elaborate and attempt to
relate to each other a vast spectrum of ideas emanating from
Christ and his teachings. It would involve an interpretation
of the Sermon on the Mount (no small task!); it would attempt
to set forth the meaning of the kingdom of God; it would
elaborate a christology in which Jesus Christ would be
attributed unrivaled authority. Associated with christology
would be the concept of discipleship. What does it mean concretely to be a follower of Jesus Christ?

IV. The Church as a Community of Peace

A peace theology would move immediately and virtually
without disjunction from christology to ecclesiology. The
church is "organically" related to the living Christ as his

"body." The church would be defined as a community which
incorporates the spirit of Christ in its own life and seeks
to make Jesus' spirit universal. The community would be
bound together by the love of Christ. The church would not
only attempt to live in the spirit of Christ but also would
attempt to express the love of Christ structurally. A community of love would seek to embody principles of organization that would stand in clear contrast to the principles
which inform the organizations of worldly powers such as
government and economic orders.

The church is a community through which the process of
redemption continues in history. For reasons unknown and
not given to God's children the coming of the Kingdom was
delayed (Acts 1:7). It did not come in its fullness with the
historical Jesus. Hence the church becomes a community of
hope taking up the promises of redemption. The church means
that the kingdom has not come. But God will eventually rule
on earth as it is in heaven. In the meantime, the church
attempts to facilitate the life of the spirit as individuals,
communities and social structures are redeemed, however partial and piecemeal. The spirit of God, which is the spirit of
shalom, seeks to unite all that has been separated, beginning
with its own community in which such historic conflicts as
those between Jew and Gentile, master and servant, rich and
poor, men and women are resolved in Christ. The church
becomes a model for reconciliation of all that is at enmity
with God and fellow human beings and organizations (Eph 2).
The church is being redeemed and becomes the agent of
redemption. It seeks to restore all that is broken by the
Fall beginning in Jerusalem, Judea, Samaria and to all parts
of the world. Its mission is represented by words that are
used interchangeably--*shalom*, redemption, restoration, salvation and unity. Later epistles such as Ephesians and Colossians include visions of cosmic unity within which "all
things" are united in Christ. The church is made the agent
of reconciliation--thus "making peace" on a universal scale.

A peace theology would elaborate the essential lines of
the New Testament worldview. It would of course seek to
make sense of the New Testament cosmology by abstracting it
from its mythical framework. Without necessarily accepting
at face value such images as angels, principalities and
powers, heavens and clouds, and other features of the ancient
cosmology, philosophical and primitive, it would, however,
uphold "Jesus as Lord"--an implication of the ascension. It
would seek to acknowledge Jesus as the authority "before
which every knee shall bow" including such reals as

governments, social and economic disorders.

Despite numerous references in Scripture to the sovereignty of God's grace and power in bringing redemption to completion, the church is beset by problems which are typical of humanity. It must make decisions of a theological and practical nature for which its own unaided wisdom is inadequate. Hence an important aspect of its coming to terms with the contingencies of history is to "discern the spirit" of Christ. Even if the church were committed to an uncompromising, if not legal, application of the teachings of Christ, questions would remain as to what the teachings mean concretely in ever-changing historical situations and what to do when none of Jesus' teachings apply. In such a situation the church seeks to "discern" the will of God by a combination of prayer, study of Scripture, discussion and reason. Discernment is not simply and *ad hoc* experience of the Christian community but a structural element in the life of the church.

Discernment applies not only to the internal life of the community but to the world as well. Since the world operates upon numerous assumptions, values and myths, many of which are less than obvious, it is essential for the church to look below the surface of the world events. Analyses of world structures as well as of discrete events are partly technical. There is no substitute for facts and experience. But as students of history know, it is amazing how the "wise men" of the world are blinded to the meaning of historical events—events which are obviously prime exhibits of "folly" when seen in historical review. A phenomenon noticeable throughout history, regardless of place or period, is, as Barbara Tuchman says, the pursuit by government of policies contrary to their own interests. She asks, "Why do holders of high office so often act contrary to the way reason points and enlightened self-interest suggests?" The church, as a peace community, would not claim to possess superior knowledge about worldly affairs, but it would have internalized perceptions, dispositions, sensitivities and values which would allow the community to discern the "spirit of the age."

V. Theology of Intentionality

The doctrine of God is obviously the central doctrine of the Christian faith. Under this doctrine traditional issues are considered such as the reality of God, transcendence, eternity, attributes and relations to nature and history. Today the very idea of "God" is being considered critically under the influences of empiricism and language analysis. Does "God talk" make sense?

A theology of peace would be obliged to take into consideration problems typical of those that belong to the history of Christian thought. However, since every theology reflects particular concerns, a theology of peace would emphasize issues relevant to its purpose. Specifically, a peace theology would concentrate more upon the intentionality of God than on the being of God. A theology of peace would seek to explore what God is doing and what God wants done. Obviously the intentionality of God cannot be separated from questions of being. However, speculative questions about what God is and where God is would be subordinated to questions about God's character and purpose for the world.

The point that would be made is that God's intention is to unite all peoples, nations, and things that are separated and are in a state of enmity. Reconciliation on a universal basis is the purpose of God and for that reason becomes the purpose of history. To be sure, intentionality of that kind invites all kinds of speculation of things no less ineffable than speculation about God's being. However speculation about how God will accomplish redemptive purposes may be of greater practical value than to reflect upon God's being. Intentionality raises questions of an "economic" sort. Is God sovereign? If so, in what sense? How does God's power impact the world? How will God's purposes be accomplished? How is his sovereignty related to the dynamics of nature and history? May we speak of the "nonresistance" of God? Is the consummation within history or above history?

Such questions could be stated less bluntly, but they are the questions of intentionality. If it were claimed that the intentionality of God were fully disclosed in Christ, the mystery of God's plan would remain no less for us than for the Apostle Paul who could declare categorically that God will "unite all things in Christ" and yet confess "O the depth of the riches and wisdom and knowledge of God! How unsearchable are his judgments, and how inscrutable his ways!"

Whether a theory of government would be considered within the doctrine of God or elsewhere would be a matter of choice. Suffice to say, government is one of the instrumentalities through which the world is being preserved while it is being redeemed. Government is essential to order. It helps to create the conditions of freedom through law within which life is possible.

Various shapes of government are bound to appear from

age to age. No one form of government may be said to be
God's will though some are obviously more desirable than
others. A theology of peace would insist that the ultimate
purposes of government and the church are the same, though
their specific functions and means vary. Both would attempt
to make life possible, to liberate, to reconcile, to pacify, to
facilitate, and in a thousand ways to harmonize. Differences
between the church and government are confessional and functional. To put it briefly, the church consists of those who
have *freely* confessed Christ and are organized as the "body
of Christ," whereas the state consists of citizens who by
virtue of natural dependencies of all kinds have entered into
relatively fixed relationships defined by law and secured by
power.

A peace theology would be particularly concerned to
emphasize the necessity of government while denying
government absolute authority and challenging ontological
claims of apotheosis. Possibly one could argue with Bonhoeffer that government is a "mandate" if one were to mean no
more than that government is essential to life and therefore
inevitable. However, government is to be regarded for what
it does rather than for what it is. If it were "ordained" by
God it would not for that reason be placed within some sort
of cosmic order. Government is created by human beings for
the sake of warding off anarchy and protecting its citizens
from the destructive powers of sin, insanity, and error.
While government needs to be organized around certain ideas
of universal value and validity, it should not be accorded
the right to define the meaning of existence.

If one were to set forth the doctrine of God from
primarily economic rather than ontological considerations,
one would have to wrestle with the problem of evil. What is
that power which resists the plan of God for the pacification
of the world? How does one explain the beauty and the
brutality of nature? How does one explain the tortuous
processes of billions of years of evolutionary change linked
by a food chain consisting of hunter and prey? Is God in
control of history? If so, how can one explain the cruelties
of history? If God is not in control, how can we be sure
that cosmic peace lies at the end of history?

These and many other questions would haunt the author of
a theology of peace. It would take a fearless, possibly
foolish, person to work out a peace theology in the face of
the evils of nature and history, and especially in light of
the enormities of the atomic arms race in which the
sovereignty of God and the possibilities of atomic destruc-

tion are interfaced. At bottom are issues concerning how to understand the inescapable fact of dualism in a world which by faith we accept as God's domain.

VI. Responsibility for the World

A theology of peace would tackle the complicated and sometimes controversial subject of responsibility for the world. The term "social responsibility" entered Christian ethical discussions some forty years ago under the aegis of the World Council of Churches, but the problems it poses have been with the church since the first century and became a dominant issue during the Reformation. With the beginning of democracy social responsibility has seemed logical and inevitable, although ever more complicated than when responsibility was calculated simply by whether one would carry a sword and accept the office of the magistracy. It is a problem of particular interest to pacifists since responsibility has been understood as doing or supporting what needs to be done to run the world including police work and military defense.

At any rate a peace theology would explore both subjective and objective implications of responsibility. It could do none other than advocate *attitudes* of responsibility. Its emphasis upon global understanding, justice, transcultural involvements, and humane treatment for all mankind would most certainly reinforce responsible attitudes.

Considerations of responsibility for the world are associated indirectly with a host of issues including the meaning of the Sermon on the Mount, discipleship, communal organization, church order, eschatological expectations, and social involvement in the world. Responsibility for the world tends to evoke responses in clusters of ideas and attitudes noted by sociologists of religion such as Ernst Troeltsch.

Clearly the most unambiguous response to social responsibility is the sectarian approach. With appeals going back to the Sermon on the Mount interpreted in such a way as to accept as normative both the form of the commandment and the spirit of the commandment and to traditions of separation from the world in Monasticism and in Anabaptism, the Mennonite community has at certain periods of its history consciously renounced responsibility for the world in deference to the formation of communities of peace and "sanity." A review of the *Concern* pamphlets of the fifties and sixties would indicate how logical the sectarian approach to the world is, given the pacifist premise. For a convinced sec-

tarian, participation in war is unthinkable. By the same
logic responsible involvement in power structures is
eschewed with a keenness of spirit and logic that most mainline Christians do not experience. The world is to be run by
"unbelievers" who, it is assumed, are able and just and who
are somehow guided and restrained by Providence. Disavowal
of responsibility is, at the same time, juxtaposed by a most
serious and selfconscious attempt to be the church--the
peaceful, law-abiding, godly counterpart to the world.

A theology of peace would most certainly treat the sectarian position with respect and seriousness. Certainly sectarianism helps to define the issues. A peace theology would
entertain many of the impulses of sectarianism. A peace
theology would address problems of social solidarity, community formation, peace witness and compromise, using sectarian lines of analysis while acknowledging the struggles
and weakness of sectariansim for peace-making in the modern
world.

A theology of peace would assume involvements in the
world of the sort that is typical of modern urban existence.
It would also assume that Christians do feel responsible for
the world. Feelings of responsibility cannot long be
resisted given the awareness of social solidarity, the importance of social structures, the interdependence of the world,
the significance of political decision-making, and the dread-
ful consequences of atomic war. One is hard put to argue
for less responsible attitudes and deeds than one's awareness
of the needs of the world evokes. If indeed one has been
made conscious of the world, whether through direct experience or through a liberal arts education, there is no turning
back. Awareness of the world for the Christian is awareness
of the neighbor, albeit those who may be most effectively
served through political policy-making.

It may be assumed that many Christians may not feel
responsible for the course of human history. They may lack
awareness of what goes on outside their immediate environment; they may be too preoccupied by family responsibilities;
they may not have the necessary qualifications of imagination, experience, education, and rationality to do anything
about the world at large. Also, there are those who feel
called to concentrate exclusively upon the affairs of the
church or community to which they belong. There is no compelling reason why every Christian must carry the burden of
the world upon his or her shoulders. However, there is no
legitimate reason why those who feel responsible for the
course of human history should not seek ways to turn their

concern into the most effective way to make an impact upon
the world. Responsibility is an implication of imaginative
love. If one's horizons were widened to include an unbounded
world, responsibility for the world would be felt. To suggest that one's feelings of responsibility for the world
should be constricted arbitrarily is the same, in principle,
as to suggest that feelings of responsibility for a drowning
child should be constricted. Obviously the complexity and
possibility of success in the former are hardly to be compared with the latter. But the moral issue is the same. One
should help to "save" the world wherever and whenever one
can. If this means helping to direct the course of human
history, all the better.

There are, however, practical considerations which
pacifists must face. When pacifists assume responsibility
for the world, they are bound to experience moral conflicts
with various degrees of seriousness. The world simply is not
run on Christian principles. Hence compromise is inevitable.
Questions therefore arise as to where to draw the line.

A relatively unambiguous expression of responsibility is
witness. By witness we mean speaking out on issues of public importance. One could include such activities as writing
to congressmen, signing petitions, nonviolent protesting, and
lobbying, under the category of witness.

In western democracies legal provision is made for witness. Hence few prophets are stoned. Nevertheless, witness
for peace may take courage, depending upon circumstances.
Parenthetically, a peace theology would be not only
"systematic." It would be "practical" as well. As such, various ways to uphold peace publicly would be set forth
"scientifically." Peace-making would occupy the place in a
peace theology that practical theology occupies in most
systematic theologies. According to Schleiermacher, the
prologomena of systematic theology is practical theology.

A vital consideration is the content of witness, for
there is a vast difference between peace witness in the form
of general statements and witness in support of specific
policies. Peace witness becomes "political" when it takes
sides. When peace witness means supporting particular
candidates, particular policies, and particular national goals
it partakes of the ambiguities of politics. Intentions and
outcomes may not always resemble one another. One may support a campaign for the Great Society and get the Vietnam
War. In power politics the "Christian" thing to do may result
in tragic consequences. Hence, to witness is to lose one's
innocence as well as one's confidence of always knowing what
is "right."

A peace theology would acknowledge that it is difficult
to draw direct lines between the Sermon on the Mount and
political witness. When moving from the councils of perfection to the realities of power politics, adjustments must be
made whether we call them "middle axioms" or something else.
By what right and by what method one would "reduce" pure
love to political reality is in itself a major issue. Suffice
to say, at this stage in God's economy, the state is not
prepared, nor can we expect the state to bear the cross,
except possibly in unusual circumstances such as refusal to
respond in kind to an atomic first strike.

One of the chief functions of political witness is the
help keep government from becoming demonic. When
government assumes totalitarian power or becomes militarily
aggressive or oppressive it is out of order. Furthermore,
while it may not be necessary or wise to demythologize
governments until their philosophical presuppositions result
in excesses of power or injustice, the church must stand
ready to claim publicly that "Jesus is Lord." Whether
excessive claims are made through Nazi superman
philosophies, theories of divine right, Marxist materialism,
or American manifest destiny, Christians must be ready to
proclaim that "all power in heaven and earth has been given
to Christ the Lord."

The possibilities of peace-making through witness is
relatively unexplored. A peace theology would set forth ways
by which peace witness could be carried out in an organized
way on an international scale. Peace witness is especially
important with the danger of atomic war leading to the
destruction of the world. The power of peace witness lies in
the fact that, at least with respect of the use of atomic
weapons, Christian and pragmatic considerations converge.
Furthermore, there is a growing public awareness today that
war is a far greater enemy of mankind than has been recognized historically.

Inevitably questions arise as to whether Christians who
feel called should be encouraged to accept full
responsibility for society through political office-holding.
Historically, mainline churches have permitted, if not encouraged, their members to accept the magistry and its many
modern equivalents. In so doing, however, they have justified
participation in "justifiable" wars. This has been done
primarily through appeals to Old Testament theology and natural law.

It is obvious that office-holding near the center of
political power is problematic. How can one rationalize

pacifist theology--not to speak of pacifists instincts--in
such a way as to make sense out of participation in structures of power that are committed to defense? What would a
pacifist legislator do in reference to the defense budget?
Would the attempt to inject pacifist idealism into "real
politics" simply be ridiculous?

Practical problems facing hypothetical pacifist legis-
lators or secretaries of state have spared us the troubles of
theoretical considerations! The "failure" of the Pennsylvania
Experiment and the general reluctance of the pacifists to run
for office speak eloquently of a fundamental contradiction
between pacifism and power politics. At the same time, there
may be circumstances within which pacifists may be able to
contribute more within politics than outside of politics.
After all, government is highly differentiated, complex, and
moves less consistently along theoretical lines than many
traditional theories of politics recognize. Especially in a
pluralistic democracy, peace sentiments need to be heard and
felt where decisions of momentous significance are made.
Furthermore, it may be assumed that Christians who are personally opposed to participation in war may express their
calling not simply by opposing the military in absolute
terms, but by speaking for enlightened policies of reason and
moderation. The pacifist would seek to support policies that
point toward peace and justice even though military
preparedness were presupposed.

A theology of peace would explore the possibility of
political responsibility in the form of participation in
government at many levels of involvement.

VII. The Claims of Universality

I would propose that Christian pacifists, especially
those of sectarian roots and sensibilities, face two opposite
and diametrically opposed obligations, both of which are
grounded in the New Testament. One the one hand, disciples
of Christ are obligated to love their neighbors with reckless
abandon--loving nonprudentially and indiscriminately, forgiv-
ing infinitely, responding non-resistantly to evil, going the
second mile, becoming poor, abandoning normal obligations to
wife and family, abandoning nets, renouncing "lording it over"
as the Gentiles do, and taking up the cross.

If these teachings were to be taken literally--indeed,
even if they were "spiritualized," they would still lead logically to some kind of separated communal life, beginning possibly with "all things in common," as in Acts, then to

Corinth, where the community, under eschatological pressures, would be advised to live with "wives as though they had none, and those who mourn as though they were not mourning, and those who rejoice as though they were not rejoicing, and those who buy as though they had no goods, and those who deal with the world as though they had no dealings with it." From Corinth the logic of *agape* love and radical obedience would move to Catholic monasteries where monks and nuns would live according to the "councils of perfection," to the Anabaptists who would insist upon living according to the "perfection of Christ," through to sectarian Mennonite communities of various sorts and conditions. In other words, radical discipleship leads one to devote his or her life and energies away from centers of massive worldly power and particularly from politics. Furthermore, sectarian ethics tends to emphasize, if not exalt, weakness, powerlessness, suffering, and finds its perfect fulfillment in the death of the martyr.

The gospel, on the other hand, would seem to point in another direction as well, namely in the direction of universality. Universality is presented in the New Testament as hope for the reign of Christ. Universality is implied by the ascension, declared in the early confession, "Jesus is Lord," and the mission to the Gentiles. Universality is implied in Paul's desire to go physically to the center of *Pax Roma*, and the universal vision reaches its culmination in the cosmic Christology of Ephesians and the Logos Christology of Colossians. The New Testament vision of history declares that in the "fullness of time" "all things" will be united in Christ.

To be sure, the vision of universality, having become the theological basis for Christendom, has inspired both the best and the worst in Christian history. It resulted in religious intolerance, the Crusades, misuse of power, and corruption. However, the question remains as to how Christians should respond to the vision of universality. Shall Christians fulfill their obligations to universality by evangelism, community formation and good works (MCC, *et al*) only, or shall they seek, however problematic, to exercise power in order to serve mankind most effectively? Shall Christians help the world to define and implement its goals through social, economic, and political power? If one were grasped by the universal implications of the Gospel, the issue becomes not only why but why not enter the power arena in order to do the greatest good to the greatest number? This is one of the most difficult issues facing Christian ethics and it is a

particularly acute one for those who belong to the peace
tradition.
Obviously, universality from a Christian perspective is
eschatological. At first blush, eschatological considerations
would seem to suggest that the "ends" of history lie entirely
in the power and wisdom of God. But the logic of "letting it
up to God" would seem to be too simple, and particularly
when, in modern history, the total destruction of the world
through atomic warfare is a technical possibility.

This is not to suggest that the church as an organization should attempt to wield temporal power as in the Middle
Ages. But the church should at least address the concept of
the Christian calling allowing positions of power and
decision-making through which the course of history may be
influenced.

The seemingly contradictory claims of separatist "perfec-
tionism" and universal involvement should be worked at in the
context of the discerning congregations. It is within the
congregation that sincere Christians may find their callings
within the dynamics of history. Without the counsel, encour-
agement, comfort, and forgiveness of the congregation, the
disciple is left alone to suffer the tensions between love
and power.

VIII. A Place for "Natural Law"

Most major traditions (Catholic, Lutheran, Reformed, and
latter-day Baptists) have attempted to bridge the gap between
Christian idealism and the world by recourse to natural law
coupled with the Ten Commandments. These traditions have
taken creation seriously since creation is thought to reveal
the will of God. To be sure, nature is less than a clear
reflection of God's intention. Nevertheless, it is generally
acknowledged that the Fall defaced rather than destroyed the
mirror, and therefore nature may supply a component to
Christian ethics.
It is impossible here even to review the positions of
traditional Catholic theologians, let alone the heated debates
between Barth, Brunner, and the reflections of Bonhoeffer in
his *Ethics.* I would suggest that theories of natural law
must be taken seriously but critically. Natural law has been
interpreted in many ways and its results are diverse. All
too often appeals to natural law have been used to bestow
divine approval upon the *status quo* and what is claimed to be
natural is more a reflection of a particular culture than a
reflection of creation. The results are generally conserva-

tive when seen in retrospect.

Suffice it to say, the value of the natural law tradition lies in the fact that it may illuminate what we are dealing with when we seek to order life within the secular realm. Its chief function is "indicative" rather than imperative. Much more would seem to be gained by approaching the natural realm functionally than by use of static concepts of natural law. After all, when we are dealing with nature we are dealing with a reality which is more flexible than the "orders" have presupposed.

The best we can say for traditional natural law is that it has been an avenue through which the philosophical tradition has impacted theology. It has opened Christian thought to wisdom, for which a precedent may be found in the wisdom literature of the Old Testament. By studying such philosophers as Plato, Aristotle, Pascal, Kant, Schopenhauer, and Nietzsche one may learn what life is like, if not what to do about it. Furthermore, in recent years the churches are increasingly forced to take the wisdom of the world seriously even when attempting to solve its own problems, not to speak of the problems of the world. Philosophical analysis may help Christians to think analytically. This is especially important since the Bible is not a textbook given to precise definitions, causal connections, and scientific correlations. Such elements of nature as number (complexity), power, continuity, change, matter, spirit, and time need to be understood ontologically if they are to be used responsibly and in conversation with the "movers" of the world. It is particularly important for Christians to acknowledge justice as a fact of nature. Justice is a universal principle of fairness that facilitates human relations among and between all races, cultures, and nations. Even though nature in its fallen state stands over against grace, justice is a point of convergence. Justice is love generalized, structured and ordered.

IX. Hope for Cosmic Peace

It is clear that a peace theology would involve all the problems of systematic theology. Not to be left unattended would be eschatology. Clearly, a theme represented by the Pauline tradition is the hope for cosmic peace. In the age to come, love and power will be united unambiguously. When love and power are united, what Luther referred to as the "left arm" of God will be united with the "right arm." In other words, nature and grace will be reconciled, particularity and universality will no longer present a problem, the church and the world will be one and all things will be put in subjugation under Christ "that God may be everything to everyone"---"the last enemy to be destroyed is death" (1 Cor 15). In the consummation the strange and incomprehensible negative relationships between ontological and moral dimensions of reality which accompanied the Fall will be reversed. For whereas sin corrupted nature in the Fall, grace will restore nature to its primal condition. Therefore, tensions, conflicts, dialectics, incoherences, and the confusions imposed by sin and compounded by complexity will be obliterated. The problems posed by the "one and the many" will be gone forever.

However, until the world is transformed, love can be expressed unambiguously only in powerlessness. Hence we look to the cross and the perfect embodiment of love rather than, say, to the Exodus. Indeed, one may speculate whether even God can inject power into the world without bringing suffering to Egyptian riders or to women and children who lived inside the walls of Babylon and to innocents who were contemporaries of Jesus. Paradise regained is the condition within which "tragic necessity" is no more and pacifists will no longer find it necessary to ponder the Bonhoeffer question as to whether it is the will of God that one insane person should be assassinated for the sake of western civilization.

A peace theology would frankly face the dilemmas of pacifism but would insist that in the "interim" between the advent of Christ and the consummation, compromises, of which there are many, would stop at the point of killing human beings. For to kill a human being is to remove him or her from the realm of repentance, renewal, and salvation.

Until the end, therefore, peace-making will not be without risk, contradictions, and disappointments. However, it is impelled by the conviction that the making of peace with justice is the meaning of existence. The church is God's people organized to make peace through the power of the Holy Spirit looking to the consummation when that which is separated will be united in Christ. "Maybe it is impossible to live in a world where no innocent children suffer; but it is possible to create a world where fewer innocent children suffer. And as we work for this, if we look to you (the faithful) and cannot find help, where shall we look." (Camus)

Notes

1. Although some would contend these days that systematic theology as a comprehensive view of reality is an intellectual exercise divorced from the complexities of modernity and even from the secular life of the Christian community, I would contend that to do peace theology systematically would, by virtue of the inherent requirement of completeness, rationality and order, let no stones unturned including the stumbling blocks. Whereas tractarians are relatively free to select their themes, systematic theologians must face all relevant facts whether they like them or not. A systematic theology for Mennonites would mean that neglected issues such as structural ambiguity, power, moral conflict, institutional sin, and social responsibilities would need to be considered with greater clarity and frankness than in the past.

To be sure, a peace theology would be constructed in light of diverse and voluminous efforts of the church to speak to issues of war and peace emanating from its life and thought, including the experience of relief workers in Central America and men and women who seek to incorporate the spirit of Christ in competitive business.

2. By orthodoxy I refer more to the task of theology, its scope and its coherence than to theological outcomes. What I am contending for is that the church needs to gather together its thoughts in a manner that may be understood in light of certain central convictions normally presented in a prologomenon. Obviously the durability of a systematic theology may not be long in light of the acceleration of change characteristic of the modern world. Nevertheless, search for continuity, coherence, and unity in Christian thought is essential to the viability of the Christian Church.

It should also be pointed out that while Scripture is of vital importance as a source of religious knowledge, a systematic theology would draw upon such extra-biblical sources such as experience, philosophy and tradition. In other words, systematic theology would not simply be biblical theology lifted to an unusual degree of coherence.

MENNONITES AND THE STATE:
PRELIMINARY REFLECTIONS

Ted Koontz

Introduction

As you will soon discover, this is not a complete, polished or "academic" paper. I have neither the time nor ability to present such a paper on this topic at this time. Much of what I will do is to tell a story--my story--which for twenty years now has had as the central theme the issue of Mennonites and "politics." Along the way and at the end I will propose some approaches for addressing the issues the story raises. The primary goal of this exercise for me is to stimulate thought and response on these matters so that someday someone will be able to write the definitive last word on the subject as I cannot now. Although some of the observations which follow represent considered judgments from which I will budge only as a result of a substantial jolt, others are closer to "thought experiments" than arguments rooted in deeply-held convictions. On all points, I welcome questions, suggestions, criticisms--discernment.

I have chosen to tell a story for three primary reasons. First, the central issue I wish to raise is that different Christian responses to the state will look appropriate from different historical, cultural, economic, and political vantage points. People see the biblical message differently from different settings. This is perhaps not a profound observation, but it is one which has been taken with insufficient seriousness in Mennonite ethics generally.[1] Since I wish to stress that positions regarding the state are shaped by people's particular settings, it is fitting that I tell you something about my vantage point and about how I got to it. Doing so will give you handles with which to criticize my perspective--but it will also illustrate my point that we would do well to pay more attention than we have done traditionally to the specific contexts out of which all arguments about Christians and the state (and all other arguments, for that matter) must necessarily come.

Part of the point here is to question what I see as a fundamental starting point in the way Mennonites have typically done ethics (or at least the way Mennonites who have written about ethics have argued we should do ethics). Recognizing that this is something of an oversimplification,

that starting point is that *if only* we could get ourselves
and others to look at the Bible honestly and objectively it
would be clear what its meaning for ethics is. Although I
believe that the Bible does provide the foundation upon which
Christian ethics must be built, that it gives us a normative
standard which can challenge our biases and call us to
repentance and change, and that it does give clear ethical
guidance on some issues, I have been impressed increasingly
with the diversity of plausible readings of the biblical
material, particularly on the issue of relationships to the
state. Another way of saying this is that our theological
and ethical views are shaped crucially by our understandings
of "the facts"--and that our views of the "the facts" are
shaped decisively by the contexts in which we live and work.
This is not, of course, a one-way street since our theological presuppositions also shape our perceptions of the facts.
But we have been overly inclined to stress this latter perspective and to assume, at least implicitly, that the only (or
at least primary) agenda for ethics is to get our theology
straight. My story will show, I hope, how different readings
of "the facts" lead to different views regarding a Christian
attitude toward the state and to somewhat different theological viewpoints (though I develop this less explicitly).

Second, and closely related, I am convinced that
understanding "the facts" is a crucial element in making
specific ethical judgments. In other words, we need to get
our facts straight as well as our theology. We have, as Mennonites, been relatively uninterested in this task, partly, I
think, because we unconsciously assume that once we have our
theology straight we have largely solved the problem of
ethics and partly because we have been suspicious that
studying "the facts" will introduce other norms that will
crowd out Jesus. Nevertheless, some reading of the facts is
inevitable in making ethical judgments. I suspect that many
disagreements which we tend to interpret as differences in
theological or ethical commitments might be just as much
rooted in different understandings of the facts.[2] I suspect,
for example, that differences in understanding the facts
about disinvestment or selective investment and the effects
of these policies may be at least as crucial as differences
in ethical or theological judgments as a cause of disagreement on which policy is right in South Africa. I have sought
to learn something about the facts of international life
having spent most of the last ten years studying international politics and war. Perhaps my reporting on my learnings will confirm the dangers Mennonites have sensed in such

study, but I remain convinced that adequate ethical decisions cannot be made if they are not rooted in adequte empirical analyis. If some of you may be skeptical of my theological views, I might say that sometimes I feel positions on these issues which disagree with mine are based on inadequate empirical views, though I recognize that there is no unanimity on the facts about international politics among scholars of the field—just as there is none about theology among theologians.

Third, I hope my telling my story will encourage others to share more fully and think more self-critically about their stories and how they shape views concerning witness to government. I suspect that discussing the meanings of our stories may be at least as helpful in moving forward a discussion regarding stance toward the state as a more typical academic approach. At the same time, I do not mean to put myself above criticism by telling a story. The theological and factual views which emerge in stories can be challenged and debated.

'Where You Stand Depends on Where You Sit:'[3]
Confessions of a Mennonite Political
Scientist (of sorts)

Phase 1: Naïveté (?)

I grew up in a General Conference Mennonite congregation which taught pacifism (at least my father, the minister, did), but in which the majority of the men had fought in World War II. From as early as I can remember I studied the Bible and learned there that Christians cannot kill.

I came to political awareness (perhaps!) in the early to mid '60's.[4] Nurtured in my understanding of the Christian faith by Vincent Harding's interpretation of the meaning of the cross and resurrection in the context of the civil rights struggle, I went to Mississippi in the summer of 1964. As a college student, I participated in an early "peace walk" to mail letters opposing the war in Vietnam to members of Congress in 1965, despite threats from Newton "townies" that they would beat us up and cover us with yellow paint if we crossed the tracks from North Newton to Newton and, more important, despite concerns from people at Bethel that the "walk" would cost the college over a million dollars.[5] In short, I was something of an "activist" and was not overly worried about whether my activism was rooted in the New Testament or in a "common sense" American Liberalism.

Although I valued the New Testament teaching on peace and
came to my own earliest convictions against the war on biblical grounds, it was not necessary to start from that point
to see that opposing injustice and war was a good thing.
Opposition to segregation and to the war in Vietnam was
fully justified on the basis of both my Christian commitment
and a simple, sensible look at what the best policy alternatives were. One did not have to be a Mennonite Christian to
know that Bull Conner was wrong on race and that Lyndon
Johnson was wrong on the war.

After several years of struggling with what to do about
my deep opposition to the war (I thought of going with MCC to
Vietnam to repair some of the damage but decided I had little
to contribute at the ripe age of 19 or 20), I graduated from
college and went to Harvard Divinity School in the fall of
1969.[6] Although I knew there was a lot of opposition to the
war at Harvard,[7] I was surprised to find that there was
almost no visible support for the war. In some important
ways I felt more kinship with the mood there than the mood
among Kansas Mennonites, many of whom supported the President's policy (while still refusing to serve personally).
This bastion of the worldly "Establishment," in which I was
learning all about Reinhold Niebuhr and the Just War tradition, was more firmly on the "right" side than most of my
Mennonite brothers and sisters![8] As you might surmise, this
was not healthy soil in which to grow a worldview that has
as its central categories "church" (i.e., everything good) and
"world" (i.e., everything bad).

After graduating from Divinity School I began working at
the MCC Peace Section Office in Akron (1972-1976). It was a
time when there was increasingly powerful political opposition to the war, leading first to the end of U.S. military
involvement and then making possible the overthrow of the
Saigon regime. It was also a time when military budgets
were sharply curtailed (in relative terms), when a new relationship with our erstwhile enemy, China, was in the making,
when SALT I was being signed and hopes were rising for significant reductions (at least) in the nuclear threat, and when
detente was offering the promise of an end to the unrelenting
hostility of the cold war years. In the Peace Section we
found much commonality with other Christian (really, mainline,
surely not evangelical) denominations on issues like the war,
military budgets, domestic welfare policies, and southern
Africa. The kinds of policy options we tended to support
were those that most other mainline church groups active in
Washington supported--and they were the same kinds of posi-

tions which many liberal political leaders supported. Again these realities were hard on a church/world dualism--and on a "sectarian" posture in relating to other Christian groups. But perhaps even more important was the subtle sense of where the "action" is, or where the inbreaking of the Kingdom might be happening, that this experience conveyed. The things that we supported were not inherently impossible in political terms. Things could change, if not into the Kingdom then in Kingdom directions, through the political process. After all, hadn't "we" transformed the face of the South (despite residual racial problems which still hung on, to be sure) and ended U.S. involvement in Vietnam (despite continuing war and genocide in Southeast Asia, to be sure)? And it had been done through *political* action. Moreover, the church (i.e., the actual visible Mennonite churches in the U.S.) often seemed more of an impediment in the way of Kingdom building than the world! There often seemed to more liklihood of getting politicians to cut military budgets in Washington than to get Mennonites to press their political leaders to cut military budgets. Though it was never articulated at the time, it may be fair to say that on an emotional level, if not intellectually or theologically, I (perhaps others too?) had been "Constantinianized:" i.e., I perhaps had come to see God's primary agent in history being the state (if only we could work a litte harder to get someone like McGovern elected the next time, etc.) rather than the church.

Despite this relative optimism about politcal activity (relative, that is, to many more traditional Mennonites) there was a sense in which I harbored a rather deepseated dislike, perhaps even hatred, of "America." I often wished I was not an American. I watched Mayor Daly and his police in action during the 1968 Democratic convention. I protested the shootings at Kent State. Although some reforms were happening, they were so small compared to what was needed. The war dragged on unconscionably long. To understate the case, Johnson, Nixon, Kissinger and Ford were not leaders who fired my idealism. Sometimes I could scarcely contain my rage when Johnson or Nixon gave one of their "My Fellow Americans..." TV speeches. McGovern was roundly defeated. Even when the war ended, the really dramatic shift in direction which I desired did not come. The grade school image of the U.S. as a shining white knight setting the world straight had been thoroughly dismantled. The opposite was true: the U.S. was the major problem in the world.

While this revulsion about "America" and my comparatively high hopes for political action in the U.S. are in some ways

in tension, they are also in at least one deep way coherent:
it is only because I had such high expectations for what
America should and could be that I was so deeply repulsed by
what it was.

Phase 2: Maturity (??)

A major shift in my orientation on these matters began
in the fall of 1976 when I returned to Harvard to try to figure out why nations act as they do in the international
arena, and especially to study the problem of war from a descriptive instead of primarily a prescriptive or normative
perspective.[9]   Being a naturally modest fellow (my Mennonite
roots, no doubt), I decided to try to solve the nuclear problem. After all, since that is hardest problem, by solving it
I would also solve other lesser war/peace problems!   The
trouble is I didn't solve it.   Instead I discovered what I
felt were profound reasons that it could not be solved. This,
together with the fact that I was starting a Ph. D. program
in an area in which I had had one previous course and with
the discovery that my father had what proved to be terminal
cancer, threw me into a deep depression which lasted most of
my first two semesters.   Learning the facts about nuclear
reality, particularly also about the political realities which
underlie the technological reality, simply *is* depressing.

What was it that I learned that made me depressed and
that challenged my earlier views?   It is obviously hard to
summarize it in a way which can have the power for you that
it had for me.   Most of it is not new, but I found the
implications to be far reaching.   I will not comment here on
the nuclear situation particularly, but on larger "lessons"
about international relations and war.

1. I learned to compare and evaluate events and policies
not only in terms of an ideal about how things should be, but
in terms of how they have been.   I learned to use a relative,
historical, measuring stick for judging the U.S., as well as
an absolute theological/ethical one.   In terms of my evalua-
tion of the U.S., my study of the history of international
politics led me to conclude that the U.S., in its actions as a
"superpower," was not uniquely evil or misled (though it is
both evil and misled)—nor uniquely wonderful (I had been, as
should be clear from the above, less tempted earlier by this
interpretation than the former one).   What the U.S. was doing
was in most important ways typical of what other "great"
powers have done.   Insofar as the U.S. has deviated from
typical actions of other recent great powers (the Soviet

Union, Germany in the early twentieth century, Great Britain
in the 19th century, Napoleon's France) it has probably more
often deviated in a more, rather than a less, "enlightened"
way.[10] Seeing the U.S. in comparative historical terms has
had the effect of both reducing my high expectations (we are,
after all, much like other great powers) and reducing my
hatred of America (we are, after all, probably not worse than
other great powers). Learning more about how nations
(including the U.S.) have behaved historically (in brief,
nastily) brought my "Constantinian drift" to an abrupt halt.
From this vantage point, if looking for signs of the Kingdom
within the church may be discouraging, expecting the Kingdom
through the action of any nation is downright preposterous.

2. This growing skepticism about the possibility of a
transformed international politics was rooted not only in a
realization that there are few historical grounds for expecting the eagle to lie down with the bear. It was also rooted
in a deepening conviction that this discouraging historical
record was not accidental, i.e., it was not mainly the result
of key countries by fluke or an unlucky choice of leadership
making the wrong decisions at key times. The problem goes
far deeper than misguided American policy--or any other
national policy. The problem is systemic, having much more
to do with the structure of the international arena than with
the peculiar evils of particular regimes. In a fundamentally
"anarchic" environment there are powerful reasons to be
fearful--and, if one is in a position to do so, to take
measures which are designed to make sure that no one will be
able to threaten you. Hobbes was right: for ordinary mor-
tals or for states, under these conditions there is

a perpetual desire for power after power, that ceaseth
only in Death. And the cause of this is not always
that a man hopes for a more intensive delight than he
has already attained to; or that he cannot be content
with a moderate power: but because he cannot assure
the power and means to live well, which he hath at
present, without the acquisition of more.
...There is no way for any man to secure himself, so
reasonable, as anticipation; that is by force, or wiles,
to master the persons of all men he can, till he see
no other power great enough to endanger him: and
this is no more than his own conservation
requireth...."[11]

This systemic problem was amply demonstrated to me in the study of international politics. While there are plenty of evil and stupid leaders on which to blame many wars, there is another sense in which many times leaders are victims of the structures in which they operate.

3. But the problem is even deeper than this. It is not only a misguided quest for security for oneself which leads nations to take actions which lead to war. Again, Hobbes articulates the problem. Despite his stress on the "security dilemma" he also recognized expansionist ambition going beyond security requirments as another important problem. "There be some that take pleasure in contemplating their own power in the acts of conquest, which they pursue farther than their security requires."[12] People, groups, and nations are sometimes (probably normally, given a sufficiently tempting opportunity) aggressive--seeking to increase their well-being at the expense of others, not only seeking to protect themselves and what they have. In other words, the problem is not only systemic, it is also a problem of "human nature."

4. These last two observations are simply evidences of human fallenness. My study of international politcs forced me to conclude that we live in a fallen world--a world that will not be redeemed by human beings in history. While we are called to redeem it, or at least to create a community which lives in a (partially) redeemed way, it is also very important for the world (and for the church) to have some mechanisms for restraining evil until redemption is fully realized.

5. While I had heard of this problem of fallenness before, I had not seen so fully the far-reaching implications of it for government and international politics. One primary function of government is to "protect the innocent." It is this function which most clearly sets government apart from other institutions and creates the basic ethical problem in relating to government. This function is made necessary by human fallenness. The central problem of government, both in domestic life and international life, is dealing with individuals or groups which seek to harm or exploit others. This is not to say that protecting innocents and restraining evildoers is the only thing, or even the main thing, which governments do or should do, but it is to say that this is the main *problem* of government--and the main reason that government is problematic for Mennonite Christians. In other words, government is that institution which has primary responsibility for dealing with the consequences of human fallenness.[13]

6. I also came to see that, in the condition of fallenness in which government operates, one of the central
mechanisms which has been most effective in restraining evil
exploitation of others is offsetting power. Potential
evildoers (i.e., probably most of us, surely all states) are
less likely to implement their evil designs (which they, of
course, most likely do not see as being evil at all) if they
see other powerful actors which will oppose their evil (perhaps only because it would interfere with their evil designs)
than if their prey is an easy target. I suspect Africa would
not have been colonized if Africans had possessed military
technology and manpower equal to that of the European
powers. I suspect the United States would not have invaded
Grenada if Grenada had had the military strength of the
Soviet Union. And I suspect the Soviet Union would not have
invaded Afghanistan if the United States had committed its
full military force to Afghanistan's defense (not that I think
that would have been a good idea!). I even suspect that "lesser" powers in the world today may well be less independent,
and more exploited, if either one of the two superpowers had
simply disappeared at the end of World War II.[14] Both the
United States and the Soviet Union would, I suspect, be more
exploitive of more small countries (each is already too
exploitive of too many) if they did not have to contend with
the offsetting power of the other. In other words, peace--
and some modicum of justice--often is served by a balance of
power. To quote John Oyer again, we need to "recognize the
role of balance of power in politics--that it does in fact
work to some extent, probably more than we like to realize
or admit. I say this because most Mennonites in my circle of
friends *never* include it in their thought on specific political issues."[15] I am *not* saying balance of power politics is
without its dangers, nor that the unrelenting buildup of arms
in which the U.S. is engaged is a good thing from the viewpoint of world peace of justice. I spend most of my time in
International Politics classes (particularly at Notre Dame)
stressing the dangers of a spiral of hostitlity and conflict
which an arms race, sparked in part by balance of power concerns, poses. This spiral, in my judgement, is clearly the
primary danger in current U.S.-Soviet relations. I *am* saying
that my study of international politics led me to the
uncomfortable (for an erstwhile liberal Mennonite pacifist)
conclusion that, in the fallen world (which certainly includes
the world of international politcs), it is possible to be too
pacifist if one's goal is to prevent war and minimize
exploitation and domination. It does not add to our

credibility in making our arguments about the dangers of the
spiral if we do not acknowledge also the dangers of one-
sided weakness.

7. Having been forced to admit to myself that power must
offset power in a fallen world, I came to ask whether this
offsetting power should not be, and could not be, a form of
power which is not militarily or otherwise "violent." I was
intrigued by the work of Gene Sharp, partly because it
recognizes the reality of power, the reality of national
independence, and the likelihood of continuing aggression.[16]
I did some study with and about him and his views on "nonviolent alternatives" for dealing with aggression and for
rectifying injustice. I came away convinced that the ability
of a regime to maintain control is very heavily dependent on
the "consent" (or, often, acquiescense) of the population and
that this fact opens the door to a powerful potential
resource for overcoming political oppression—particularly if
the oppressive regime is indigenous and cannot rely on heavy
external military support (e.g., Iran). I also came to the
conclusion that while the search for mechanisms to exercise
power nonviolently ought to be pressed, such mechanisms are
not likely to be as fruitful in deterring and defeating some
kinds of aggression as military threat or military resistance
(i.e., where the aggressor has little sense of identification
with the population or has the technological capability and
political will to destroy at a distance). Thus while the
kinds of power which Sharp explores are important and worth
examining further, they do not, in my judgment, do away with
the need for military forms of power in all cases.

8. A final (so far) effort to escape the conclusion that
governments may sometimes in some sense be "justified" in
using violence or fighting wars came through encountering
Robert Johansen and the "world order" school of thought of
which he is an intellectual leader. Bob was President of the
Institute for World Order (now World Policy Institute) when
we were in Princeton (1980-81) and is a Church of the
Brethren international relations scholar. We were members of
the same small group which met weekly as the part of the
Princeton Historic Peace Church house church. In very general terms, the world order movement takes seriously the
"systemic" problem identified earlier by exploring ways to
eliminate or radically modify the "anarcy" which prevails in
international relations. Put simply, the idea is to "domesti-
cate" international politics, i.e., make it much more like
domestic politics by having some centralized authority which
could adjudicate disputes and enforce settlements among

nations. Serious plans are advanced for what a new world
order might look like and efforts are made to lay out
mechanisms for getting there.[17] My reaction to these
efforts, put very briefly, is that I would like to see international politics re-formed in the general ways which they
point to, but feel they have been unable to demonstrate
realistically how the transition can be made. World order
thinking in general starts with a vision of what should be,
but never quite connects with the present realities--most
particularly, the reality of national *independence* (despite
"interdependence") and the very obvious and persistent reluctance of most nations (both political leaders and populations)
to surrender their independence for the sake of what world
order thinkers hope will be a more peaceful world. Perhaps
the central weakness is that in addressing the systemic
causes of war, world order thinkers have inadequately
addressed the "human nature" causes--causes which may
prevent re-forming the system.

Perhaps these comments are sufficient (perhaps "overkill"
is a better term!) to demonstrate that "sitting" at different
vantage points has caused me to think differently about war
and expectations of the state. I have said little about how I
"made sense" in biblical or theological terms of these shifting views but I did struggle with that question throughout as
I sought to see the biblical message as both normative and
applicable in all of this. Needless to say, the way I
understood the biblical material changed as I continued to
read and ponder it as I was undergoing these other changes
in my vantage point. Those shifts could be elaborated but I
suspect that some of the correlated ways of interpreting the
biblical material may be clear implicitly. In any case, I
will not elaborate them here, nor claim that it was shifting
views on biblical interpretation that caused my other shifts.
It was primarily other things which forced me to rethink my
understanding of the Bible--something which I suspect is true
of most reinterpretations of the Bible, though it is not
always recognized or admitted. Judgments about what is the
right thing to do and what is the correct theological view
change when understandings of the facts change. I do not
mean to say here that there is a one-way street in the opposite direction than I had noted earlier--that factual readings simply determine theological views and ethical actions.
Rather there is a dynamic interrelationship in which changes
on one level effect changes on the other. My primary
changes were coming during this period in my understandings
of the facts. Perhaps this appears to subordinate my

theological views to my other understandings derived from
other sources. I would only note that I think my earlier
theological views were no less influenced by my earlier
reading of the facts and that this seems to me true of most
of us. Also, despite the flexibility in interpreting facts
and in theological views which I have outlined, I would hold
that there is a limit to the fluidity of perspectives which is
acceptable. That is, some readings of the facts seem clearly
implausible (this was the problem I faced when I started
studying international politics--I came to see my previous
reading of reality as being impossible to sustain with
integrity) and some theological positions seem clearly
incompatible with the biblical message (thus despite my factual analysis that violence may sometimes be necessary for
the state in carrying out its ordering function, I do not
conclude that Christians should participate in that violence
because I cannot with integrity reconcile that with what I
take to be a central part of the biblical message).
Nevertheless, my understanding of the facts has altered my
conception of what should be expected from the state, the
main topic upon which I wish to focus in the concluding part
of this paper.

Rethinking a Two-Kingdom Ethic

It is no doubt apparent by now that my thought has led
me to a renewed appreciation for some sort of "dualism" or
two kingdom ethic. I make no pretensions of developing a
systematic or comprehensive view here. In this section I
wish rather to outline very briefly some central notions that
are a part of my emerging perspective.
1. **The church is the primary vehicle of God's action in
history.** Mennonite thought has been right on this point in
criticizing views which look to the state (or some other
body) as God's primary instrument. This perspective includes
stressing the alternative community, creating new and more
redeemed models for handling a variety of problems, as the
primary means of achieving meaningful social change. While I
think this view is still affirmed, at least rhetorically, in
Mennonite social ethical thought, I sometimes wonder whether
"we" (here meaning mainly people who teach and write about
these issues) really believe it--or at least whether we are
communicating it. While I strongly affirm a Mennonite witness in Washington, for example, I see that kind of political
involvement as derivative from and subordinate to the wider
mission and service work of the church. I interpret my role

as a political scientist in the Mennonite church as being not in any sense normative, but as filling a small and secondary role in the total life of the church. (To use the body image, perhaps I and others with my calling are a finger nail on the left little finger![18]). I am sometimes puzzled and troubled by the apparent magnetism "Washington" (both actually and symbolically) has for a new generation of Mennonite youth. Judging from my very limited experience at Goshen, I would say that "the best and brightest" of our youth are more likely to go to Washington to work in a congressional office or a (good) "lobby" than to Nigeria with a mission board or MCC--or into a pastorate. What are we communicating about where Kingdom business is transacted?

2. **The church's integrity in its own life and mission is essential to its direct "political" witness.** The focus on the church is essential not only because it is the primary locus of God's action but also because a more explicit witness to government will be fruitless unless it is rooted in authentic church experience, arising from direct engagement with a needy world and able to point to more kingdom-like alternatives--already embodied in the church's life--than those the government is currently pursuing. Even I, as a Mennonite sometimes get a bit cynical about our prophetic calls for changes in government policy when I see us doing no better (or little better) within the church. Do we favor government policies which would distribute wealth more equitably and criticize the current Administration for adopting policies which do the opposite? I surely do, and I think it is right to do so. But how do we deal with economic disparities within the church itself? Do we in the church do even as much to assist poor black Mennonites in Chicago, for example, as the Reagan Administration does? Do "rich" Mennonites *give* as much to help the poor as the government *takes* from those same rich Mennonites? On another issue, more closely related to violence and coercion, I am unconvinced that we have developed and modeled redemptive ways of dealing with conflict which could give credibility to our witness to government against its violence. If we cannot do a better job of this within a voluntary community of non-resistant believers, how can we expect the government to hear us when we call upon it to resolve disputes nonviolently in a world where most affirm no commitment to the way of peace? All of this is to say that those concerned with witness to government still need to give priority attention to the quality of the church's life and work.

3. **The appropriate overarching norm for the life of the**

church is agape. This involves (though it of course means much more) at least renunciation of violence. At a minimum, disciples of Christ may not kill.[19]

4. **An appropriate ethic for the state is different from an appropriate ethic for the church.** It seems that this issue of the sense in which, if any, there are different norms for the state than for the church is one on which there is a good deal of confusion--or disagreement. Here I mean to follow and expand on the discussion in *Justice and the Christian Witness: A Summary Statement.*[20] Perhaps the clearest recent official expressions of differing views come in the General Conference Mennonite Church (GCMC) statement *The Way of Peace*[21] which stresses that "God does not have two standards of morality--one for government and one for Christians" and the Lancaster Conference formulation: "We believe in two kingdoms--the kingdom of God and the kingdom of this world. The state is ordained of God to maintain law and order in this world. Force and the sword are recognized by the Scriptures as tools of the state which God uses to promote justice."[22] I am not certain how much of the argument about norms for the state to attribute to real disagreement and how much to misunderstanding, so I will try to state my view as clearly as possible in order to minimize any additional misunderstanding--though if I succeed in minimizing misunderstanding I may also maximize disagreement!

a) I do not mean that *ultimately* God has two different wills. I would agree that finally God wants everyone--and every institution--to live by the ethic of Jesus.

b) Why then should one say that now it is in some sense "right" for the state to act in a way which is different from that ethic of Jesus? Because in the present historical situation (characterized by the problems of sin and evil described earlier) the state's task of protecting the innocent entails accepting a norm which cannot rule out the possible use of coercion, sometimes even violence. I agree with John H. Yoder (in his appreciative comments about Reinhold Niebuhr on this point) that it is the weight of sin which holds down the performance of the state.[23] The point at which I may disagree with some recent Mennonite thought is on the question, "Whose sin?" That is, I think the reason the state must use some coercion, and sometimes, at least potentially, violence is that it is charged with protecting innocents from the sinful exploitation or aggression of others and, as suggested earlier in my discussion of learnings from international politics, there are not always non-coercive or nonviolent options which will protect the innocents.[24]   If other actors (i.e., individuals, corporations, other states, etc.) were not sinful in seeking to exploit or hurt others it would be possible for the state to function nonviolently (and indeed it often, in many contexts almost always, does so). But because the state cannot count on all actors always refraining from harming others, the state must be prepared to restrain such harm and it may sometimes be able to do so using coercion or violence and unable to do so using less objectionable means. In other words, the primary sin which necessarily pulls down the performance of the state is the sin of other actors, not the state itself.[25]   The force, coercion or violence used by the state when it actually is restraining evil and protecting the good can on one level be labeled "sin," in the sense that it falls short of the ultimate norm revealed in Jesus. But insofar as that coercion or violence really does restrain evil and protect the good (while meeting an additional criterion I have hinted at and will discuss later) the state's behavior can be called "right" (or whatever other term you prefer indicating moral acceptability, given limited options all of which are less than what is desired), given the state's function in human society, a function I see suggested in passages such as Romans 13.[26]

c) All of this suggests that it is possible for the state to be too nonviolent. I believe this is possible—though it is *surely not the main problem of most states most of the time!* I am not certain what the percentage is, but am quite confident that well over 99% of the time states err on the side of using too much violence or threat of violence in seeking to protect the innocent (not to mention all of the times they protect the evildoer and exploit the innocent). Overwhelmingly, the state needs to be called to reduce its level of violence, simply in order to be a good state. Nevertheless, if I understand him correctly, I have come to disagree with John Yoder's model of witness to the state insofar as it suggests that if the statesman, as statesman, did not have his vision of the true norm obscured by a cloud he would see that the proper norm of action for the state is *agape*.[27] As noted above, I have no quarrel with this if what is meant is an ultimate vision of what it is right for everyone to act upon. But as I understand it in Yoder's work (I think this is also true of most other Mennonite writings on this theme in recent years), *agape* is what is really ethically required of the state here and now. The need for "middle axioms" or any norms other than *agape* arises not because those norms have any inherent "normativeness" about them or

are derived from the function of government in human society,
but simply because they express all one can hope a statesman
might see and understand, i.e., they are the only way to get
the statesman to move toward *agape*. From this perspective,
as I see it, if the statesman would choose to reject all
violence, even if it meant someone else would do greater and
more indiscriminate violence against innocents he could protect if he was willing to use violence, this statesman would
be acting in a morally superior way to one who would use
limited violence to prevent innocents from greater violence.
It may be argued that this is a purely hypothetical
situation--and I surely grant it does not describe most cases
of state violence! Nevertheless, I think there are numerous
real-life cases of this sort, including cases of sectarian
violence or rioting, where "firm" action (including the threat
and probably the use of some violence) by the government can
greatly reduce the carnage and where action based on *"agape,"*
if that means ruling out any threat or use of violence, can
increase it. It can be argued, for example, that the United
Nations should have intervened militarily sooner and with
more force in the Congo civil war and that part of the
reason it did not do so was Dag Hammarskjold's near-pacifist
convictions. Here is a case, I think, where something like
agape (at least deep moral reluctance to use military force)
caused a political leader to fail to act "rightly" as a
statesman in a concrete here-and-now situation. This is not
to say that Hammarskjold erred more and more often because
of his convictions than other statesmen do because of their
(typically) more militarist convictions. I believe the
reverse is true. But it is ·to say that governments (or
supra-govermental organizations like the U.N.), in their
peculiar role in fallen human societies, may occasionally be
too pacifistic. It is also to say that a moral standard other
than *"agape"* is needed to guide state behaviour in a world
which is fallen (if *agape* means ruling out all threat or use
of violence) and that that other moral standard should be
viewed as having more status than a "middle axiom," at least
as I have understood the meaning of that term.[28]

   5. **The proper norm for the state is to protect the good
by restraining evildoers with the least possible coercion or
violence.**[29]

        a) The part of this criterion which calls upon the
state to "protect the good" is a way of saying that not all
violence by the state is cut of the same moral cloth. State
action, including violent action, which serves "justice" has a
different moral standing than does action which perpetrates

injustice. Though the norm I am proposing suggests that it
may be "acceptable" for the state to sometimes use violence,
it gives the state no moral license to use violence (or any
other means, for that matter) in support of injustice. The
requirement that the state act to protect the good (rather
than evildoers) is, of course, already grounds upon which to
challenge a great many state actions.

b) The part of this criterion which calls for "least
possible coercion or violence" suggests, following Yoder and
Niebuhr, that there is no static norm for the state. Rather,
this is a relative standard. In situations where there is a
relatively stable and just order, the level of violence (probably even the level of coercion) needed by the state to do
its "good protecting" function will be very low, perhaps
approaching zero. This will typically be true of societies
in which governments have a high degree of "legitimacy" (i.e.,
where people voluntarily acknowledge the government's right
to make decisions on behalf of the whole community because
of a sense that the government is fair, accessible, etc.) and
of societies which are well integrated (i.e., where there is a
high degree of agreement on basic values, rights,
responsibilities, procedures for settling disputes, etc.). In
the absence of these conditions, the level of coercion and
violence needed by the government to perform its "legitimate"
functions typically will be much higher. This seems to me
evident if one compares the level of coercion and violence
needed to protect innocents in some parts of Boston to that
needed to do the same in Goshen, Indiana.[30] Similar com-
parisons might be made internationally. Military preparations to defend against attack from Canada are entirely
unjustified in the United States (I'll let Canadians speak to
whether the reverse is also true!) in light of the level of
integration or interdependence existing between the two
societies. Because a whole web of ties links the two
societies and assures peace between them, developing military
means to assure peace and to deter aggression is both
preposterous and wrong. Given the absence of integration
and interdependence in relations between the United States
and Soviet Union (and the possibility of aggression, resulting largely because of this lack of integration and interdependence) some military preparations to deter aggression
are neither so preposterous nor so wrong. This standard is
relative in the sense that it would condemn a level of
violence (and preparation for it) in Goshen (or in U.S.-
Canadian relations) equivalent to what may be legitimate in
Boston (or in U.S.-Soviet relations).[31] It is also relative in

the sense that there is no theoretical ceiling on the level
of nonviolence and noncoercion to which a state might be
called--provided it protects the good.   There is no
"inherently" (or definitionally) necessary minimum level of
violence a state must perform in order to be the state. In a
perfectly integrated society with a perfectly legitimate
government, it should be possible for the government to perform that function without violence or coercion.   Under those
conditions this standard would condemn outright a policeman
with a billy club.   In other words, under those conditions,
the norms for the state and the church in practice would be
the same (at least on the issue of violence).

c) At the same time, this relative norm, as suggested
earlier, implies that it is possible for the state to be too
pacifistic if it is operating in a situation where society or
societies are less than perfectly integrated and governments
(or supragovernmental institutions) are viewed as less than
perfectly legitimate.

d) A further implication of this relative norm is that
it is morally incumbent upon governments to increase the
level of integration and legitimacy existing in and between
societies.   The "least possible" amount of coercion or
violence is not a static quantity, as I noted earlier.   This
suggests that if states really are to use the least possible
coercion and violence, they have a moral responsibility to
work not only at using the "least possible" in a crisis right
now (e.g., a race riot) but also to make strenuous efforts to
assure that "less" (or none) is needed in the future.   In
other words, this standard suggests that working toward the
creation of political "community" is morally required of
governments, because it is only as the degree of political
community is increased that the degree of coercion and
violence needed to "protect the good" can be decreased.

These considerations mean that the scheme I am working
with can be represented graphically (following Yoder) in this
way:

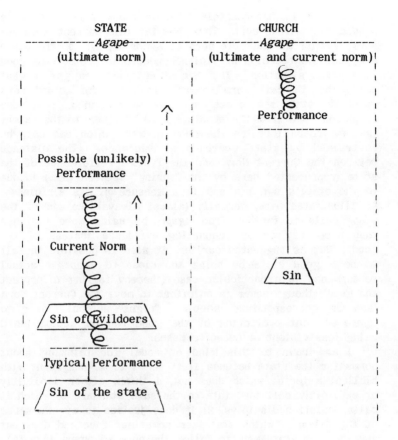

The arrow on the upper right represents the pull toward
the ultimate norm of *agape* (or at least nonviolence) inherent
in the model as the state must take seriously the "least possible" part of the norm in working to create a community in
which cohesion is maintained on the basis of consent and
common bonds rather than coercion and violence. The "Possible (unlikely) Performance" line illustrates a situation
(normally but not always hypothetical) where the state uses
too little coercion or violence and because of this fails to
protect the good. The "Current Norm" line is the actual,
relative norm which the state should use at the moment--
restraint of evil with the least possible coercion or
violence. Note that this norm is itself moveable, as stressed
in the text and as illustrated by the arrows on both sides of
the Current Norm. Where this Current Norm actually is in
any specific case will depend on how heavy the weight of Sin

of Evildoers is, because this determines how much violence is needed to restrain evil. Thus, how far this current, relative norm is from the absolute norm of *agape* depends on the minimum possible coercion or violence needed to protect the good in a given situation. The "Sin of Evildoers" weight is what holds the "Current Norm" down. That is, the actual norm which the state should act on at the moment in a given case is pulled down from the absolute norm of *agape* to the extent that evildoers threaten the good in ways which can only be restrained by state coercion or violence. The distance between the Current Norm and the Typical Performance of the state (represented here by the "spring" between them) is due to the state's own sin and is a measure of its sinfulness. As illustrated here, normally (almost always) the sin of the state pulls it farther from *agape*, by using more violence than necessary or by supporting evildoers instead of the good. But as suggested earlier, it also is possible to fail to be a good state by being too close to *agape* in actual performance in a particular case (thereby failing to protect the good), though never in an effort to move the Current Norm (and the corresponding immediate "right" action) closer to *agape* so that protection of the good can be accomplished using less violent or coercive means.

I am drawn to this kind of model for thinking about norms for the state because 1) it seems to me congruent with biblical material which does not, I think, either implicitly or explicitly call the state to the same standard to which it calls Christian disciples, 2) it does justice to my own sense of the dilemmas which statesmen sometimes face and does not ask them, as statesmen, to follow the norm of agape in a fallen situation (though we should also call statesmen as individuals to become Christians and, if there is no consistent way to be both Christian and statesman in a particular situation, to stop being statesmen), and 3) it allows plenty of room for a prophetic critique of government. These first two reasons seem to me to be in basic continuity with "traditional" Mennonite thought. But the third, I think, is radically different from the church/world dualism in Mennonite ethics which many recent writers have criticized, a dualism which saw the world as fallen and therefore sometimes appeared to feel there was nothing to say to the state by way of prophetic critique. I agree with those who wish to speak a prophetic word to government. What I have sought to do is to begin exploring the normative framework out of which such a prophetic critique should come, a framework which recognizes that the state's function in God's economy is different from that of the church.

Notes

1. We have been more ready to note how the settings of *others* have shaped their understanding of the Christian message (mostly by distorting it) than how our settings have shaped and perhaps distorted our own understandings. We see this clearly in Augustine or Luther or Niebuhr, or perhaps in our criticisms of an earlier generation of "apolitical" Mennonites who were shaped, for example, by the experience of Niebuhr and World War II, but do we see as clearly how we have been shaped by the civil rights movement, Vietnam, liberation theology, etc? I make no claim to exemption from this danger in what I present here. Rather, I seek to deal with it by being open about where I sit and asking for discernment concerning the distortions which may arise from that vantage point. I'd invite others to be self-conscious and open about their vantage points and the dangers of distortion which may be inherent in them.

2. This is a point I made briefly in "Theology, Ethics, and the 'Facts'," *The Mennonite*, 22 December 1981, 744, in reaction to the last Peace Theology Colloquium. I should also note that by "the facts" I do not mean only factual bits of information, but the social theories (e.g., Marxism) which we use to integrate and give larger patterns of coherence to our views about social reality.

3. *Graham T. Allison, Essence of Decision: Explaining the Cuban Missile Crisis*, (Boston: Little, Brown and Company, 1971), 176, credits Don K. Price for this aphorism. The point of this saying in Allison's book is to stress how the institutional interests of different units of the government shape the "stands" on issues which leaders who "sit" at the top of those different units take. As will become evident, my meaning here is somewhat broader than that.

4. The surest sign of this awareness was that by 1964 I no longer saw the only Democratic member of my class in Hillsboro as hopelessly uniniformed—perhaps even heretical—maybe even unpatriotic!

5. A compromise was reached which saved us from some of the wrath of the townies and of the college administration. We carried out our revolutionary action of petitioning members of Congress at the North Newton post office instead of the Newton post office.

6. I had planned to go to AMBS, but had a scholarship that would pay expenses at any seminary. My frugal Mennonite impulses made me feel it would be poor stewardship to

"waste" it on such an inexpensive school! Besides, I thought it would be good to get out of the Mennonite world for a while.

7. The previous spring anti-war activists had taken over University Hall, and when we arrived we found that the shop windows in Harvard Square were boarded up, having been repeatedly broken in peace demonstrations.

8. This view was reinforced by the fact that Massachusetts was the only state to go for McGovern in the 1972 election, while Kansas went about 69% for Nixon, and Mennonites in Kansas probably voted at least as heavily for Nixon as other Kansans.

9. I did this despite the warnings of Don Smucker that the Government Department there was apt to pollute me. What follows may be just the evidence Don needs to demonstrate that his warnings were indeed right.

10. I think John Oyer is probably right in his observation, based on his post-war MCC service in Europe, that "American propaganda was much too mild compared with the realities which it tried to describe, both German and Russian." (Unpublished manuscript, "Anabaptists, the Law and the State," 15. To be published by the Marpeck Academy, Washington, D.C.) He adds, "We compare U.S. performance against our own *ideal* in politics. We ought to compare U.S. performances with those of other superpowers, now and in the past. How would Rome...or the Egyptians of the 8th or 6th centuries BC, or Moscow *now* handle Managua? (Russel Baker says Rome would have marched down and whomped the bejeebers out of the Nicaraguans—I'd add as they did to Germans, including the ancestors of most of us in this room...)" 22.

11. Thomas Hobbes, *Leviathan,* ed. C. B. McPherson (New York: Penguin Books, 1968), 161, 187. For an excellent and readable survey of international politics theory, focused on the problem of war, which stresses the international environment as a central element of the problem see Kenneth N. Waltz, *Man, the State, and War* (New York: Columbia University Press, 1954).

12. Hobbes, 184-185.

13. To be sure, governments are very often agents which attempt to harm or exploit others, rather than agents which restrain it. When they are, they fail to be what government should be and there is no doubt about what the Christian response should be: to oppose and condemn the evil which government does and to seek to change that governmental evil. I believe that this is often the problem with which we are in reality confronted (e.g., U.S. policy in Central

America) and that we often fail to act so as to confront this evil. I favor, and practice, this kind of calling government to task for its sins, though I may have some quibbles with the methods some use in doing so. For the practical, pastoral teaching needed in the Mennonite world today this may be the primary message—be willing to see and confront the evils of governments, especially one's own. While that is an urgent problem on a practical level, it does not, I think, raise many difficult theoretical issues. The primary question is simply whether or not we will be willing to do what we ought to do. For this paper and this audience I have chosen to focus on what I think are the hard theoretical questions, but this should not be taken to mean that I believe the other issue is unimportant.

14. It is interesting in this connection to observe the parallelism between (and optimism of) Soviet and U.S. apologists. In attributing all of the world's ills to the other side, both groups imply that everything would be fine if they could just have a free hand to remake the world. I think both sides overlook their own tendencies to domination and exploitation—tendencies which are held in check at least in part by a relative balance of power.

15. Oyer, p. 23. To some degree we have become more aware of this need for power to balance power within the church and have worked harder in recent decades than in much of our earlier history at creating structures in which power is distributed widely (perhaps *too* widely for efficient operation). This principle of diverse power centers checking one another is also widely accepted in American political theory—including, I think, by Mennonites. It is ironic, in this context, that the view seems to be implicit (it is not explicit—perhaps this is a misreading on my part) in much Mennonite thought and writing on international issues that if only the U.S. would stop being belligerent (or stop building nuclear weapons, etc.) things could be turned around. Why a balance of power is not needed to restrain evil and exploitation on the international level (where the moral ties which bind groups together are weakest, ties which reduce the likelihood of exploitation and the level of coercion required to make life together possible) when it is needed in a national community and even in the church, is a mystery to me.

16. See especially *The Politics of Nonviolent Action.* Boston: Porter Sargent, 1973.

17. See Johansen's short proposal *Toward a Dependable Peace.* New York: Institute for World Order, 1978, for one

Peace. New York: Institute for World Order, 1978, for one example.

18.   While we have chosen an image that makes us sound more expendable than I perhaps really believe in order to emphasize the supportive or secondary role we play, it is only fair to note that I would disagree with those who might view me and others interested in politics as tonsils--often "red," inflamed, painful--a part which might best be cut out of the body!

19.   How far they can move into using "coercion" as they seek to work for justice is an issue on which much more work needs to be done.   I find interesting, but highly problematic, Ronald Sider's treatment of this issue in *Christ and Violence* (Scottdale, PA: Herald Press, 1979), chapter 2.   Duane Friesen moves in similar directions in *Christian Peacemaking and International Conflict* (Scottdale, PA: Herald Press, 1986).

20.   Adopted by the Mennonite Church and General Conference Mennonite Church, Bethlehem, Pennsylvania, 1983, 35.

21.   Adopted by the GCMC in 1971.

22.   Adopted March 1979, published in *Pastoral Messenger*, April, 1979, reprinted in John H. Yoder, *Christian Attitudes to War, Peace, and Revolution* (Elkhart, IN: Mennonite Cooperative Bookstore, 1983), 408.

23.   Yoder, *The Christian Witness to the State* (Newton, KS: Faith and Life Press, 1964), 66-73.

24.   I am surely aware of the fact that coercive or violent options do not always protect innocents either.   When they do not they should not be used.   I am also aware of the fact that many times violent options are used when nonviolent options are available which may work as well or better. When noncoercive or nonviolent alternatives are available they should of course be used.   All I contend here is that there are some cases, though many fewer than most people believe, where government coercion or violence may protect innocents and where nonviolent alternatives may fail to do so.

25.   It should be clear that I am here describing why the best of possible states may still need to use violence and in that context am locating the fundamental reason the state may need to use violence with the sinfulness of others.   I am, of course, keenly aware of the fact that states are often as much a source of unnecessary, sinful violence and exploitation as are other actors, that states are a source (probably the primary source) of exploitation and harm, not only (or even mainly in historical actuality) institutions which protect the innocent.   Again, however, this poses no ethical

problem in making a moral judgment concerning that kind of action by the state. It is simply and unambiguously wrong.

26. My thinking about this problem of how action can in one sense be called sinful and in another sense right has also pushed me to begin thinking more broadly about what I have come to think of as an ethical of fallenness. I would like to see Mennonites give more thought to this issue because I think often our ethics have been focused more on articulating what should be (in some full sense) than in helping us sort out what to do when the alternatives we face seem far removed from the norms we espouse. That is, how do we make ethical judgments in situations when the ethical vision we hold seems impossible to attain because of our past sins or mistakes—or perhaps because of factors over which we have had very little control? Perhaps a couple of examples will illustrate my concern. Suppose one has just become President of a Mennonite institution when reductions in enrollment force cutbacks which seem to require dismissing staff who have been promised continuing employment. What should one do? Or how does one think ethically about the breakup of a marriage—and act ethically (can one—in any sense?) in the midst of it?

27. *The Christian Witness to the State*, p. 72. Perhaps there is no disagreement, depending just how *agape* is defined. But if it means never using coercion or even always ruling out violence as an alternative I would disagree that it is the correct norm for the state in the historical period which Paul Ramsey has aptly labeled "not yet the plowshares."

28. If I am convinced of all this it might be asked why I do not simply reject pacifism and thereby be done with an untidy dualism. Part of the answer is suggested in my earlier comments about the centrality of the church. I will not burden you with the rest of the answer in this already burdensome paper!

29. I hope it is clear that in all of this I am not attempting an overarching understanding of the state and seeking to provide guidance in all of its activities. I am rather focusing on that aspect of the state, or government, which is most problematic from a Mennonite Christian ethical perspective and seeking to articulate a normative standard only for that aspect of the state's activity. That is, I surely see promotion of social justice and welfare, for example, as important parts of the state's role, but I do not see them as presenting the kinds of theoretical problems for understanding the state and its standards that arise when confronting the problem of violence used by the state in its

"ordering" function. I should also add that I think there are additional constraints on the kinds of violence that are "acceptable" even for the state, constraints laid out in the "just war" tradition. I will not address those additional constraints in this paper, but they are important in my total understanding of this matter.

30. I recognize, of course, that part of the reason for the greater "need" for violence in Boston may be due to the fact that the police there are perhaps often perpetrators or supporters of injustice. But I don't think that is the only reason. Perhaps another illustration will make this point. In Goshen there is a small, unused, fortified building on the corner by the courthouse. I was told it was built to defend against John Dillenger's bank robberies in the Midwest and for a time was manned by police with machine guns. When confronted with an "aggressor" such as Dillenger police in even a relatively tranquil town like Goshen may be forced to resort to greater threat of violence. I would also point out that the level of "coercion" needed to run Mennonite institutions also varies with the degree of "legitimacy" accorded to the "authorities" and the degree of "integration" of those within the institution. Threats of expulsion, etc., were not needed (presumably) 50 years ago at Goshen College to enforce rules against on-campus drinking (in fact, the rules were also probably not needed).

31. It might also be noted that there may be a significant difference in the level of coercion or violence needed to hold together different alliance systems. Although the NATO alliance is by no means a "voluntary association" in the sense that the church is (or should be) voluntary, it is probably true it relies less on U.S. military threats against NATO members to maintain its unity than the unity of the Warsaw Pact relies on Soviety military threats (and actions) against Warsaw Pact members. NATO relies more, I think, on deeply held common interests and values, thus enabling the U.S. to avoid stark threats of military force against members as a means of keeping them "in line." One of the problems of NATO currently, I think, is an increasing gap between the interests and values of the U.S. (at least as perceived and articulated by recent administrations) and those of other NATO members. If the gap continues to develop, the U.S. may find itself increasingly confronted with the need to "manhandle" its allies in Soviet fashion or to allow the alliance to disband.

A RE-ASSESSMENT OF SOME TRADITIONAL
ANABAPTIST CHURCH-STATE PERSPECTIVES

John H. Redekop

A. INTRODUCTION

There are doubtless many reasons why the Anabaptist branch of the Reformation has, on balance, remained small and relatively weak. A commonly assumed reason is the heavy demand which accompanies the acceptance of obedient discipleship. Persecution by larger branches also played a part as did the resulting dispersion and eventual defensiveness. To the extent that migrations transformed an indigenous religious group into an ethnic minority, the dispersion was doubly important. Of course, not all migration resulted from persecution. Some major migrations were triggered by economic considerations which at times were an expression of another widespread factor, namely, loss of conviction and commitment. Much of the ineffectiveness and retardation of the Anabaptist movement can be explained by the recurring collective waywardness.

While the above reasons were all important and widely accepted there is another reason which tends to be ignored. I have in mind the question of what we have generally posited as the essence of Anabaptism, especially in twentieth century North America. We have made much of church-state relations, often describing Anabaptism, mainly in those terms. By doing so, we have not only distorted the essentials of Anabaptism, but have probably also greatly impacted the otherwise natural growth of the phenomenon. This observation brings me to my central concern. *The general thesis of this paper is that the dominant twentieth century Anabaptist perspectives on church-state relations, especially in North America, have been inadequate.* The focus has been too narrow and the implied or stated significance of the state has loomed too large.

Certain assumptions should be stated unequivocally at the outset.

1. The doctrines of Anabaptism are rooted in the 1st, not 16th century. Conrad Grebel, Menno Simons, and their associates did not add to divine revelation. They rediscovered truths and applied them in new situations.

2. God created humankind to have a people who could
respond to God out of their own free will and with whom God
could have a relationship. In the evolution of God's interaction with humankind, this establishment of peoplehood,
whether focused on Eden, on Israel, or on the church, has
never hinged on church-state dynamics or tensions.

3. The church is the contemporary equivalent of the
People of Israel in the First Covenant Age. An affirmation
of this assumption, and the consequent acknowledgement of the
universal character of the church, provides an antidote to
the cult of state-bound or nation-bound Christian structures
and emphases.

4. The important Christian ethical issues are constant.
We need to emphasize that point lest we define ethical
dilemmas primarily with reference to recent or transient
social or political structures.

5. The notion of the believers' church is theologically
and logically antecedent to, and thus takes precedence over,
the notion of the peace church, or that of the suffering
church, or that of the love-permeated community. Figure 1
sets forth a schematic formulation of this idea. The emphasis is important because we need to be clear on the point
that what a church is, takes precedence over what it
encounters.

B. THE PROBLEM

Our basic problem is that our key Anabaptist norms have
been drawn largely from the 16th century without a thoroughgoing reinterpretation and re-application of those norms in
light of the changed situation in the 20th century. We
revise very reluctantly. We cling tenaciously to a 16th
century expression of theology as well as assumptions about
society.

We have tended to stress church-state structures and
functions, an approach which has some merit. But we must
also address the larger scene as well as acknowledge altered
reality. Some of us have drawn attention to new roles.[1]
Such emendation is useful but inadequate. We need to move
beyond the category of state, whether ecclesiastical,
imperial, dictatorial, democratic, negative, positive, wel-
faristic, or providing. The required agenda is much broader.
Even as we rethink and revise classical or medieval definitions and notions, we must remind ourselves that we are
refurbishing only one room in the house.

Let me state the question candidly. Why do contemporary

Figure 1   The Believers' Church —— A Perspective

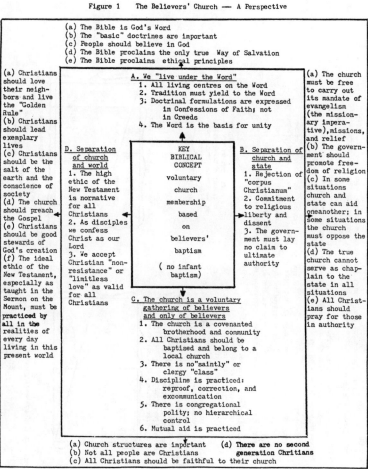

(a) The Bible is God's Word
(b) The "basic" doctrines are important
(c) People should believe in God
(d) The Bible proclaims the only true Way of Salvation
(e) The Bible proclaims ethical principles

(a) Christians should love their neighbors and live the "Golden Rule"
(b) Christians should lead exemplary lives
(c) Christians should be the salt of the earth and the conscience of society
(d) The church should preach the Gospel
(e) Christians should be good stewards of God's creation
(f) The ideal ethic of the New Testament, especially as taught in the Sermon on the Mount, must be practiced by all in the realities of every day living in this present world

A. We "live under the Word"
1. All living centres on the Word
2. Tradition must yield to the Word
3. Doctrinal formulations are expressed in Confessions of Faith; not in Creeds
4. The Word is the basis for unity

D. Separation of church and world
1. The high ethic of the New Testament is normative for all Christians
2. As disciples we confess Christ as our Lord
3. We accept Christian "non-resistance" or "limitless love" as valid for all Christians

KEY BIBLICAL CONCEPT
voluntary church membership based on believers' baptism (no infant baptism)

B. Separation of church and state
1. Rejection of "corpus Christianum"
2. Commitment to religious liberty and dissent
3. The government must lay no claim to ultimate authority

C. The church is a voluntary gathering of believers and only of believers
1. The church is a covenanted brotherhood and community
2. All Christians should be baptised and belong to a local church
3. There is no "saintly" or clergy "class"
4. Discipline is practiced: reproof, correction, and excommunication
5. There is congregational polity; no hierarchical control
6. Mutual aid is practiced

(a) The church must be free to carry out its mandate of evangelism (the missionary imperative), missions, and relief
(b) The government should promote freedom of religion
(c) In some situations church and state can aid one another; in some situations the church must oppose the state
(d) The true church cannot serve as chaplain to the state in all situations
(e) All Christians should pray for those in authority

(a) Church structures are important
(b) Not all people are Christians
(c) All Christians should be faithful to their church
(d) There are no second generation Chritians

NOTE: The centre is crucial and distinctive for the believers' church. A,B,C, and D follow logically, are normal traits of the believers' church, and are given much emphasis. (The numbered items are only illustrative). The illustrative items in the outer area, and some of the middle area items, are not unique to the believers' churches but tend to characterize all Christians.

© J.H.Redekop

Figure 2   State, Society, Political Systems

A. Liberal Democracy   B. Dictatorship

anarchy   modern   democratic

conservatism   liberalism   socialism

Key trait: lack of free and periodic elections

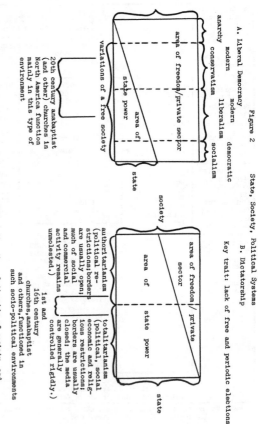

society

area of freedom/private sector

variations of a free society

area of
state power

area of
state

20th century anabaptist
(and other) churches in
North America function
mainly in this type of
environment

society

area of freedom / private
sector

area of
state power

state

authoritarianism   totalitarianism
(political re-   (political, social
strictions;borders   economic and relig-
are usually open;   ious restrictions;
much of social   borders are usually
and commercial   closed; the media
activity remains   are generally
unmolested.)   controlled rigidly.)

1st and
16th century
churches,anabaptist
and others,functioned in
such socio-political environments

Notes:

1. There are other ways of categorizing and depicting the relationship of society and
state. This one emphasizes freedom as the key variable.

2. In this context state power refers mainly to political and economic intervention.

3. Not all state intervention reduces the extent of freedom, individual or group. This
diagram suggests the general, overall effect.

4. This diagram is useful but it oversimplifies reality. While churches, especially
minority believers' churches, flourish best as the private sphere of freedom increases,
they can also flourish under dictatorships. Further, throughout history many church
movements have associated themselves with state power and have more or less served as
an arm of the state.

5. Generally speaking, the greater the degree of private sector freedom, the greater the
degree of believers' church opportunity, impact, and accountability.

Anabaptists stress church-state issues so extensively? (Almost 70% of my fairly extensive library of Anabaptist books and pamphlets deals with church-state, war and peace titles. It seems to be typical of numerous library collections.) I suggest that we stress what we stress because we are still caught up in the struggles and structures of the 16th century. We have had much difficulty separating theology from the historical struggles which were precipitated by the enunciation of that theology. We have been inclined to equate essence with arena, and the initial experience with the norm. The result has been a "backward" mindset and considerable frustration. It is therefore high time that we "rescue" Anabaptist doctrine and ethics from the lingering irrelevancy of a 16th century milieu.

It may be argued that Anabaptists need to be taken up with church-state issues because such issues were important for the Head of the church. Now it is true that Jesus had much to do with the state, indeed, state authorities "did him in." But Jesus had amazingly little to say about the state, particularly in comparison to what he had to say about religious leaders and the public generally. Admittedly, some of his followers wished it to be otherwise but his greatest tension was not with the state. In fact the novel, non-resistant, love ethic had very little to do with the state and nothing to do with military service at that time. Jesus' Jewish audiences had no role in governance and were not permitted to serve in the military. Whatever those audiences, or Jesus for that matter, had in mind when the love ethic was enunciated, the concern was not how one should respond to the matter of military service. The hearers--men, women, and children--were hearing a practical ethic that was relevant to all of them in all walks of life. In other words, Jesus was instructing his disciples and other followers how to live in society, not how to relate to government. That distinction holds true despite the fact that in Jesus' imperial and totalitarian setting the differentiation between state and society was both limited and arbitrary. (See Figure 2)

It is sometimes argued that Paul developed certain Christian imperatives more completely. That is doubtless true in many respects, but concerning church-state relations, Paul elaborated rather than extended, even in Romans 12 and 13. Given his Greek background Paul was familiar with the complexities of citizenship roles, but time and again, in explaining the important issues in the Christian life, he chose not to dwell on them. In line with Jesus' emphasis, he also stressed living in the brotherhood and in society.

If the major part of our problem is that we are still preoccupied with a 16th century agenda, then the second part is that this "major part" is not acknowledged, let alone understood, by most contemporary Anabaptists.

C. AN EXPLANATION OF THE PROBLEM

In the 16th century the incipient development of the modern state system and a reassertion of princely power, albeit within a framework of ecclesiastical rivalry--not much had changed since Cannosa--made church-state relations a top agenda item for both mainline and radical reformers. The authorities whom the radical reformers defied were both civil and religious. Conrad Grebel, Menno Simons and their followers could not avoid becoming enmeshed in church-state issues. And, of course, the more popular, but less thorough, reformers had no intention of abandoning the fusion of church and state. The only difference on this score among Luther, Zwingli, Calvin and the rest was how that interrelationship was to be expressed. State religion and conflicts over state religion permeated life. Therefore the early Anabaptists said and wrote much on the topic. Small wonder, then, that Anabaptism came to be perceived, alongside Catholic fusion, Lutheran dualism, and Calvinist theocracy as one of the major options concerning church-state relations.[2] Given the subsequent era of church-state warfare in Europe, the battles over the options, literal and verbal, persisted.

The European preoccupation with church-state relations was exported to the New World. In New France it took firm root with the result that for three and a half centuries that region remained a bulwark of ultra-montagne Catholic church-state fusion and conservatism. Since there was no Anabaptist presence in New France/Quebec during those centuries, and since there were no important church-state struggles, the matter is of little consequence for our purpose. In the diverse English-speaking colonies, the situation was more complex. Not only were many of the colonies in constant turmoil over church-state issues, but also, in Pennsylvania and subsequently elsewhere, large numbers of Anabaptists were caught up in the disputes and struggles.

The American Revolutionary war gelled the U.S. mindset. Although the immediate catalyst was taxation policy, the larger issue revolved around freedom and quasi-absolutism. In the rubric of freedom, guarantees involving religious liberty and the prevention of the establishment of religion were central. That agenda persisted. Throughout the past two centuries U.S. legislatures and courts have repeatedly, almost constantly, dealt with issues of church and state. Two strands of thought, related yet almost contradictory, developed simultaneously. To ensure liberty for all, there was to be a "wall of separation" between church and state. But a "lowest common denominator" quasi-Christian civil religion also developed, one which to this day makes the election of an atheist or even a Jewish person as president inconceivable.

For American Anabaptists these developments were very important. The national debates over church and state seemed to parallel, even overlap, their own questions. The emphasis on a supposed "wall of separation" suggested notions of a separate people, even though the only common element is the word itself. And for some, especially in later years, the idea of Christian-Americanism somehow legitimized their often vicarious involvement in the national debates. Thus it came about that in the United States, the locus of the great 20th century Anabaptist Renaissance, issues involving church-state relations have remained important, if not central, for Anabaptists. Cold War confrontation with atheistic and dictatorial communism has also helped to perpetuate agendas as well as to blur distinctions. The atheism reinforced notions of Christian-Americanism and the spreading Soviet dictatorship made court decisions about religious and other freedoms seem all the more important.

Although Canadians did not develop an indigenous notion of Christian-Canadianism nor a doctrine about a "wall of separation", the American norms have had increasing influence north of the border. Accordingly, Canadians are generally familiar with the arguments and sympathetic with the rationales. To date Canadian Anabaptism has not developed a distinct perspective.

In summarizing these developments from the 16th to the 20th century the following assessments seem warranted. It is understandable, maybe even logical, for the Catholic and mainline Protestant churches to be preoccupied with church-state relations. After all, they have generally sought to establish and perpetuate state religion or at least favored treatment, both in Europe and in the New World. Only secularization has seriously modified those proclivities. For Anabaptists, however, there was no similar rationale or theology to explain the heavy emphasis on church-state concerns. Aside from wartime problems, the explanation must lie in the preoccupation with the 16th century and in the rather

uncritical acceptance of categories and tensions from mainline religion and from secular authorities.

D. SOME PRACTICAL CONSEQUENCES OF DOMINANT
    TRADITIONAL VIEWS

One of the important consequences of emphasizing the
church-state relationship as a central, if not integrating
concern of Anabaptism is that we tend to use it as a starting
point or reference point for other ethical considerations. A
recent book by the seminal Anabaptist theologian, John Howard
Yoder, illustrates the point. The opening sentence of *What
Would You Do?*, a book which deals with the question of how
individuals react to violence, reads, "Sooner or later, in
almost any serious discussion about peace and war, someone
is sure to ask that standard question: 'What would you do if
a criminal, say, pulled a gun and threatened to kill your
wife....'"[3] The reference to peace and war is significant.
One wonders if Jesus would have cast the question that way
or whether he would have referred to a neighbor or a
stranger.

Of course, church-state relations are significant and it
is important that we understand our situation. J. H. Yoder
and other writers have helped us to that end. Yoder's *The
Christian Witness to the State* stands as a convincing
explanation.[4] So do several of his other books interestingly
entitled, *The Politics of Jesus*[5] and *The Original Revolution*.[6]
Americans, in particular, understand the nuances in such
titles. The title of Guy F. Hershberger's seminal work suggests a similar mindset: *War, Peace, and Non-resistance*.[7]
But a church-state or even a political focus is too narrow,
too confining. It is only one aspect of a more encompassing
"way of the cross." It is one of the fruits, not the root.

Let us reflect on some specific inadequacies resulting
from an emphais on the church-state, or even the more
broadly political, aspects of Anabaptist thought.

1. The tendency towards an emphasis on structures
rather than relationships.

2. The tendency to apply principles of justice and
reconciliation too much in one area government. There are
reasons for this state of affairs. A major one is that the
state has harassed and persecuted the faithful church in various countries for centuries. But that fact does not mean
that we should recast and narrow the thrust of the Gospel to
suit our purpose.

3. The tendency to apply one standard to government and

another to the rest of society. Thus many Anabaptists get all worked up over war taxes but seem to overlook funds misused just as badly in the private sector. Why not focus on the breweries and distilleries instead? Many more people are killed and maimed on our highways each year by drunken drivers than die in military service or become "enemy" casualties.

4. The tendency to distort God's call to repentance, conversion, and discipleship. A tendency to suggest that church-state issues are more important than they actually are.

5. The tendency, largely unintentional, to suggest that Anabaptists have an alternate Christian prescription for political action and church-state relations and problems generally.

6. The tendency to describe separateness in political terms. Some, perhaps much, of our discussion of what it means to be a separate people sounds disquietingly similar to the niceties of constitutional jurisprudence. We need to remember that to be a separate people is not a political experience.

7. The tendency to have peace conferences only in wartime, or when war threatens, and mainly for men. Does the way of peace apply only to adult males who are healthy?

8. The tendency to allow the Christian peace stance to degenerate into a secular prescription for peace as opposed to war. Clearly there is an overlap. We need to address war and peace just as we must address other social issues. In our day, with a nuclear holocaust threatening, it probably is the most important social issue. A radical Christian answer is an essential consequence of an Anabaptist commitment but it is not the essence of Anabaptism. Therefore we should not suggest that political peace was primarily in mind when Jesus was described as the Prince of Peace. Peace among humankind is not synonymous with peace with God.

9. The tendency to assume that all of humankind has experienced politics. What about the primitive Innuit, Apaches, or Maoris who had no specialized political structures? Does the full Anabaptist message not apply to them?

10. The tendency to think that we are being faithful when we are not. Opposing the evil in government, or of government for that matter, is not necessarily Christian. When it is Christian, it is fruit not root.

If this preoccupation with church-state affairs is inadequate for what it does, then it is equally inadequate for what it fails to do. Specifically it tends to ignore or minimize private sector evils and problems involving labor-management, taxpayer-welfare recipient, landlord-tenant, and many other relationships. Problems such as racism, exploitation, ecological desecration, and media pollution also need to be addressed.

We need to remind ourselves that however important church-state problems are, they are not part and parcel of the Anabaptist message and must not persist as an over-arching concern. A peculiar church-state stance is not the key distinguishing trait of Anabaptists.

There was not always a state system. Throughout much of human history most people have not lived in states. State is a subcategory of world. Paul's reference to powers of this world, rather than of the state, is noteworthy (Eph 6:12). The central issue all along has been church-world or, more accurately, God's people versus society.

The overall consequence of a preoccupation with church-state affairs has been a constraint of our peace witness in time, in scope of relevance, in arenas of participation, in breadth (age and gender) of Christian accountability, and in extent of impact. The inadequacy is beginning to be remedied; a more basic conceptual correction is needed.

E. THE URGENCY OF COURSE CORRECTION

A number of factors make a thoroughgoing "correction" in Anabaptist emphases, especially in North America, important; the situation is urgent.

1. The traditional manifestations of the state are undergoing change. The distinction between civilian and military is becoming blurred as is the difference between governmental and private sector.

2. Some traditional, especially some institutional, manifestations of the church are being superceded.

3. We are becoming part of the state: in education, in business, in the bureaucracy, in many professions, as tax-payers, as researchers, as citizens, indeed, even as the loyal opposition, at least in those polities with a British parliamentary system. We have become part of that which we have criticized. Boundaries are vanishing. To a considerable degree, at least in some polities, the military has been demilitarized, the political has been depoliticized, and the imperialistic has been sanitized. At issue is not just the increasing Anabaptist participation in the political arena, although that is an important political agenda in its own right, but the politicization of society, both as a whole

and in many of its supposedly voluntaristic parts. For most contemporary political jurisdictions the traditional dichotomy is passè.

4. We are beset by a raft of new ethical dilemmas--from broken homes to bankruptcies--which do not involve the state.

5. Increasing numbers of North American Anabaptists are being taken in by nationalistic Christian fundamentalism and need to be reminded that there are ethical considerations beyond church-state affairs which warn against wrongful compromises in such affairs. Uncivilized civil religion requires counteraction.

6. The modern state is not the only large actual or potential oppressor. Multi-national corporations and cartels, immense labor organizations, and transnational terrorist groups, to name three, are equally important structures warranting a critique. A church-state orientation is therefore too simplistic.

If we do not address these matters with greater clarity, then, as the modern state becomes more pervasive, more interventionist, and simply larger, an inadequate Anabaptist church-state emphasis may seem, to many, to be correct.

F. POSSIBLE MEANS OF COURSE CORRECTION

We need to advance on several fronts.

1. We must remind ourselves and all who will hear that consistent Anabaptists are not so much participants in church-state tensions and confrontations as an alternative community.

2. We need to remind ourselves that the modern democratic state is profoundly different from the dictatorial states experienced by the early church in the 1st century and Anabaptist reformers in the 16th; it provides vastly more opportunities to witness in and to it, as well as to society in general, and therefore, even as society becomes politicized, we are much more accountable. (See figure 2)

3. We need to emphasize that the starting point for Anabaptism is God's desire to establish a people and that an informed and discipled believers' church is the expression of such peoplehood. The parameters of this emphasis are far-reaching. It means that in describing the environment in which God's people are shaped, challenged, tempted, and in which they serve, grow, and witness, we shift from state to society. For it is primarily in society that we encounter

the ethical questions that perplex us, the tensions over
which we agonize, and the opportunities that await us.
In times past we had peace conferences that often reinforced unfortunate cleavages and sent a distorted message.
Adult males, in the main, met to discuss how adult males
could practice nonresistance. God's "people" does not consist only of adult males nor is the message of love mainly
related to war and peace. We need conferences, as well as
other approaches, that challenge and instruct men, women, and
young people to be separated people of God in society. The
question of military involvement thus becomes one of many
and not necessarily the most important. Peoplehood is primary; it is antecedent to all else. It is open to all of
God's people, it requires the involvement of all of God's
people. By consciously shifting our focus from state to
society we should quite naturally be able to eliminate the
traditional gender bias of the Anabaptist nonresistance distinctive. The love and peace in society applies equally to
all who constitute the peoplehood. A further associated
benefit would be less perception of the church as paralleling
political boundaries.
    4. We need to remind one another of the importance of
process in shaping peoplehood. The group, or a part thereof,
is the counselling and reference point for all. The process,
the dynamics of developing peoplehood, works to counteract
individualism, to eliminate alienation, to replace self-
sufficiency with the higher ethic of mutual servanthood, and
to permit each to benefit from the insight of all. As long
as we are preoccupied with the state as our arena of development, the concept of peoplehood will remain misshapen and
its achievement unnecessarily difficult.
    5. Once we have emphasized that the primary focus for
implementing Jesus' ethic is society, a category which covers
all parts of the earth and all of history, we must stress
that Anabaptism is as relevant for an urban as for a rural
setting. We have been relatively, but only relatively, successful in describing and achieving separated peoplehood in
rural situations. But the gospel was not given only for
rural folk. The early churches were city churches. With a
recovery of the emphasis on society rather than state, and on
the involvement of all, urban formation of peoplehood should
become less difficult.
    6. We need to emphasize the primacy of distinctions
between moralities over distinctions between structures. The
two moralities, of course, are the Christian and the sub-
Christian. State morality, because of its ultimate monopoly

concerning life and death issues, is in some respects unique, but it is still part and parcel of the sub-Christian, society-wide, ethic.

7. Because of the blurring of boundaries and the partial transformation of categories as described earlier, we need to modify, if not abandon, a simple two-kingdon mindset. Thus the new agenda should not so much stress what church and state should do, or what church and society should do, but what the two are becoming.

8. We must come to see that the refusal to pay war taxes, for example, deals more with symptoms than with substance. It may well be a commendable reaction to irresponsible militarism, but a refusal to pay a tax for a tobacco subsidy or a grant to breweries and distilleries would be equally commendable.

9. Given the fact that our reference point is God's desire to relate to a committed people, Anabaptists should probably re-emphasize the notion of purity of peoplehood. That means, for example, addressing the issue of Christian-unbeliever marriages. Such concerns are important to God-- maybe more important than church-state concerns. They were already very important in Old Testament times. From Genesis to Revelation such concerns far outnumber any references to the way in which God's people should relate to the state.

In developing these nine corrective emphases and undertakings two points must be kept in mind. First, we do not reject the excellent contributions of our leaders, teachers and prophets who have done much to rekindle an interest in Anabaptism and who have done a masterful job of addressing church-state issues. We build on what has been done. Second, we must be open to different, even more radical, correctives than have been mentioned in this paper.

G. CONCLUSION

This paper has asserted that the main arena of Christian ethics, as enunciated in the 1st century and rediscovered in the 16th, is not church-state interaction but church-society interaction. It has suggested further that the primary Anabaptist concern should be to function as a people of God, a believers' church. We have reviewed the historical development of an over-emphasis on church-state relations and spelled out some means of correcting that situation.

If the thesis of this paper is valid and if the suggested corrections prove effective, then we will become more similar to the early church, a church in which the "way of the cross," as discipleship and peoplehood, applied to all Christians and was immediately relevant for all.

NOTES

1. *See John H. Redekop, "The State and the Free Church,"* in *J. R. Burkholder and C. Redekop, eds., Kingdom, Cross and Community* (Scottdale, PA: Herald Press, 1976), 179-195.

2. See Thomas G. Sanders, *Protestant Concepts of Church and State* (New York: Holt, Rinehart and Winston, 1964).

3. John Howard Yoder, *What Would You Do?* (Scottdale, PA: Herald Press, 1983), 13.

4. John Howard Yoder, *The Christian Witness to the State* (Newton, KS: Faith and Life Press, 1964).

5. John Howard Yoder, *The Politics of Jesus* (Grand Rapids, MI: Eerdmans, 1972).

6. John Howard Yoder, *The Original Revolution* (Scottdale, PA: Herald Press, 1971).

7. Guy F. Hershberger, *War, Peace and Nonresistance,* third edition (Scottdale, PA: Herald Press, 1969).

POWER: AN ETHICAL ANALYSIS FROM A
CHRISTIAN PERSPECTIVE*

Duane Friesen

I. Introduction

Before we can assess power from an ethical standpoint we must determine what we mean by power. Definitions of power are shaped by the particular academic discipline using the term. There is a significant difference in approach, for example, between Paul Ramsey's discussion of power in *The Just War*, Rollo May's psychological approach in *Power and Innocence*, and Karl Deutsch's discussion in *The Analysis of International Relations*. One method we could use would be to define one kind of power (political power, for example), and then ethically reflect upon that kind of power without claiming to speak to the whole range of types of power. The other approach is to try to penetrate deeper behind the various particular definitions of power to get at root meanings. One here risks the danger of generalizing from what is in fact particular. However, I prefer this approach for two reasons: 1) One of the purposes of the discipline of theological ethics is precisely to help us reflect on the entire range of the experience of power in terms of a view of God and human responsibility; 2) The focus upon power in one arena (politics) can make us blind to equally important ethical issues of power in other arenas (church, school, family). It is easy to critique abuses of power in realms more distant from us, not noting the dilemmas of power we face as parents, teachers, administrators, pastors, etc. (See Appendix for a summary of levels of power in human relations.)

II. A Theological Perspective on Power

I want to begin by claiming that power is the creative and positive force which defines our humanity as made in the image of God. From God we receive our power of being, which is a creative power to be co-creators with God. This power is expressed in the creation of culture, in institutional life

*Significant portions of this paper were taken from three different chapters in a to be published book by the author entitled: *Christian Peacemaking and International Conflict: A Realist Pacifist Perspective*. The book has since been published by Herald Press, Spring, 1986.

where the central feature of human activity is social interaction which involves us continuously in relationships of
power.

If I were to approach power in a typical Mennonite way, I
would treat power as a "problem" of the "world." We would
begin with a dichotomy between love and power, and reflect,
using the categories of Reinhold Niebuhr, on how we should
live with the tension that exists between the Christian ideal
of love and the reality of power in the world. I think this
Niebuhrian approach leads us to a dead end for two reasons:
1) because it begins with a false dichotomy between love and
power, and 2) because it understands power too narrowly and
too negatively. Thus I will begin at a very different point.

We begin with the affirmation that human beings are
social animals. We find our meaning and value not in isolation, but in relationship to each other. This emphasis is
expressed symbolically in the man-woman relationship of the
Genesis creation stories. Human sociality serves no mere
instrumental purpose. Man and woman are called to partnership, to be co-workers, to depend upon and care for each
other.

This co-humanity is even linked with the image of God.
"So God created man in his own image; in the image of God he
created him; male and female he created them" (Gen. 1:27-28).
We become who we are in social interaction, and it is this
relational quality of human life that is itself a reflection
of the nature of God.

Human sociality is made possible by our capacity to
create symbols and interact socially through speech. The
human symbolic capacity is what above all gives us our special place in creation. This symbolic capacity enables
humans to create culture, to create social institutions which
enable human beings to give order to human life. Other
animals do not create culture or institutions. The patterns
of life they need to survive are either programmed into them
genetically or learned directly from other animals they
imitate. Human symbolic capacity enables us to delineate
patterns of behavior into symbolic forms, in various forms of
speech, writing, diagrams, plans, system of rules that can be
transferred from one geographical location to another and
from one time period to the next without anyone ever directly
observing the behavior. The symbol "represents" the behavior
pattern. This symbolic capacity enables human beings to be
creators of culture, for symbols enable humans to bind time--
to remember and be affected by a past we may not have even
experienced and to project ourselves into the future by

imagining alternatives not yet in existence. This capacity to "represent" through symbols to ourselves a plan for future behavior which we have not yet acted out nor has been acted out in the past makes possible human culture and human institutional life. In coordination with other persons, human beings can visualize, plan and then act to create something new in the universe. For example, an architect can "represent" on paper a building. The architectural plan is not the building itself, but it can tell a builder what to do even though he has never seen a building like it before. A group of people can imagine or visualize a way to organize themselves in order to get a task accomplished. They do not need to have experienced such behavior before they can go out and act on the basis of a mental model or image of the future.

As creators of culture and of human social institutions, human beings reflect the image of God in them. They are co-creators with God. They literally construct their world. In this sense human beings are empowered by the very power of God. God makes available to humans the power to transform the world. They are placed by God in a world that is still in the process of formation. As partners with God, as beings created in the likeness of God, they are given the task of being co-creators with God.

Human social and cultural life develops over the process of time. According to Ashey Montague, "As the forms of life grow more complex, the weight of the power to adapt to circumstances, which eventually becomes conscious thought, grows also, and eventually outweighs the power of instincts, until finally, in human beings, instincts count for little behavior if any, and thinking and learning for almost all of it."[1] Thinking and learning in human beings makes us distinctively historical and cultural beings.

The more we are defined by history and culture, the more necessary it is for us to cooperate and coordinate our efforts. It is reasonable to assume that rudimentary forms of political behavior emerge simultaneously or parallel with the development of human social behavior. To say that humans are created as social beings with language as their distinctive mark is at the same time to think of humans as political beings. As beings create culture, which becomes more and more complex over time, the planning, organization and coordination of social behavior becomes more and more central to human life. Political behavior is, then, an essential component of God's creation of human beings. In other words, the coordination, structuring and organization of human

social life for the sake of human survival and human
creativity is an essential component of what it means to be
human.

Human sociality is expressed not simply through I-Thou
relationships of two people or the "Gemeinschaftlich" relationships of small groups where people know each other face
to face, but it is also expressed through and in the context
of patterned institutional relationships. Persons perform
functions, play roles as part of a larger cooperative human
effort. The more complex this organized human effort
becomes, the more explicit and self-conscious becomes the
organization of social behavior. Eventually certain persons
take on defined roles of leadership, coordination and organization.

To be human, then, means to be acted upon by others, to
be pressed to conform to patterns of behavior and speech.
One takes on the patterns of others--the language, habits,
attitudes, metaphors, rituals, and gestures. To become
socialized means to have one's behavior "ordered" so that it
is coordinated and patterned to fit into the group as a
whole. In this sense, behavior is "determined." From this
perspective coercion is an aspect of being a social animal,
and is not entirely a negative or sinful aspect of social
life. The word "coerce" comes from the Latin root "co" and
"arcere" which means "to shut up" or "to press together." To
be social means to be pressed together, shaped, structured,
patterned into behavior that coordinates with others.

The previous analysis provides a point of view that
enables us to avoid misconceptions about social life that
have been held by pacifists and non-pacifists alike. Coercion is an inherent component of social life, and should not
be assumed to be necessarily a violation of the good.

A theology of creation which has not thought through
what it means for humans to be social animals believes that
the "ideal" is the anarchist "golden age" of spontaneous
harmony. Love is often defined as a completely spontaneous
harmony between human beings. This view fails to recognize
that social life entails roles, structure and organization.
An anarchist view is anti-institutional, and can provide no
real basis for a theology of power. To long for a "golden
age" where human social life is spontaneously harmonized,
where all relationships between human beings can be face to
face, I-Thou relationships, is essentially an asocial view of
human life. Frequently Jesus is defined as one who spoke
primarily to one-to-one relationships. This view of Jesus
arises out of an anarchist definition of love that is essen-

tially an asocial view of human life. But if we are social beings, we are called to a task, to order our lives through institutions. This is absolutely essential, for example, to the task of the peacemaker who must create institutions which can solve human problems of conflict and injustice. This means, too, that politics is not to be understood only as in institution of the fall. If we take Karl Deutsch's definition of politics, "the more or less incomplete control of human behavior through voluntary habits of compliance in combination with threats of probable enforcement,"[2] we are not describing a different, more corrupt, form of social behavior different in kind from other social behavior. Deutsch's definition simply recognizes both the voluntary and coercive element inherent in all social behavior.

Another source of confusion is a result of the dichotomy we draw between freedom and determinism, between autonomy and heteronomy as if these were two realities fundamentally opposed and contradictory to each other. Consequently, if one is to be free, (i.e. completely uncoerced) one must conclude that all forms of coercion are bad, an indication of human sinfulness. Again this confusion arises because of the failure to understand ourselves as social and thus historical beings. As Gordon Kaufman put it:

> On the one hand, freedom involves predetermination: by decision we mean precisely a movement in the present moment through which the future course of events will be determined... If a father's decision did not significantly shape the future of his son, in what sense would he be free with reference to his son? ... On the other hand, predetermination involves freedom. To 'determine' (cf. 'terminate') means to set limits; to predetermine is to set limits prior to the event. Predetermination thus presupposes the power to anticipate an event and to set certain bounds within which it will occur. But such power significantly to bind the future is precisely what is meant by freedom.[3]

To be human, then, also means to be free, to be able to shape the future through decisions one makes in the present. Thus politics which denies this side of human sociality, is a violation of what it means for humans to be created as social beings. When politics operates so as to destroy that human capacity, then we have a politics of the Fall. This coercion turns into a violation of the meaning of being human, and politics becomes "violent." The doctrine of creation affirms the truth of the polarity that we are social beings pressed

into (coerced) patterned, structured behavior, and at the same
time free to create, shape and modify this same environment.
Power in this framework is the capacity to effect
results, or as Rollo May puts it, the capacity to effect or
prevent change.[4] As social beings we continuously experience a field of forces acting upon us. We seek to influence,
persuade, move others, as we respond, react, resist the movement of others upon us. Force and counterforce is the stuff
of social life--parents and children, husbands and wives,
teachers and students, employer and employees, nations toward
each other, corporations and consumers, business competitors,
pastor and congregation. Power is essential to life. To be
without power is death. To be powerless is to become less
than fully human. To strip persons of their power is to
dehumanize them, which is what prisons literally do to people
since they fundamentally restrict a person's capacity to
effect or prevent change. Thus we can turn Lord Acton's
statement on its head. Lack of power tends to corrupt.
Absolute lack of power corrupts absolutely.

But this discussion of power is incomplete from a
theological perspective. The human exercise of power is
corrupted by sin. Socially legitimate expressions of power
are turned into patterns of exploitation and violence.
Institutions intended to serve the good of human beings
become destructive powers in human life. In the language of
the New Testament, the powers that have been created in
God's image become principalities and powers which place
humans in slavery and bondage to them.

The purpose of Christ is free persons from bondage to
these powers so they can live in a new community (the church)
where power is again exercised as God intended it in the
world as created by God. In Christ, for example, human
beings are no longer in bondage to the division of male and
female (sexism), the divisions of Jew and Greek (eth-
nocentrism or nationalism), or the divisions of slave and free
(patterns of exploitation and class conflict) (Gal 3:28).[5]

Christ's lordship over the principalities and powers not
only frees persons from bondage to the powers, but the
church, both corporately and through its individual members,
is set free to contribute toward the restructuring of these
powers. In the midst of the principalities and powers the
church should make its witness, a witness which brings both
critical judgment upon the failure of the powers to serve
humane purposes and a creative contribution to the structure
of social and cultural life. In other words Christians
become creators of culture after the image of God, but now on

the basis of their new creation in Christ. The Christian position is thus neither total acceptance nor total rejection of the social structures, but the Christian approaches these structures with a discriminating ethic. Sometimes Christians may find that they can cooperate with institutions. Other times they can expect to face difficulty and conflict which may require that they bear the cross of suffering and perhaps even death. We must, however, keep the cross in perspective. The cross arises out of conflict with the powers in the midst of the goal to seek the welfare of the *polis*. The cross itself arises out of the prior motivation of compassion, a compassion which leads Christians to seek liberation, justice, and wholeness for fellow human beings. Though Christians must be prepared for the cross (the cost of discipleship must be counted), the goal of their action is the reestablishment of friendship among fellow human beings, a friendship which is righteous and just.

Serious distortions of the gospel can result if the cross is not viewed as a consequence of compassion for the welfare of the *polis*. The one distortion is pacifistic withdrawal and the other is the violence of fanatical confrontation. For example, the position of some Mennonites of withdrawal form the world results from an ethic of suffering without a corresponding compassion for the world. Christians also often commit the error of relating to the powers with the violence of fanatical confrontation. It is easy to slip into messianic delusions without the servanthood spirit of Christ, because it is extremely difficult to remain compassionate as one confronts the injustice, self-interest, and status quo defensiveness of the powers that be. The temptation to strike out with hate, to expose and humiliate the opponent is great. When that happens, the opposition can only respond defensively, with stronger opposition. This produces and even greater self-righteous contempt for one's opponent.

The Christian who is genuinely interested in liberation, for both oppressor and oppressed, seeks to create space for the opponent to respond creatively. The ultimate purpose for confronting the powers is to create space for change, so that the enmity can be broken down and friendship based on justice can be established. Jesus' encounter with Zacchaeus must have done that. Both Gandhi and Martin L. King, who ultimately fought for reconciliation and friendship with the opponent, demonstrated a remarkable capacity for patience and flexibility so that the opponent could respond creatively.

III. Power and the Social Process.

James Luther Adams defines this creative use of power as:

> the capacity to participate in the shaping of social decision. Its sphere of operation may be in the family or the small group; it may extend to the larger groups of the church or the professions or industry; it may embrace the total community, the government and the nations. Power in this context is the capacity to participate in creative controversy -- in short, to change the profile of participation. As such it is the principal freedom available to men. But it is a freedom that requires organization. The history of freedom (and of unfreedom) is largely the history of effective organization. Not that the individual is insignificant, but rather that if his contribution is to make an impact upon communal decision, it will require organization. Otherwise, the individual (so far as public affairs are concerned) will remain socially uncreative; he will remain a eunuch. Power, then, as we understand it here, is the ability to make oneself heard, the capacity to cause others to take one's concerns seriously. It is the capacity to make one's concerns felt as "an impact in the communal decision-making process." It is also the capacity to listen. It is the capacity to respond creatively to others, to the needs of others. In all of these dimensions power engenders conflict, for in crucial matters of public policy one encounters competition for a share in power.[6]

As Adams suggests, then, power involves two dimensions: (a) the ability to *produce an effect,* i.e. to bring something onto being or to maintain what has been actualized against the threat of non-being; and (b) *the ability to undergo an effect,* to be open and receptive to knowledge or to someone's request or need, to be able to adapt to one's environment. An analogy from football is perhaps helpful. A lineman in professional football needs to weigh at least 250 pounds to be able to move an opposing force. The quarterback is effective, however, by his ability to "read" the defense and respond accordingly. Definitions of political power often build only on the first aspect of power. Max Weber defines "power (*macht*) as the probability that one actor within a social relationship will be in a position *to carry out his own will despite resistance,* regardless of the basis on which this probability exists."[7]   Hans Morgenthau says: "When we speak of power, we mean man's control over the minds and actions of other men.   By political power we refer to the mutual relations of control among the holders of public authority and between the latter and the people at large."[8]

These definitions of Weber and Morgenthau tend to equate power and violence, since one basic meaning of holding public office is that those in authority have control over the instruments of force.   But this is surely not a sufficient definition of political power.   Control over the minds and actions of human beings may in exceptional cases be accomplished by brute force, but that only can happen if the people who are controlled allow that to happen.   A political system is not able to last very long if it does not gain a basic compliance by those it seeks to control.   It cannot do this unless the large numbers of people a political system controls see to a large extent the political system as "beneficial" to them, or at least as sufficiently beneficial that it does not pay to resist.   Even the most brutal system must be somewhat responsive to the needs of those it seeks to control.   A political system cannot achieve control over people if it is not fundamentally responsive to those it seeks to control.   According to Karl Deutsch "the voluntary or habitual compliance of the mass of the population is the invisible but very real basis of the power of every government."[9]

This leads me then to suggest a very different understanding of political power than that advanced by Morgenthau.   Instead of defining power as dominance or control over others by the holders of public authority, power can more appropriately be defined as the ability of groups and persons from below to shape and control their environment.   This does not mean that people in key positions of public authority do not also have power.   As individuals they have significantly more power than ordinary individuals not in public office.   But their power is often overestimated when one considers the potential collective power of ordinary people when that is organized.   It is the organization of the masses into collective power that underlies nonviolent social action, and explains why it can often be effective even against physical violence.   Gene Sharp views the power of nonviolence as twofold: (1) residing in a people's capacity to do what they are not expected or required to do; and (2) their withholding consent from what they are supposed to do.   Governments depend on habits of compliance by people.   Their power is pluralistic and fragile because governments depend on many sources for reinforcement.[10]

The organization of people to do what they are not supposed to do, or not to do what they are expected to do, involves the deliberate creation of controversy in order to shape social decision. Such use of power is effective because of both the stubbornness and willingness to persist despite obstacles in its way, and the ability to adapt and respond imaginatively to circumstances as they occur. Both Gandhi and M. L. King were masters at integrating these two dimensions. King had both the stamina to carry through in the long struggle in Birmingham and at the same time to modify strategy in the short run in view of changing circumstances in the mayoral race in the city. Since the exercise of political power depends to a degree on the consent of the governed, people can by withdrawing that consent control and even destroy an opponent's power by nonviolent means, even when that opponent's power is exercised in an extremely repressive and violent way. Nonviolent action is a technique of struggle. It assumes the opponent will resist, and that those who employ nonviolence must expect suffering and loss. A common misconception of nonviolence is that it presupposes the inherent goodness of people. Rather, as Martin L. King puts it, in his book, *Why We Can't Wait*, "We know through painful experience that freedom is never voluntarily given by the oppressor; it must be demanded by the oppressed." He draws upon Reinhold Niebuhr's insight in *Moral Man and Immoral Society* that privileged groups seldom give up their privileges voluntarily. Individuals may tend to act morally, but groups tend to operate more out of self-interest and tend to be more immoral.[11] Pressure must be brought to bear upon privileged groups so that change will take place.

Why and how nonviolent action works is based on the concept of asymmetrical actions according to Sharp:

> The use of nonviolent means against violent repression creates a special asymmetrical, conflict situation, in which the two groups rely on contrasting techniques of struggle or weapons systems. To have the best chance of success, the nonviolent actionists must stick with their chosen technique. An extensive, determined and skillful application of nonviolent action will cause the opponent very special problems, which will disturb or frustrate the effective utilization of his own forces. The actionists will then be able to apply something like jiujitsu to their opponent, throwing him off balance politically, causing his repression to

rebound against his position, and weakening his power.
. . The nonviolent actionists deliberately refuse to
challenge the opponent on his own level of violence.
Violence against violence is reinforcing. The nonviolent group not only does not need to use violence,
but they must not do so lest they strengthen their
opponent and weaken themselves.[12]
We do not have time to go further into Sharp's extensive
elaboration of the nature of this nonviolent weapons system
and the dynamics of nonviolent change.

IV.   Ethical Criteria in the Use of Power.

Because expressions of power are corrupted by sin, we
must carefully discern how power can be exercised in the
world by Christians in a way consistent with the spirit of
Christ's liberation of persons from the power of sin so as to
restore them to their God intended purpose. What we need to
do is develop criteria for the use of power in such a way
that these criteria can serve as "middle axioms" to bridge
two gaps: 1) between the first century and our situation; and
2) between the theological context of the NT world and the
life of human institutions. In this brief paper we cannot
spell out just how that is done, but can only point out here
that this is an important task that needs more explanation.

Due to limitations of space the following is simply a
summary of ethical criteria which these need to be elaborated
much more fully.

A.   Does the use of power reduce other human beings to
impotence, or does it enhance their power to effect change?
The following are examples from human institutional life
which illustrate this issue:

1.   Good teaching empowers students to become
learners themselves, no longer totally dependent on the
teacher.

2.   Good administration empowers others in an organization to participate as fully as possible in the shape
of that organization.

3.   Effective ministry equips lay persons to be
effective ministers.

4.   Development strategies enable people to become
gradually more in charge of their lives.

5.   Political structures invite broad participation in
decision making.

B. Does the goal or end toward which power is being used
contribute to:

  1. Shalom—well-being for persons, the community and
the physical environment in a holistic sense?
  2. A more just society?
      (a) Allocating benefits to all, particularly the
      least advantaged members of a society.
      (b) Shared participation in the allocation of
      resources.
  C. Is the use of power truthful, or does it involve
manipulation? Manipulation is the process by which people
are made to act against their will without realizing it.
Such can happen by appeals to fear, anxiety, emotion; by the
use of argument that involves appeals to authority without
giving reasons why a course of action is appropriate (appeals
to law or the Bible can involve such manipulation); or by *ad
hominum* arguments that attempt to discredit an idea not by
arguing against the idea, but by attacking the person or
group who holds the idea.
  D. Does the use of power injure or harm the persons who
are the recipients of someone's or some group's effort to
change or resist change of a situation? To what degree does
it enhance an individual or group's well-being?
  1. By intending their good?
  2. By protecting their dignity?
  E. Is there a reasonable chance of success? Is it
reasonable that the exercise of power can in fact accomplish
the change or resist the change being contemplated. In other
words, is the use of time, energy and money a wise choice, or
is it wasting scarce resources?
  F. Is the power exercised nonviolently? Here I will
reflect more extensively on the issue of violence and coercive force. Nonviolent action makes use of force, both persuasive and coercive. The key ethical question is whether
coercion is inherently violent, or whether a distinction can
be made between violence and coercion. We have already laid
the groundwork for a distinction in our theological treatment
of the subject. Scholars have debated this question for some
time and have not achieved much clarity. William Miller, who
has written extensively on the subject of nonviolence, at
times distinguishes between coercion and violence:

  Physical force is a factor in violence, but not a
  determining one. There is an area of considerable
  ambiguity in which questions of proportion and
  legitimacy arise to distinguish between acts that are
  clearly violent but morally justified and those that
  are not justified, and between those that include
  physical force but not violence.[13]

Yet later in the same book he seems to speak as if all forms of physical force include some measure of violence. Reinhold Niebuhr also at times acknowledges the validity of the distinction between force and violence when he says:
It is possible to justify the use of such force [he is here referring to Gandhi's boycott of Britain, the Chinese boycott against the English in Hong Kong, and the strike of the industrial worker] without condoning violence of any kind. The distinction between violence and such other uses of force as economic boycotts is not only in the degree of destruction that results from them but in the degree of redemptive force that they possess.[14]
At other points, however, where Niebuhr contrasts his vision of the pure anarchistic and political non-resistant *agape* love of the New Testament with a politically oriented nonviolent strategy of social change, Niebuhr says the difference between violence and nonviolence are not fundamentally morally different because both violence and nonviolence are coercive.[15]

Violence and force can be distinguished only if we keep in mind the root meaning of the word "violence," injury to persons. The following continuum between persuasion at one end of the spectrum and coercive physical force at the other end can help clarify the difference between force and violence.[16]

1. Persuasive Power. These are actions that try to effect the action of the other without denying their freedom either to accept or reject a point of view.

2. Coercive Power of Social Pressure (threatened or actual). These are actions which put pressure on a person or group to act in a certain way rather than another because of likely sanctions against the person ranging from disapproval, social ostracism and estrangement from others, political defeat, to strikes and economic boycotts. Pressure permits persons to continue to act according to their desires as long as they are willing to take the consequences of their action. Forms of pressure have been accepted by pacifist groups such as the "ban" or "shunning" or other forms of church discipline to pressure persons into repentance and reconciliation with the community. This is not simply persuasion because the costs to the person who is not reconciled, such as ostracism or severance from the community, are clear. This use of power is very difficult to separate from violence because it seems to be or certainly is perceived by the per-

son or group receiving the pressure to involve harm toward
them. I would continue to describe this pressure as nonviolent so long as it: a) intends the restoration of or reconciliation with the party to whom pressure is applied; and b)
is likely to activate a reconciling result.

    3. Coercive Power of Physical Force. These are actions
which physically restrict persons from continuing to do in an
actual physical sense what they have been doing, or make
them do something in an actual physical sense that they
would not otherwise do. These forms of physical coercion
range all the way from certain forms of punishment of children, to the physical prevention of suicide and criminal acts,
to the use of drugs and other forms of psychic manipulation
which make it impossible for the person to behave any other
way. I would apply the same standards as I did to category 2
above.

    I maintain that any of the above (including persuasion)
can be violent,and that all of the above (including physical
coercion) may be nonviolent. The key issue is whether the
persuasive or coercive acts are intended and likely to
restore the person or group to wholeness. It is usually
assumed that an act of physical coercion is a violent act.
That is not necessarily the case. One can readily imagine a
situation where someone is about to commit suicide and one
physically intervenes to prevent that person from killing
himself. The justification for such an action is based
actually upon the principle of nonviolence. Because of one's
respect for the value of another person's life, a life over
which they may have momentarily lost control because of
extreme emotional turmoil, one intervenes to prevent injury
to the person. One does this under the assumption that were
the person in rational control, he or she would not want to
injure her- himself.

    One may also justifiably use physical coercion to prevent
a violent criminal act. On the one hand, one should do what
is possible, short of violence, to intervene and restrain
someone physically in order to prevent them from injuring
another person. One may justifiably restrain persons
engaged in or about to commit criminal acts of violence also
for their sake. Physical restraint protects persons from
doing irreparable damage to themselves. Persons who commit
violent acts against others do damage to their moral conscience and may feel deep remorse later over their action.
They may severely damage their future life prospects because
of eventual long- term incarceration and loss of freedom.
Thus the police use of physical force that is properly

restrained and aims to protect and preserve the life of both the community and the criminal for the purpose of the enforcement of a just law is not necessarily violent. Some here might object and say that any loss of freedom is a violation of a person. I think such a view fails to understand the meaning of our social identity and entails an overemphasis upon individualism. To assert that unless we are totally free we are being treated less than humanly is in fact a denial of our humanity as social beings. It is in being "pressed" by others that we become more fully human.

We should also not assume that all forms of persuasion are nonviolent. A person who goes into another culture with the Christian gospel and preaches in such a way as to utterly condemn another culture and its way of life may violate the dignity and self-esteem of such persons. Even though persons of this culture can freely decide for or against the Gospel, the injury can be done to people by verbal condemnation. Thus persuasion and violence can coexist. Persons who claim to be nonviolent because they are not being coercive or physically destructive can be violent through verbal abuse or other kinds of symbolic action. The destruction of a group's symbol (i.e. a flag), or the violation of a community ritual (like not saluting a flag) can be violent acts. Such actions, therefore, require just as careful and conscientious justification as an act of physical coercion. This does not mean that just because an act is subjectively offensive to another person or group that it is a violent act, though I would acknowledge that it is often difficult to draw the line between something perceived as violent and actual violence.

In summary we can say that both persuasive force and coercive force can be used either violently or nonviolently. The key question is whether the force used harms people (in which case it is violent) or whether it initiates a *process* that can lead to the restoration of human beings and eventually to reconciliation.

G. Because we have said that we *should* attempt to be successful in our use of powers, we also need to clarify the relationship between the ethical principle of nonviolence and nonviolence as an effective social strategy. Nonviolent action is not right only for pragmatic reasons, because it works and is effective. The ethical justification of nonviolent action arises out of two moral principles: the obligation to work for constructive goals of justice and *shalom* and the obligation not to injure persons in the process. These two ethical principles underlie nonviolent

action as a *social strategy.* That nonviolent action is also
a workable strategy is not an argument that it is morally
right because it is workable. It is morally preferable to
the use of armed force because it enables us to pursue justice without injury to persons. It also happens to be the
case that it is often effective as a political instrument.

What is the role, then, of judgments about effectiveness
in Christian ethical thinking? At one extreme are those who
operate by essentially pragmatic or utilitarian standards.
We ought not violate the principles of justice and nonviolence for the sake of what works, for the sake of what we
believe will produce a better future. At the other extreme
are those who reject "effectiveness" as a category
altogether, who argue that Christians are simply called to be
faithful to the crucified and resurrected Servant Lord and
not try to "look for the right 'handle' by which one can 'get
a hold' on the course of history and move it in the right
direction."[17] John H. Yoder, who takes this position in *The
Politics of Jesus,* does so for three reasons.

1.   The problem with "effectiveness" reasoning is that
for the sake of a good cause, one is able to justify "the
sacrifice of the life and welfare of one's self, one's neighbors and (of course!) the enemy." (234) Yoder rejects "effectiveness" as a moral yardstick which permits us to sacrifice
these other values.

2.   Secondly, Yoder rejects this position because he
believes that we cannot predict very well the effects of our
actions. He supports his view with Reinhold Niebuhr's notion
of "irony": "that when men try to manage history, it almost
always turns out to have another direction than that in which
they thought they were guiding it." (235) The basic reason
for this is that a host of other free agents also act with
similar assumptions about managing history.

3.   Thirdly, Yoder argues that "effectiveness" thinking is
basically behind the denial of the relevance of the New
Testament for social ethics.   Since the New Testament does
not speak in terms of managing history but in terms of
faithfulness, then we moderns, if we want to manage history,
will need to get our standards for social ethics from other
sources. The New Testament affirms, says Yoder, that history
is meaningful, but its meaning is to be found in the statement of the book of Revelation: "The Lamb that was slain is
worthy to receive power."

> John is here saying, not as an inscrutable paradox but
> as a meaningful affirmation, that the cross and not
> the sword, suffering and not brute power determines

the meaning of history. The key to the obedience of God's people is not their effectiveness but their patience (13:10). The triumph of the right is assured not by the might that comes to the aid of the right, which is of course the justification of the use of violence and other kinds of power in every human conflict; the triumph of the right, although it is assured, is sure because of the power of the resurrection and not because of any calculation of causes and effects, nor because of the inherently greater strength of the good guys. The relationship between the obedience of God's people and the triumph of God's cause is not a relationship of cause and effect but one of cross and resurrection. (238)

I agree with Yoder that the meaning of cross and resurrection points to an inherent connection of means and ends. For the sake of some good end we are not justified in using immoral means. Martin L. King summarizes my position with his statement: "Constructive ends can never give absolute moral justification to destructive means because in the final analysis the end is preexistent in the means."[18]

I also agree with Yoder that the belief that we can manage history to make it come out our way is a serious illusion, one of the signs of human sin. Such a position fails to take seriously human finitude and sin. Many other actors with many different motivations and values make up the direction of history and it is simply beyond our power to manage history as a whole. The illusion that we can make history come out right leads to the kind of fanaticism that uses destructive and violent means. The assumption that we can bring in the kingdom within history through our own effort fails to take seriously the eschatological tension we live under. Faith in the Lord who transcends history means we can abandon fanaticism because we wait patiently for the full realization of the kingdom which is still to come through God's miraculous power.

But in the context of eschatological expectation we are expected to be faithful within history. At this level Yoder's language about the illegitimacy of judging an action in terms of its effects is misleading. We are called to act in history in specific arenas of life. We are placed in history, empowered by God, to become shapers of human culture and creators of human institutions. How can I make any moral judgment about an action if I do not know how it will affect another person or a situation? How can I make any judgment at all about how to choose between alternative courses of action if I do not have some capacity to predict what the consequences of my action will be? An action cannot even be judged violent or not if I do not know how it will affect other persons, whether it will injure them or not. The Christian is called upon to work for justice for the poor, to defend the fatherless and the widow, to be a minister of reconciliation in the world. Compassion for the poor implies that Christians must have a concern for laws, policies, social structures and general environmental conditions that are destructive of human health and well-being. We need to be able to assess how alternative laws, actions, policies, programs, and institutions will affect people in order to know how to act in their behalf with compassion. Sometimes problems are created when naive, well meaning Christians believe they are acting out of love in obedience to their Lord, but fail to assess carefully what they are doing, why they are doing it, and what the likely effect of their actions will be.

At this level the question of effectiveness and the careful social scientific inquiry which tries to predict the consequences of a course of action is absolutely essential in enabling a Christian to fulfill the Christian ethic of discipleship. In this respect the probablistic studies of social scientists have an important bearing on Christian ethics. Since John H. Yoder argues that the church should act compassionately in the world in such programs as mental health or overseas development, I doubt that he would disagree with me. The problem is that his language confuses the issue as if he were rejecting "effectiveness" altogether. Faithfulness to Christ cannot be fulfilled without attempting to measure one's effectiveness and predict the consequences of one's actions in the specific and concrete decisions one makes in the process of acting in the world. The more Christians become involved in the transformation of structures, the more they will need to concern themselves with the effects of their actions. This is appropriate so long as two principles are kept in mind: first, that means and ends are interconnected, that a righteous cause cannot lead to the use of immoral means; and second, that Christians have an attitude of humility and patience recognizing that the ultimate fate of history is not in their hands but in God's. Abraham Heschel expresses in a profound way, I think, the proper perspective with his statement:

> We are continually warned lest we rely on man's own power and believe that the "indeterminate extension of human capacities would eventually alter the human

situation." Our tradition (Judaism) does not believe that the good deeds alone will redeem history; it is the obedience to God that will make us worthy of being redeemed by God... Yet the Hebrew tradition insists upon the mitzvah (obedience to God, the good deed) as the instrument in dealing with evil. At the end of evil days, evil will be conquered by the One; in historic times evils must be conquered one by one.[19]

V. Peacemaking and Power

I would like to conclude by reflecting briefly upon what this approach to power means for peacemaking. Mennonites traditionally have been preoccupied with how Christian faithfulness places one in constant tension with an unjust and violent world. However, how would we approach peacemaking if we were, instead, to see human conflict as an opportunity to use our imagination and our energies to find creative solutions to human problems?

In his book, *Making Peace,* Adam Curle provides a useful typology for analyzing conflict and determining what means are appropriate given the basis of the conflict. He distinguishes between three sets of variables. The one variable, which he calls "balance" and "imbalance" between two parties, refers to the relative equality or inequality with respect to the parties engaged in conflict. What is the capacity each party has to effect or prevent change? An imbalanced relationship exists between parent-child, teacher-student, Israel and the Palestinians, etc. A relative balance exists between two friends in conflict, or two nations like the Soviet Union and the United States.

The second variable is the degree to which parties are "aware" or "unaware" of the conflict. Most people or groups are usually very much aware of "balanced" conflicts. In "unbalanced" situations a lack of awareness of the situation often prevails: children who do not understand how they are being repressed by abusive parents, a wife who blames herself for her husband's unfaithfulness, or students who do not enjoy learning because they do not realize that their professors are dictating the content and style of their learning. One nation or group within a nation may be severely repressive of another nation or group who is not aware of the repression. In the 20th century we have seen a fundamental revolution in awareness of peoples of the so-called "third world" *vis a vis* their status in relationship to the former colonial powers of the West.

Thirdly, Curle distinguishes between peaceful and
unpeaceful relationships. He defines an unpeaceful relationship as one in which the conditions of a relationship impede
human development. What constitutes human development, of
course, needs fuller definition, but we cannot go into that
here.
We can diagram these relationships as follows:

	Unpeaceful Realtions		Peaceful Relations
	Low awareness of conflict	Higher awareness of conflict	
Balanced		Soviet Union—United States Syria—Israel	European Common Market
Imbalanced	Colonial people prior to independence Blacks prior to civil rights struggle	Underdogs who are confronting groups with more power Palestinians, Revolutionaries in El Salvador	State/Federal Government France/Monaco

Curle then defines the processes of peacemaking that are
appropriate for each type of conflict. In a low-awareness
imbalanced relationship, education for consciousness raising
may be the first step toward a peaceful resolution, what liberation theologians have also called "conscientization."
Once that has happened, then various forms of confrontation
may be required to enable the weaker group to put the issues
before the stronger party. A peaceful orientation would seek
to find nonviolent means of confrontation so as to avoid a
situation of violence or war. It is in this context that the
advocacy role of a third party may be helpful.
    Conciliation is a word to describe those processes which
lay the psychological foundations for bargaining and negotiation to take place. Conciliation seeks to change perceptions
and reduce tensions so that the rational processes of
bargaining can take place. Though conciliation is probably
necessary in some stage of almost any kind of conflict, it
may only be helpful at certain times. Particularly in situations of unbalanced and unaware conflicts, conscientization
and confrontation (advocacy in the case of third party inter-
venors) must take place first in the peacemaking process. In
fact, confrontation may produce reactions that are the opposite of conciliation by creating conflict and hostility
between the parties. Hostility, as such, is not necessarily

bad if it is part of a total process where the issues are confronted by the parties in a conflict. At some point, then, conciliatory processes will need to be utilized to move the peacemaking process toward resolution.

Bargaining or negotiation is the process in which two parties to a quarrel try to reach an agreement in which they maintain their own most important values without excessive concessions to the other party. This state of the peacemaking process assumes some kind of balance between the parties (at least the recognition of each other as appropriate negotiating parties who have crucial values at stake where imbalance exists). It assumes a relative degree of rationality. Third parties may play a key role here as mediators between the two parties, to foster communication and to enable the parties to find options and reach agreements.

The final stage in the peacemaking process is what Curle calls "development." By this he means the restructuring of the unpeaceful relationship along positive or peaceful lines. This is now the new structure of relationship, the new agreement between the parties that removes the old structure and puts a new structure in its place. Curle says that development can take many forms, but he regards one principle as fundamental to the restructuring of relationships in the developmental sense:

This is the principle felicitously named 'autonomous interdependence.' According to this principle, development signifies a relationship between groups, states, governments and communities, or groups within communities--in which each recognizes and respects the autonomy of the other, its right to organize itself according to its cultural and political preference; and at the same time each admits its dependence on the other for such matters as trade, communications, the sharing of scarce resources, the exchange of skilled persons, security, weather forecasting, and so on.[20]

Too often governments use only the very primitive methods of threat and counterthreat. Most people believe that the posture of threat and use of force demonstrates strength. We need to stand this thinking on its head and expose the misunderstanding that underlies it. The resort to threat and the use of force is a sign of the *weakness* not strength of a nation. A nation which uses violent force no longer knows how to solve a problem with its neighbor. It has lost the imagination of how to solve problems peacefully, how to get its opponent to do what it wants them to do. Threats also often reinforce the stubbornness of one's opponent. The teacher who must constantly resort to threat and force in the classroom is one who does not know how to control the students in other ways. Most parents know that when they get angry and hit their children it is because of their weakness, their inability to get their children to do what they want them to do. Similarly a nation which uses a posture of threat and force as its primary mode of operation in the world is a nation that is demonstrating a lack of imagination, a weakness at solving problems. We ought to be immediately wary of politicians who campaign on platforms of threat and force, because they demonstrate a loss of intelligence and imagination to accomplish the purposes of government, to solve problems with one's neighbors by engaging in the conflict resolution process that will end up in the structuring of a peaceful relationship.

In summary, then, the task of Christians, fully aware of their creative potential as co-creators with God, is to utilize power creatively and effectively. We should see ourselves not only as persons called to judge the world as prophetic critics (though that role too has its place), but to be creative agents of change, to use conflict creatively in order to make peace where there is violence and injustice. In this way we can exercise our power creatively in the shaping of social decisions, rather than seeing ourselves primarily, as individuals and as a church, in sharp tension with the world. Though tension with the world is also a reality, we as Mennonites have distorted our overall theological perspective by focusing primarily upon power from the standpoint of the doctrine of sin. We need to look at power more positively, to balance out our view of our task as Christians by emphasizing more forcefully that we are creative agents of change in the world in our partnership with God, our Creator.

Appendix

Some Levels of Power in Human Relations

1. Life Cycle Changes
   From childhood dependency to enhanced power and control back to increased dependency in old age. The ethical issue is how dignity can be maintained for elderly persons as they gradually lose power over their lives.
2. Power Differential in Social Roles
   a. Family
      1) Husband-Wife
      2) Parent-Child
      3) Siblings
   b. Student-Teacher. Below are examples of "professional" power, one of the most unbalanced relationships in terms of power, yet an arena seldom assessed ethically by academia.
      1) A faculty member writes a letter of recommendation that either hinders or helps a person to receive position of employment.
      2) A faculty discussion of a student in the coffee room creates an attitude toward that student, but the information is not shared with the student.
      3) A faculty member determines what shall be studied in a course. In an ethics course he prefers to work on issues of war and peace because he knows the subject. The students in the class have other interests, but are not allowed to shape the course content, or the style in which the class is taught.
      4) A faculty member gives a student an "F" in a course that causes the student to be inelegible for scholarship aid and to participate in athletics.
      5) A professor requires that students attend class with the threat of a lowered grade if attendance is irregular.
      6) A qualified person is denied a faculty position at an institution because an influential faculty person objects to hiring that person.
      7) A teacher determines what constitutes quality work on students exams and papers.
      8) A scholar uses his expertise on a subject to demolish the viewpoint of a novice in the field.

9) Persons in a professional academic organization
    determine the basic agenda and methodology of
    the enterprise such that a new perspective is
    "frozen" out.

10) On a doctoral exam one professor seeks to get
    at his rival by the line of questioning directed
    to his rival's student.

11) An erudite professor makes his students feel
    how little they know and how incapable they are
    of understanding the complexity of an issue.

12) A professor in a professional field appeals to
    the demands of an accrediting agency to get the
    faculty to pass a program.

13) A teacher determines what books a student shall
    buy and read in his class.

14) Professors who have reputations have material
    readily published because it sells.

15) An influential faculty member feels so strongly
    about an issue that a committee of the college
    decides not to bring an issue to the faculty
    because it is not worth the "hassle."

16) Tenure.

   c. Employer - Employee

3. Power Differential in Terms of Class, Race, Sex, Economic
    Status.

4. Power in Voluntary Organizations in Terms of Author-
    ity/Status. Below are some examples of power issues
    from the arena of church life, also not usually discussed
    as an arena where power is an issue.

   a. A pastor who gives powerful sermons that persuade
       his people to change.

   b. The Board of Deacons accepts or denies membership to
       persons based on certain moral criteria.

   c. One group in a church organizes themselves to vote
       in a policy they favor.

   d. A person gives money to the church or church agency
       under the condition that it be used for a particular
       purpose.

   e. A minister is given a favorable vote by his con-
       gregation.

   f. A highly qualified woman is not able to serve in the
       ministry because her denomination does not allow
       women to serve.

   g. A person develops a "reputation" among influential
       people in the church such that he/she is frozen out
       of any role in the church.

h. Another individual serves in responsible positions on six committees in the denomination (or church) because of his positive reputation.

i. Because of a person's "authority," his stated view on a key issue can sway the views of many people.

j. A pastor determines the style and format of worship in the congregation.

5. Power to shape Public Opinion or Command Allegiance of People.
   a. Sports or entertainment "stars."
   b. Media, advertising.

6. Power in Political Organizations (Taken from Karl Deutsch's, *The Analysis of International Relations*). Deutch defines politics as "the more or less incomplete control of human behaviour through voluntary habits of compliance in combination with threats of probable enforcement" (19). While force is integral to politics, when voluntary compliance is not given, "the voluntary or habitual compliance of the mass of the population is the invisible but very real basis of the power of every government" (19). The most brutal regimes who are willing to use armed force as a normal practice depend for their survival on the compliance of a significant percentage of the population. Deutsch further differentiates power in the following ways:
   a. Power *potential* is inferred from resources.
      1) Military resources
      2) Knowledge and expertise
      3) Economic strength
      4) Will to prevail
   B. Weight of power as inferred from *results*—i.e. how a particular course of action changes or effects an outcome. Deutsch argues that in the modern era governments have tended to increase their power over their own populations (taxes, draft, enforcement of laws) relative to what governments in the past could do, but their weight of power in world politics has been declining ever since 1945 (29).

Also, two other qualifications must be made:
      1) The more highly specific a positive outcome is, the more alternatives are excluded by it and thus the more difficult it is to bring about with limited power. It is more easy to reduce the probability of an outcome not desired. For example, the U.S. may be able to prevent a

regime from keeping or taking power, but may
find it much more difficult to bring about the
kind of government it desires. (Vietnam?)

2) The power to acheive results consists of both
   goal *attainment* and *control* over one's environment. It is more difficult to steer and stop a
   truck than a small compact car. Nations with a
   vast amount of power potential may be able to
   overcome all obstacles in their path, but do it
   in such a clumsy way that specific positive
   results cannot be achieved. Or they may have
   such momentum (resources committed, reputations
   at stake, a committed public) that they are
   trapped in their past of policies and cannot
   turn around quickly enough to respond to alternatives (arms race).

c. *Domain* of power is the set of person whose probable
   behavior is significantly changed by its application. Sometimes geographical area and a particular
   population belong to the same set. Rulers of nation
   states aim as much as possible to bring these sets
   together. Of special interest is where the set of
   persons affected crosses national barriers. Here we
   can see the power potential of the church or peace
   movement as a transnational force gaining adherents
   who withdraw their loyalty to their own nation
   states. Or we see how obedience to economic incen-
   tives leads multinational corporations to behave in
   ways that are not within the domain of national
   states. We can also understand domain as the
   amount of land, capital goods or resources controlled by person or groups. The weakness of many
   "third-world" countries or peoples in these
   countries is their lack of control over this domain.

d. The *range* of power Deutch defines as the "difference
   between the highest reward (or 'indulgence') and the
   worst punishment (or 'depreviation') which power
   holders can bestow or inflict. Though rulers could
   have many people in thier domains, the range of
   power over some may be smaller than others. Over
   those who wanted nothing and feared nothing, who
   were indifferent to pain or gain, their power would
   be small indeed" (39). Deutch says the range of
   power has tended in modern times to decrease in
   domestic politics. (Excessive rewards or extreme
   punishments to gain the subjects' fear are no

longer tolerated in most places). In international
politics the opposite seems to be the case (use of
economic rewards or threats of masive armed
destruction), though these approaches are expensive
and often have had quite limited effects in achieving dependable results in foreign policy.

e. The *scope* of power is the class of behaviour relations and affairs to which someone or a group is
subject. The scope of parental control over young
children is large, a church college over its students considerably less. Laissez-faire theorists
seek to decrease the scope of governmental control,
whereas socialists seek to expand it.

Deutch concludes his discussion by noting that the word
"power" is a symbol, "a symbol of the ability to change the
distribution of results, and particularly the results of
people's behaviour" (45). He draws an analogy between power
and money. "Just as money is the currency of economic life,
so power can be thought of as the currency of politics.
Power is the currency or medium that makes easy the
exchange of more or less enforceable decisions for more or
less dependable support" (46). In politics (and, I think, in
many other institutions) this exchange process occurs in two
stages--a government, regime (or administration of another
institution) assumes general responsibility for making and
enforcing decisions. In turn, they gain support for the decisions they make. Even if persons or subjects disagree in
particular cases, people tend to give support to the
government in general because it is regarded as the "legitimate authority." This "legitimacy" implies consent, however,
and can be undermined if the "authorities" in a government
(or head of an organization) misuse or abuse their
responsibility. Thus Deutsch critiques the view of political
power held by Machiavelli who saw power in only competitive
and quantitative terms, i.e. the appropriation of power for
onesself to ward off other competitors. Politics in any
country, or any group of countries, means not just the
appropriation of power in a quantitative sense, but "the
ability" of the whole political community *to coordinate* the
efforts of its members, to mobilize their support, and to
redirect their patterns of cooperation" (51). Such a view
must recognize the limits of power. The use of armed force
is not, from this perspective, the "essential" expression of
political power, but is just the opposite--a symbol of lack
of control and coordination, or lack of power.

Notes

1. *The Nature of Human Agression,* 160-161.
2. *An Analysis of International Relations,* 2nd Ed., 19.
3. *Systematic Theology: A Historic Perspective,* 336-337.
4. *Power of Innocence,* 99.
5. For a fuller discussion of Christ's relationship to the powers see my book, *Christian Peacemaking and International Conflict,* 91f. Also see John H. Yoder, *The Politics of Jesus,* 135-162.
6. James Luther Adams, from an unpublished paper, "Hits Win Ball Games: The Creative Thrust of Conflict."
7. Quoted in the *International Encyclopedia of the Social Sciences.* See "power."
8. *Politics Among the Nations,* 26.
9. *An Analysis of International Relations,* 19.
10. Gene Sharp, *The Politics of Nonviolent Action,* 8.
11. Martin L. King, *Why We Can't Wait,* 80.
12. Sharp, 109-110.
13. William Miller, *Nonviolence: A Christian Interpretation.*
14. Reinhold Niebuhr, *Love and Justice,* 250.
15. The ambiguity in Niebuhr arises out of the contrast he makes between love and nonviolent social change. When Niebuhr talks about love as a passive non-resistant *agape* of self abnegation or withdrawal from the world, then love stands in sharp conflict to any use of force. He then tends to equate non-violent and violent force. On the other hand, when Niebuhr speaks of love as a redemptive process in the world (much closer to my understanding of love, and I think, much closer to the NT perspective) then he views violent force and nonviolent force as opposites, the latter being much more congruent with redemptive love than violent force.
16. There have been a number of different classifications of types of nonviolence. William Miller distinguishes between nonresistance, passive resistance, and nonviolent direct action. The problem with Miller's classification is that at one level the distinction between nonresistance and the other two types of nonviolence is defined as a theological or philosophical difference, and at another level the distinction between passive resistance and nonviolent direct action is more a difference in strategy of action. The latter two tend to merge into each other as groups readily move from one level to the other. C. J. Cadoux has a much better classification with his distinction between noncoercive and

coercive types of actions, with the coercive types broken down into two types: noninjurious and injurious. His classification is not as helpful in elaborating the various types of non-violent coercive action. More descriptive of the techniques of nonviolent action is the classification of the sociologists, Clarence Marsh Case, who distinquishes between various kinds of persuasion, nonviolent and violent coercion. (See Cadoux, *Christian Pacifism Re-examined,* 45; Miller, *op.cit.* 46f; C.M. Case, *Non-Violent Coercion,* 397). More recently Gene Sharp has classified non-violent action in terms of its political methods. In reflecting upon what means of classification is best, we need to be careful to distinquish the variable we are trying to keep in mind when making our classification. Classifications like Miller's are most confusing since they mix variables and are inconsistent in the use of variables; while Sharp's classification is most clear, though it is one dimensional. I think there are at least four key variables that are operative as we seek to distinguish types:

1) The religious or philosophical orientation; 2) the continuum from persuasion to coercion; 3) the continuum from nonviolence to violence; and 4) the methods of nonviolent action. At the religious level, there are many types of non-violence as John H. Yoder has pointed out in his book, *Nevertheless: The Varieties of Religious Pacifism,* where he describes 18 different types. I do not want to hazard any kind of classification here except to counter the assumption that there are primarily two types: a pure religious pacifism of Christianity which is nonresistant, and a non-violent social action which is pragmatic. This is Reinhold Niebuhr's typology, a typology which did not permit him to see and describe clearly an active nonviolence that is principles and rooted in the Gospel (as in Martin L. King, and also in his contemporary A. J. Muste--see Alan Letts dissertation comparing Niebuhr and Muste), a pacifism which is not simply pragmatic or based on the liberal optimistic assumptions of progress, but also which does not withdraw from the world in a political isolationism as does nonresistance as he described it.

17. John H. Yoder, *The Politics of Jesus,* 234.
18. *Stride Toward Freedom,* 92.
19. *The Insecurity of Freedom,* 145-156.
20. Adam Curle, *Making Peace,* 261.

Proposal for an
ANABAPTIST PEACE GUARD
(second draft)

Ron Sider

[This paper builds upon Sider's speech given at the 1984 Mennonite World Conference (Strasbourg), which was printed in the program book. Ed. note].

I. Goal

The Mennonite and Brethren in Christ churches in North America should establish a carefully trained Anabaptist Peace Guard (APG) of 100-500 people. The fundamental goal of the APG would be to use the techniques of nonviolent direct action to promote peace, justice and freedom in situations of conflict between nations or large societal groups within a nation by placing a body of well-trained, praying Christians in the midst of warring parties or groups that support warring parties.

II. Theological Foundations

An APG will seek to create *shalom* rather than rest content with the tranquility of an unjust status quo. Like Jesus and the early church, it will challenge what is wrong in current society because Jesus' disciples are called to be peacemakers in Jesus' new Messianic Kingdom.

Shalom in the Bible means right relationships—first with God, then with the neighbor and also the earth. An APG will seek to model, witness to and promote that three-fold *shalom.*

Although its primary purpose is not evangelism, the members of APG will witness to a right relationship with God through the cross of the Risen Lord Jesus by their own redeemed lives, their demonstrated eagerness to let Christ be Lord of their total life, and their readiness to share the Good News wherever opportunity arises.

Sinful rebellion against God has produced distorted relationships with the neighbor. These include oppression of the poor, totalitarianism and war. Therefore, an APG will seek: to transform unjust social structures, thus creating justice and wholeness for both oppressed and oppressor; to foster religious, political and legal freedom that respects the dignity of free persons created in the image of God; and to end killing, so that justice, liberty and peace may embrace.

The teaching and example of Jesus Christ means that Christians should never kill another human being.

In light of the teaching of Jesus Christ, the promise of the coming kingdom, on the one hand; and on the other, the increasing potential for massive devastation of modern weaponry, and the ever escalating cycles of violence in human history, we believe that God wills human society (including governments) to exert every effort to explore non-violent ways to reconcile hostile parties, social groups and nations.

III. A Few Preliminary Presuppositions

1. Only One Strategy

There are scores of ways that Mennonites and Brethren in Christ are working all over the world for peace, justice and freedom.   These include MCC, MDS, mediation services, the work of mission boards, local congregational activity in the inner city, activity against the nuclear arms race, etc. This proposal for an APG using the techniques of non-violent direct action in no way seeks to ignore or supplant the others.   It is merely *one additional approach* that we have not yet explored very much.

2. Humility: No Desire to Reinvent the Wheel

Others are doing it already.   Close consultation for learning and cooperation with Witness for Peace, etc. would be imperative.

3. Ecumenical Concerns

From the beginning, all Christians and those of other religious persuasions would be encouraged to develop parallel organizations that could cooperate with an APG.

4. No Martyr Complex

The goal is faithfulness, not glory or martyrdom.   It is immoral to seek death.   But it is also immoral to be unwilling to risk death for the sake of obedience to the Crucified and Risen Lamb.

IV. Name

1. Issues at Stake

a.   The name needs to communicate clearly the basic focus and concern both to Mennonites and Brethren in Christ and to others.

b.   The name needs to avoid negative connotations (e.g.,

"Peace Force" sounds militaristic).
  c. The name needs to suggest the nonviolent direct
action focus.

2. Possibilities
    a. Anabaptist Peace Guard
    b. The Lamb's Reconcilers
    c. The King's Reconcilers
    d. Reconcilers of the Kingdom
    e. Jesus' Conciliation Movement
    f. Anabaptist Peace Team
    g. Mennonite Peace Team
    h. Christians for Nonviolent Reconciliation
    i. Love Guard
    j. Cross of Christ Guard

V. Illustrations

How would such an APG intervene? That is best answered
concretely. The following scenarios are *illustrative* only.
Before an APG actually intervened, sophisticated complex
analysis would be essential.

In each case, it is assumed that a highly trained Guard
(with six months training) of 100-500 persons already exists.
Such a group would be immersed in the techniques of nonviolent direct action. They would be deeply mature
Christians filled with the Holy Spirit, experienced in inter-
cessory prayer, backed up by thousands of local prayer
chains, and expecting to experience signs and wonders. They
would also include persons with the most sophisticated socio-
economic political analysis available.

A. International
    1. South Africa
The purpose of the move into South Africa would be to
urge an immediate sharing of just political power and access
to economic life in a political democracy with freedom and
justice for all. The decision to move into South Africa
would come only after: 1) careful consultation with all seg-
ments of the church in South Africa and a clear invitation
from the major leadership of at least the non-white churches;
2) intensive analysis by economists, political scientists, and
experts in logistics and diplomacy so that the best strategy
is employed.

Several hundred members of the APG, accompanied by prominent Christians from all parts of the world, would attempt

to move into South Africa by land, from Mozambique, Zimbabwe, Swaziland, Lesotho and Botswana. Some could also move in by boat along the South African coast from bases in Mozambique. Hopefully such action would be accompanied by non-violent internal resistance to apartheid. Prior intensification of a worldwide boycott of South Africa by business and cultural groups would be important. The entire approach would be that of Christians coming in the name of the Risen Lord Jesus to plead with the Christian leaderhsip of South Africa to repent and change.

The members of the APG would fly to Lesotho, Swaziland Mozambique, Botswana and Zimbabwe and take up positions at the border of South Africa. Twenty-four hour prayer chains both at the advance camps and around the world would be central to the activity. Activities would be widely publicized and hence the world press (TV, radio, and papers) would be present. When all was ready for the initial attempt to cross the borders, fifty prominent Christian leaders of international reputation would join the the APG.

On a given day, two different teams of about fifty people each would attempt to cross the borders from Lesotho, Swaziland, Mozambique, Botswana and Zimbabwe. They would explain to border officials that they come prayerful in the name of Jesus to talk and pray with church and government leaders and ask to be allowed to travel to Pretoria. If refused, they would explain their peaceful nonviolent commitments and then move slowly into South Africa, forcing the South African officials to arrest them. (The presence of the press and internationally prominent Christians would make it highly unlikely that anyone would be injured at this stage). If arrested, two other groups would move in the next day.

A wide variety of defensive tactics for repelling the peaceful witness would be used by the South African government and vigorous analysis and Spirit-filled discernment would be needed to improvise appropriate responses.

The basic entry by land might also be accompanied by an attempted entry by ship and air. From a base in Mozambique, a medium size ship (large enough to carry fifty Peace Force members and their supplies plus members of the media) could try to land a group each day at some point on the South African coast.

It is quite likely that Christian leaders in South Africa would plan related nonviolent demonstrations within the country. That, however, would be solely at the judgment of the church there.

Part of the strategy would be to work with those already

asking Western banks and other businesses to boycott South
Africa until a constitutional convention is called. Those
that refuse would be picketted and boycotted. Nonviolent
demonstrations at all South African embassies and consular
offices around the world would further support the effort.

2. **Nicaragua** (the text for this section has been
omitted in view of the changed political situation. Ed.)

3. **El Salvador**
A smaller team of 10-50 could attempt to rebuild villages
destroyed by war and live with widows and children to comfort, protect and assist with agricultural development and
other rebuilding.

4. **Laos**
A team of 10-30 members of the APG could go to Laos to
unearth and neutralize unexploded ordinance in Laos.
Laotians chould not be left to undertake this difficult task
alone. Careful training in the culture, ordinance-
neutralization, etc., would be essential.

5. **Guatemala**
Apoyo Mutuo (Mutual Help) is a group of Guatemalan
(largely Christian parents) organized to protest the dis-
appearance, torture and murder of their children by security
forces and death squads. They hold prayer vigils and peaceful marches to appeal for the release of persons who have
disappeared. Although they have no ties to political groups,
the government denounced them as subversive in the spring of
1985. Very soon thereafter, two of their six women leaders
were killed.
Peace Brigades International is sending individuals to
Guatemala to accompany the remaining four members of the
Council of Apoyo Mutuo twenty-four hours a day. An APG team
of 5-20 people could provide a similar protection to other
members of Apoyo Mutuo or similar groups in other places.

6. **Chile**
A group of Chileans with strong support from the
Catholic leadership have developed an anti-torture organization. Their strategy is simple. They locate the torture
centers used by the Pinochet government and then hold prayer
meetings in front of these torture centers, appealing to the
government to stop the torture. All those involved are
trained in the techniques of nonviolence and they have had

striking examples of police officers who were deeply moved
by the love expressed by the members of this group as they
were arrested.
Outside involvement is welcome. An APG team of 20 persons could assist such an organization.

7. Sharing the Concept
Joseph Liechty from Ireland said that although the
original proposal for Northern Ireland was entirely wrong,
nevertheless, one or two people with experience in Witness
for Peace or an APG could come to live in Northern Ireland,
become familiar with the context, begin to explore whether or
not local perceptive, involved Christians would see an
indigenous Peace Guard as desireable. If it caught the
imagination of local people, a local Peace Guard might
emerge.
Teams of two or three people could be sent to several
places (e.g. Middle East, Chile, etc.) for this kind of long
term exploration.

B. North America
1. Nonviolent Direct Action
Teams of 5-10 people could develop nonviolent direct
action programs on a range of issues in the U.S. and Canada:
a. Things like the current nonviolent direct action
campaign in South Africa. This could include, if deemed wise
after careful analysis and consultation, an attempt to stop
the sale of Krugerrands, etc.
b. Native Americans
c. Nuclear weapons development at both government and
corporate centers of research and production.

2. Education and Interpretation
a. In the Churches. Teams of 2-5 people could develop
educational tools, travel and speak in Mennonite and Brethren
in Christ churches to share with the entire body the biblical
understanding of shalom, the current work of APG, and the
information gained in different parts of the world.
b. Press and Government. Highly skilled teams with
expertise in media and politics could work in key places
like Washington, Ottawa, New York, etc. to share the information gained by the nonviolent direct action teams both in
North America and abroad.
Ahead of time, it is impossible to predict how any of
these scenarios would unfold. For our purposes here, that is
not essential. The purpose of the scenarios is not to

pretend to know the massive detailed information that would
be necessary before any intervention began.   Rather it is to
illustrate possible types of action in order to enable the
churches to understand the basic concept, and make a faithful
decision.

VI. Underlying Principles

The following underlying principles would guide the work
of the APG:
1.   The central purpose of APG is to *glorify the Prince
of Peace.*
2.   In all its activity, the APG will use only *nonviolent
methods* grounded in an Anabaptist theology of the cross.
3.   The APG is *international* in outlook and does not seek
to promote or undermine any nation or group although in
specific situations a particular aspect of the policy of one
nation or group will be challenged.
4.   The APG is *non-partisan.*   Therefore it always, at
every phase of its activity, seeks to establish and maintain
dialogue with all parties to a conflict.
5.   The APG is a *peace-making body, not a political
party.*   Therefore it never attempts to impose a specific
political, constitutional or economic proposal, but rather
seeks to create a context where the warring parties themselves can peacefully negotiate just solutions appropriate
for their unique setting.
6.   The APG is *not neutral* on questions of justice and
freedom.   Although it never seeks to impose a particular
solution, the APG is not indifferent to the biblical call for
justice and freedom for all people.   Therefore, the APG
always seeks to act in ways that promote religious and
political freedom including freedom of worship, speech, democratic elections and equality before the law.   It also seeks
to foster economic justice where all are genuinely free to
enjoy adequate food, housing, clothing, education, health care
and meaningful work to earn their own way.

VII. Criteria for Intervention

The following criteria for intervention would be important:
1.   The APG would intervene only after a careful attempt
to dialogue with, understand, and affirm the legitimate concerns of all parties to a conflict.
2.   The APG would intervene only after at least one major

party in the conflict had issued an invitation and agreed to give the APG the freedom to operate in their area.

3. The APG would always seek to operate in the territory of both sides to a conflict and would decide to operate exclusively in the territory of one side only after the APG's offer to operate on both sides had been rejected.

4. The APG would intervene only when it believes that it can operate according to Jesus' nonviolent example in a way that will probably promote peace, justice and freedom.

An APG might undertake a number of different kinds of interventions: interpositioning (placing themselves between warring factors to deter or stop violence); recording and reporting violence; temporary police work; dramatization of an injustice like apartheid.

The power of an APG would come from international public opinion, the mandate authorizing the action, the moral power of self-sacrificial, nonviolent caring for others, the APG's discipline and coordination, and the information that APG media people woud disseminate.

VIII. Training

Four to six months of intensive training would be essential. Four areas would be especially crucial: spiritual discipleship; the techniques of nonviolent direct action; physical fitness; the culture and history of the area of action. Much of the necessary information is already available. But it would need to be assembled for a new purpose.

Growth in spiritual discipleship would be a central expectation of the months of training. Public worship, biblical study and theological reflection would be essential. Participation in prayer chains would be universal. Regular weekly communication with one's supporting prayer chain in one's local congregation would provide strength. Individual spiritual advisers would help each person grow in the inward journey of personal prayer, devotional reading, fasting, journaling, silent retreats and meditation. People like Richard J. Foster would be needed to help construct the curriculum for spiritual growth.

Careful training in the techniques of nonviolent direct action would also be a central part of basic training. In the nonviolent campaigns of Gandhi, King, the Shanti Sena, Witness for Peace and many others, a vast body of knowledge, techniques and training skills are available. Training manuals have been written and experts in nonviolent training have emerged. Their expertise would be essential to develop a sophisticated training process that would include role-playing scenarios of intervention, ambush, crowd control, and massacre; practicing complex maneuvers of large numbers of people; and prompt obedience to orders from those in command. (Terminology for the equivalents of officers will need to be developed.)

The physical fitness of an APG ought to equal that of the marines. Tough training would produce people able to trek for long distances, survive in rugged inhospitable terrain, and sleep for months in tents. The expertise of people in charge of training for the armed forces would be essential here as it would be in the area of maneuvers, logistics and structures of command and communication.

Finally, extensive study of the geography, history and culture of the area of activity would be essential. All "officers" would need to read and speak the local language with considerable fluency. Every member would need to have some command of the local language. Experts in the geography, history, politics, economics, diplomacy, religion and ethnic complexity of the region would be needed to develop both an adequate six month training program for all volunteers as well as a sophisticated strategy for the APG's leadership and decision makers.

The proposal for an APG hopes (and eagerly expects) that other Christian groups as well as people from other religions will develop similar nonviolent Peace Guards with which the APG could cooperate closely. It also assumes that for such a novel ideal of such high risk to succeed, a fairly homogenous group with a common history, spirituality, liturgy and theological perspective is essential. Therefore, the Mennonites, if they decide to proceed, will develop an Anabaptist Peace Guard that reflects the unique Mennonite and Brethren in Christ perspective.

IX. Two Options for Beginning

1. 500 people in the first group of trainees.
2. 100 people in the first group of trainees.

1. The 500 Option
In this option, probably 300-400 would be trained for six months for one location--e.g. Nicaragua or South Africa or another scenario that was deemed better.

Perhaps 50-100 would be trained at the same time to test initially the concept in other areas--e.g. Laos, Chile, Guatemala, El Salvador, US and Canada. As many as 50-100

would be assigned to direct action projects in North America.
Ten to fifty would be trained for education and interpretation although they would need to spend time on location
in direct action. Rotation of people from direct action to
education/interpretation would provide first hand vividness
and integrity.

Pro

a. If we start too small, the project will be seen as one
more small idea of a group of fringe dreamers and will not
touch the larger church. Only if the project is large enough
to signal a major new thrust will it really catch the
imagination of the heart of the church.

b. Witness for Peace has demonstrated that small groups
can make a modest difference as a witness. They have also
proven that that difference is only token. What we need now
is to test what the impact of hundreds rather than dozens
would be.

Con

a. Five hundred would be costly.

b. A major mistake at this size would create great dis-
illusionment.

c. Five hundred skilled volunteers may not be there.

2. The 100 Option

If 100 persons were trained at once, they might be distributed as follows:

-50 in the US and Canada (most for nonviolent direct
action but as least ten for education and interpretation
teams for congregations, government and media).

-25 in Nicaragua (with Witness for Peace, perhaps as an
allied, cooperating group with its own identity).

-25 in the other teams testing places like Laos, El Salvador, Guatemala, Chile.

Pro:

a. Less costly

b. Mistakes would be less devastating

Con:

Fifty people in Central America or South Africa is *not*
large enough to take the next step in nonviolent direct
action. It would merely mean adding to Witness for Peace
rather than testing the next state. Whether we like it or
not, success depends in part on media attention which depends
in part on size.

THE CONCEPT OF "WARRIOR GOD" IN PEACE THEOLOGY

Ben C. Ollenburger

We are to practice peace, but in the Bible our God is called a warrior. This apparent contradiction has now come to constitute a problem for those wanting a theology that undergirds our practice of peace. In this essay I will not attempt to solve the problem, but will attempt rather to understand the conditions under which the concept of God the Warrior can be a theological problem. Such an inquiry seems appropriate just because biblical concepts themselves are capable of posing problems only for certain kinds of theology. If some clarity is gained regarding the relation of biblical concepts to theology, we may be better able to understand what kind of concrete problem God the Warrior poses.

I

It may be thought unwise to pose the issue in terms of biblical concepts of God. Biblical theologians and scholars have often objected to the use of the term "concept" because it implies a style of thinking that is supposed to be foreign to the biblical texts, whose stories, poems, and proverbs cannot legitimately be reduced to modern styles of conceptual thought. There is some immediate force to that objection, but I think that the choice of the term "concept" is a happy one.[1] To indicate why I think so it will help to distinguish among (1) motifs, (2) symbols, and (3) concepts. These distinctions are somewhat arbitrary, but I believe that they can help to clarify some matters in the discussion.

It is possible to delineate within the Old Testament texts a "God the Warrior" motif. A motif can be understood, for our purposes, as an image of relatively fixed linguistic character employed in various literary contexts. In the motif under consideration, God is described in martial terms, often acting within a divine council and with the aid of a heavenly army or "host." The battles fought by God the Warrior are generally waged in the cosmic realm, and their effects are seen on earth. Depending on the specific text, the cosmic or earthly realm may receive greater emphasis. In Exodus 15, the decisive actions take place in the earthly (or aquatic!) realm and God's action is directed against Egyptian and not exclusively cosmic enemies. In some later texts, the book of Daniel for example, the decisive battles are clearly cosmic. In other texts (many in Judges and other historical texts) the motif of God the Warrior is relatively undeveloped, though it remains clear in most texts that God is the decisive actor.[2]

The motif is common in near eastern religions. One reason it is not always clear how the motif is being employed, in Exodus 15 for example, is that in Canaanite religion the god's enemies are personified as deities such as "sea" and "river," the chaos waters. Elements of this appear also in the Old Testament, as in Psalm 74, where the sea is personified as "dragon" and "Leviathan," names also used in Canaanite texts to designate the forces hostile to Ba'al.[3] In Exodus 15 as well, the "sea" and chaos waters play an important role, but here they are more nearly the allies rather than the enemies of God. In whatever way the motif is employed in specific cases, and however fully its mythological components are represented in specific texts, it is safe to say that in the Old Testament the motif is used to speak of God's power and victory in battle--whether against cosmic forces (Isa 24:21-23), against Israel's enemies (Exod 15), or against Israel itself (Isa 8:1-15).

A lot of fuzzy talk has surrounded the term "symbol," and I probably cannot avoid engaging in some here. When I use that term in speaking of God the Warrior I mean only to specify that the function of any motif varies according to the way in which it is employed in a specific text or tradition. Symbols are combinations of various motifs, and these combinations are themselves variable. A motif may come to constitute a symbol when it is dominant or focal with a relatively fixed pattern of other motifs. Furthermore, symbols never operate in isolation but in relation to other symbols. Thus, it is better to speak of a network or system of symbolic relations.[4] What I am describing here is a literary phenomenon--the way various linguistic elements (combinations of words and sentences) enable a text to make its point(s). I am not speaking of symbols in order to say something thickly philosophical.[5]

Normally, the three terms I am distinguishing will be used with reference to three different contexts in which God the Warrior is used. That is, "motif" will refer to the function of God the Warrior in various kinds of literature; "symbol" will refer to its function in first-order religious discourse; "concept" will refer to its function in second-order reflective discourse, such as that of philosophy or systematic theology. Without contesting that approach, I am here attempting to differentiate these levels of reference within the biblical texts themselves.

The point to be made here is that God the Warrior achieves its symbolic function in relation to something else, namely, the symbol of God as King or, more precisely, of Yah-

weh as king.[6] God the warrior functions in Old Testament
texts not for its own sake, but in relation to God's kingship, and more properly, in relation to the specific kingship
of Yahweh. It is of God's royal character that God the Warrior is predicated. As a symbol, God the King itself functions in relation to other symbols. One such symbolic system
is constructed around David, God's elected king. These can,
of course, be brought into relation with one another, but it
is always of decisive importance to determine the structure
of the symbolic system. To put it more simply, we do not
know how to take God the Warrior apart from exegesis.[7]

The current fascination with metaphor sometimes obscures
this, because we tend to think that a given metaphor carries
its own meanings or automatically evokes a given meaning
from us, which, once we have gotten it, renders the texts
superfluous except as the occasion for getting it.[8] However,
the meaning of a given metaphor--and God the warrior can be
taken as one--can vary almost infinitely depending on its use
in different texts. My talk of motif and symbol, as opposed
to metaphor, is meant to emphasize that exegesis seeks to
determine the literary function of a text's linguistic elements (metaphors and similes, for example), rather than dis-
placing the texts in favor of some metaphorical disclosure
that they may occasion. God the Warrior is first of all a
literary phenomenon. We experience this phenomenon first of
all by reading texts.

Thus, for example, in Psalm 18 God the Warrior is brought
into relation with God the King in order to emphasize the
power of the earthly king. In other texts, especially in
Isaiah, God the Warrior is brought into relation with God the
King precisely to critique the power and prerogatives of the
earthly king. There is within the biblical texts, in other
words, the possibility of a systematic theological debate
about the proper force of a focal symbol--or about precisely
which symbol, warrior or king, is focal. The debate could be
carried further were New Testament texts brought into consideration, because there, too, God the Warrior is a motif
brought into relation with God the King, especially in the
book of Revelation.[9]

One cannot properly speak of the Old Testament concept
of God the Warrior apart from the larger symbolic construction of which it is a part. For that reason, it is also
important to relate God the Warrior to God the Creator. It
is in the dual roles of warrior and creator that the royal
God is portrayed as acting in the Old Testament. That is
clear from the texts I alluded to earlier, in which God's

action is somewhat ambiguous between war and creation. For example, in Psalm 74 the action that is enjoined upon God in verses 12-17 is creation: God's establishment of primordial order is recalled as an appeal to engage in that kind of activity once more. The world in which the Psalmist lives is chaos because God's enemies have triumphed--they have destroyed Jerusalem. In the language of this Psalm, the envisioned defeat of God's enemies, the historical enemies who destroyed Jerusalem, is also the recreation of the world. It may be simplest to say that in the Old Testament texts God's royal acts are depicted as those of a warrior/creator.

To speak of God the Warrior is also to speak of God the King and, hence, also of God the Creator. Since in the Old Testament creation is almost always spoken of in terms of order, to speak of God is also necessarily to speak of justice and righteousness, the two Hebrew terms that are most nearly equivalent to what I have spoken of as "order." Therefore, it is important that we be clear, though it may seem self-evident, that to speak of God the Warrior is to speak of God--that to speak of God the Warrior is to speak in a particular way of God's "universal dominion in justice and righteousness," as Rolfs Knierim has phrased it.[10] At least, we may say, it is not to speak less than that.

Paul Ricoeur has proclaimed that "symbols give rise to thought." We should go on to say that when symbols are employed to orient thinking they are treated as concepts. Symbols are not merely replaced by concepts, except perhaps in some forms of philosophy and theology; rather, they are treated conceptually insofar as we (and not only the texts) make them the instruments (and not only the objects) of thought. But this does not mean that concepts are the end of exegesis--what exegesis ends up with; rather, they both orient exegesis formally and provide it with its concrete subject-matter. As Ricoeur has also said, "symbols give rise to endless exegesis."[11] To put it another way, concepts are instruments; they "lead us to make investigations; are the expression of our interest, and direct our interest."[12] Or, to quote Stephen Toulmin, "Concepts are the necessary instruments of effective thought." To employ a concept entails the mastery of a skill. As he puts it, "to accept a scientific concept...commits one not merely to the symbolic employment of certain technical terms and forms of calculation, but to their practical use within the explanatory procedures of the science concerned."[13]

This applies equally to theological concepts and biblical ones. God the Warrior is employed in the biblical texts in

the service of thinking about sometimes very specific issues
in specific situations. Often these specifics are difficult
to uncover. But it is clear that in the judgment of some--
certain prophets, for example--others had not quite mastered
the concept of God the Warrior, including the symbol system
into which it is integrated. Isaiah was convinced that Ahaz
and Hezekiah had not quite mastered it; Jeremiah was equally
convinced that Hananiah was similarly deficient, and Micaiah
ben Imlah was certain that Ahab's four hundred prophets had
the same conceptual handicap. Samuel tried to warn the
Israelites that their understanding of the concept "king" was
skewed, because they did not understand how properly to use
that term in relation to the concept of God the King. Jesus
took similar pains to clarify for his disciples the concept
"benefactor," as it was used by Gentile kings but misapplied
in their own case.[14]

Soren Kierkegaard once said that "God is not a name but
a concept."[15] Like other skills, proper use of the concept
"God" can be forgotten.

When employed as the instruments of conceptual thought,
or when subjected to exegesis, symbols are quite adaptable.
To this the texts of the Old Testament bear witness. Particularly important in this regard is the shift in the use of
God the Warrior in later Old Testament literature, and especially in Daniel. I want only to mention this, but not to
underestimate its importance. The shift is evident in Psalm
74, to which reference has already been made. Here and elsewhere the distortions that have come to afflict God's created
order are not regarded as repudiating decisively God's royal
and universal dominion, but as forming the context in which
faithful perseverance testifies to the hope (and fear) of the
warrior's coming. It is important to note this, because this
development creates the space, in one sense or another, in
which God the Warrior can be incorporated in the New Testament.

II

This discussion of concepts is meant to bring us to the
larger topic of God the Warrior in peace theology. The first
point to be made, of course, is that any responsible
appropriation of this concept will entail its mastery--"its
practical use within the explanatory procedures of the
science concerned." As a biblical concept, it can only be
mastered by sustained attention to the ways in which it is
employed in the various biblical texts where it occurs.[16] In
contemporary theology God the Warrior has little practical

use in any explanatory procedure. Biblical terms are often
employed, but biblical concepts seldom, either because they
have been forgotten, or because they do not figure in the
explanatory procedures--the theology--with which we work.
On the other hand, biblical scholars have concentrated
primarily on the contours of this motif, or symbol, or concept, and on its putative historical development, implicitly
assuming that this research answers the relevant theological
questions. If it did, the discussion would have been brought
to a close, assuming that the historical questions have been
correctly answered. Since the discussion appears still to be
open, it is worth considering why God the Warrior continues
to pose a problem for peace theology, and in what *kind* of
theology this and other biblical concepts can really be
materially problematic.

In the first place, certain assumptions are often made
about the way in which religious symbols function within the
communities which foster them. At this level, the assumption
that God the Warrior constitutes a theological problem may
entail as its corollary that those communities that fostered
this image would be themselves given to warrior-like
activity, activity that the symbolism was designed to legitimate or motivate. If this functionalist assumption were
granted, and if reasons were offered for preserving this
symbolism--because it is in the Bible and the Bible is somehow important in and for theology, for example--then it is
clear that God the Warrior would constitute a problem for
peace theology.

This assumption and its corollary can be addressed as an
anthropological and historical issue. In other words, our
guesses or theories about how religious symbols function in
those communities that foster them can be checked by turning
to anthropological and historical materials. Millard Lind's
work is one way in which such assumptions can be checked.
In his work, and particularly in *Yahweh Is a Warrior*, Lind
has checked certain biblical texts and has found, to his
satisfaction, that in the communities that produced those
texts God the Warrior did not function to legitimate or
motivate warrior-like activity, but to correct or repudiate
it.

Lind's work is instructive not just because he has
achieved certain significant exegetical and historical
results, but because he has challenged the assumption that
God the Warrior is inevitably or even primarily a symbolic
call to arms. He has called into question, in other words,
the assumption that a particular symbolic pattern necessarily

reflects, in a direct and predictable way, specific social norms and values.[17] Because of Lind's work we ought to be cautious about our ability to predict just what kind of society with just what kind of values a specific piece of religious symbolism will support. At Ugarit, for example, Ba'al is the central deity in the religious myths, but apparently plays no substantial role in the cult. Dagan, the central deity of the cult, is almost absent in the myths.[18] The pantheons of some patrilineal societies are matrilineal.

In that respect, Lind's work is superior to that of G. Ernest Wright. It is superior just because Lind paid closer attention to the way God the Warrior functioned for Israel than did Wright, who assumed, sometimes in contrast to what he had observed in the texts, that God the Warrior must have a primary role to play in motivating or legitimating the martial character of the Israelite community. Lind argued this assumption to be wrong by pointing to the texts that showed it to be so--and interpreting them according to certain historical assumptions that he and Wright share.

The point of this is that we cannot know beforehand what any discrete piece of symbolism means all by itself, even though people as diverse as Alfred North Whitehead and Gibson Winter claim to have this knowledge.[19] All of the biblical symbols are (naturally) embedded in texts. We come initially to understand a biblical symbol by seeing how the texts use that symbol conceptually. If we are to understand God the Warrior in the biblical texts, we will have necessarily to do with exegesis--and not just the kind practiced by those trained as historians. The symbol or concept is *this kind* of problem only if the texts are. By the same token, the elimination of offensive images, or their supplementation by more humane (or liberating, or egalitarian, or pacific) symbols will not necessarily reflect communities of a particular character. Any proposal to replace a symbol would have to be expanded to the elimination of certain texts and their replacement with new ones--as Rosemary Radford Reuther has recently suggested. A symbol is meaningful only in relation to a narrative which teaches us how the symbol is to be taken, whether the narrative is the Bible's or our own, explicit or presupposed. Feminine images or metaphors of the divine, for example, entail a community of no particular character specifiable beforehand. The goddesses Ishtar and Anat were invoked by kings of highly militarized and stratified societies going to war, and given credit for their military victories. God as friend is associated with David, the most hierarchical and militant leader in Israel's history, and with North American Evangelical pietism.[20]

III

The preceding discussion has attempted only to show that a certain style of argument for the automatic inappropriateness of God the Warrior for peace theology is not compelling. The argument that we have considered is primarily anthropological and historical, however, and it is still unclear what are the theological conditions under which God the Warrior would constitute a genuine problem for peace theology.[21] Part of this unclarity is due to uncertainty about what is meant by "peace theology." Does this designate a particular theological *method,* alternative to others currently available? Is peace theology a dogmatic exposition with peace as the central and defining *locus?* Is it primarily *praxis,* including both ethical/political engagement and theological reflection upon it? These questions, which hardly exhaust the options, are not mine to answer here; they are stated because these and other questions need to be answered before much can be said about what kind of problem God the Warrior will or can pose for peace theology. One way to proceed in the interim is to look at one or more contemporary methodological proposals and to ask whether within them God the Warrior could conceivably constitute a theological problem and be taken with conceptual seriousness.[22]

Among the more widely discussed contemporary proposals in theological method are those by Gordon Kaufman, David Tracy and Edward Farley.[23] God the Warrior could constitute a problem for them. This matter is difficult to judge in the first place because these scholars have pursued a somewhat apologetic course, seeking more to establish the public criteria on which their substantive exposition will be grounded (and if grounded, then justified), than engaging in that substantive exposition.

In the second place, the matter is difficult to judge because it is unclear how their central categories are defined in relation to the Bible. When Kaufman urges us to reconstruct the image of "God" on the basis of the language of some cultures and societies where he has heard that term used, rather than on the basis of one Testament or the other, as used in one church or another, or in one religion or another,[24] there seems to be little chance that God the Warrior would be allowed to constitute a problem. Furthermore, God the Warrior is not an image of God that one would choose to construct, since it is obvious to Kaufman that it could not nourish the humanization that is the regulative criterion for the construction of such images.[25] If God the Warrior is to

be taken seriusly in peace theology, that theology will have
to adopt a theological method other than the one proposed by
Kaufman.
     Things are not so clear with respect to Tracy and Farley.
Tracy's proposal is more obviously related to the biblical
texts than are those of Kaufman and Farley, and certain of
the categories with which Tracy works rely on a narrative
reading of the biblical texts. More specifically, his discussion of apocalyptic could be expanded to uncover one dimension of God the Warrior symbolism, namely, its apocalyptic
dimension in the New Testament.[26] However, Tracy's remarks
on apocalyptic leave the matter at a purely formal and functional (limit) level, and his methodological proposal
threatens to allegorize the texts by making their interpretation, and especially the Christ event, the particular occasion
of a general limit experience, or of a kind of reflexive disclosure (limit experiences disclose themselves as such).[27]
Thus, it is unclear how God the Warrior (or even the Old
Testament) could constitute for him any kind of serious
theological issue, or how a peace theology for which God the
Warrior *is* problematic could employ his method.
     Farley gives explicit place to "the faith of Israel" in
"ecclesial duration," and Israel's faith continues to be
embedded in "ecclesia" (he avoids the term "church").[28]
However, the faith of Israel is only accidentally related to
the Old Testament, and Farley rejects any notion of canon or
of a criteriological function of Scripture, no matter how
nuanced or enlightened. Again, if no criteriological function,
to use Farley's terms, is assigned to Scripture, then it is
hard to see how God the Warrior could constitute a theological problem, or what kind of problem it would turn out to be.
Furthermore, the faith of Israel is preserved in ecclesial
existence only insofar as it "has a certain entelechy toward
a universalized modality of divine presence."[29] God the Warrior appears, one guesses, only at the beginning of this
entelechy and could perhaps be used as a negative example
with which to contrast the more properly universalized
modality of God's presence in Jesus. This eliminates the
problem by undermining the assumptions on which it can be a
problem.[30]
     These three proposals, which are hardly unrepresentative
of contemporary theological debate in North America, thus
provide us little help in understanding the problem that God
the Warrior, as a biblical concept of God, could pose for
theology, or for peace theology. The proposals of Kaufman
and Farley do not allow for such a problem to arise; and

except in his brief discussion of apocalyptic in the New
Testament, Tracy gives little clue what kind of problem it
would constitute if it could arise.

This aside on Kaufman, Tracy and Farley is part of a
larger discussion about the assumptions under which God the
Warrior could be problematic, and hence really be a concept,
in peace theology. One of those assumptions is
anthropological--an assumption about the way symbols function. That assumption was taken up in the second section of
this essay. I talked briefly about theology in this third
section because the problem God the Warrior actually poses,
the way it will be taken seriously, depends on a theological
method--a theological way of taking biblical concepts and,
hence, biblical texts. We may conclude thus far that if
peace theology is to deal with the problem of God the Warrior as a biblical concept, it will have to go beyond an historical analysis of the texts, and beyond the kind of
theological methods proposed by Kaufman, Tracy and Farley.

IV

Is there, then, a theological proposal that is in principle capable of taking God the Warrior with conceptual
seriousness? I suggest that there is, and I will attempt to
sketch such a proposal by drawing on the original "Mennonite" theologian and on another who is decidedly un-
Mennonite.

It has often been observed and remarked that the Anabaptists spoke and thought in the vocabulary of the biblical
texts. Anyone who has read Menno Simons can attest the
truth of that observation. I will not go so far as to suggest that we must adopt this practice, though that would perhaps cure us of some theological headaches, but will suggest
that the Anabaptists, who are notorious for lacking a
systematic theology, had sufficient mastery of the biblical
concepts--had, in other words, sufficient skill in using
them--to be able to construe the world in terms of them, and
that this is a mastery worth acquiring and a skill worth
achieving. It may even be the basis of a theological method.
Some of the research on Anabaptist understandings of Scripture has tended to obscure this by focusing primarily on disagreements with Catholic, Reformed and Lutheran opponents.
From this research we have learned that the Anabaptists made
a radical distinction between the Old and New Testaments,
whether this amounted to an "Aufhebung" (elimination) or
merely an "Abwertung" (devaluing) of the former.[31]

There are, however, other things to learn from the way

the Anabaptists used Scripture--not just in formal debates or
confessions, but in identifying and situating themselves in
relation to a story whose central character and active agent
is God. This theological reading of Scripture is evident in
Menno and can be exemplified with reference to his "Meditation on the Twenty-Fifth Psalm."[32] In the preface to his
meditation and in its body Menno identifies himself
autobiographically, using the framework of the Psalm and its
vocabulary to do so. This meditation proceeds according to
the individual verses of the Psalm, but in the process Menno
draws into the Psalm the whole of the biblical narrative *and*
the world in which he is oppressed.

It is in the language of the Psalm that Menno locates
himself and his fellow believers over against the lords and
princes of this world who rebel against the God to whom
Menno directs his confession. Thus the biblical narrative,
which Menno draws partly from the Psalm and partly from
other texts, absorbs the world into itself and provides the
perspective from which Menno understands himself and the
conflicts in which he is engaged. The text not only absorbs
the world but catches up all of history, in such a way that
Menno is able to identify himself in relation to the individual characters of the biblical narrative. Most interestingly,
the characters with whom Menno identifies are all from the
Old Testament. Chief among these is King Jehoshaphat, with
whom Menno identifies explicitly. But he goes on to mention
Abraham, Jacob, Joseph, Moses, Israel, David, Hezekiah, and
Daniel and his friends as exemplars of the experience Menno
shares with Jehoshaphat. All of these are cited by Menno as
saints who were estranged, exiled, persecuted or distressed,
placed their faith in God and were not disappointed. It is
by means of these narratives that Menno construes and interprets the world, and it is by understanding himself within
the contours of that world so interpreted that Menno is able
to understand, articulate, and commend the kind of faithfulness that has characterized and ought to characterize God's
people.

The context of these meditations is Menno's and the
church's persecution at the hands of the authorities. But
Menno does not seek to understand the texts on the basis of
his experience, nor does he try to generate a theological
understanding of suffering on this basis; rather, it is in
light of these narratives that Menno understands his experience. To put it more pointedly, it is because he has
understood himself so completely according to the specific
language of the Old Testament narratives that he *can have*

this experience--not just an experience of suffering, but precisely the kind of experience that comes to those who risk exclusion and persecution on behalf of loyalty to God's "adorably great name" and God's "truth." The textually embedded biblical concepts just are, for Menno, the "instruments" of which he makes use in "the explanatory procedures" of his theological "science."[33]

This same way of reading Scripture, of using biblical concepts as explanatory instruments, is evident in Menno's "The Cross of the Saints." The focal concept here is obviously the cross, which is posited by Menno as the concept that most adequately explains the world and its history. The treatise begins by associating God's faithful, here called "the new Eve and her children," with Christ's cross, and differentiating them from their persecutors on this basis. Menno follows this use of "second-order religious concepts" with a lengthy (15 pages) recitation of "biblical examples." Here he mentions fifteen examples from the Old Testament, expounding some of them at length. In the structure (or horizon) provided by these stories, Menno gives form to the concept of the cross with which he began. Moreover, it is only after citing these and several New Testament examples that Menno turns to the central character of his narrative, "the Lord and Prince himself." He makes clear that it is precisely on the basis of these Old and New Testament stories, into which the whole world and its history are drawn, that the cross of Christ is to be understood.

Menno does not confuse the issue here by supposing that history somehow progressed along revelatory lines, culminating in the "Christ-event;" he is clear that Christ was present in the suffering of God's righteous ones from the beginning.[34] Menno's point is rather a narrative one: our understanding of Christ and his cross is predicated on a proper understanding of the larger story in which they are located, and--perforce--by means of which we locate ourselves and are either comforted or condemned. It is the cross that illumines the stories and gives them their meaning, but it is *the stories* understood from the standpoint of the cross that construe the world in such a way that talk about the cross continues to be intelligible--and not only intelligible, but indispensable to understanding Christ, the world, and faith.

That is not the whole story. In "The Cross of Saints" Menno does not assume that the cross is self-authenticating-- that the example of Christ's suffering offers us a portrayal of authentic, self-giving humanity which we intuitively recognize as such. The reason that Menno can present the cross as a genuinely explanatory concept is that Christ and the cross are conceptually linked with God the Warrior. The narratives Menno cites show not only that the righteous suffer, but also that "the Almighty Lord and Ruler of all things punishes the haughty, bloodthirsty tyrants, each one in his own time," and that this Almighty Lord "can guard His elect and help them out of all distresses...even as he has clearly shown and demonstrated to all Israel at the Red Sea, to David...to Elijah and Elisha, to Daniel in the lions' den, to the young men in the furnace, and to many others with great power."

This linkage between the cross and God the Warrior is also stated with reference to Christ and his people, who hope for the return of "Christ Jesus...as an Almighty Sovereign, a conqueror, and a glorious king before all the tribes and peoples, unto the last judgment." The whole world, its future and his history, are here compressed into a narrative extending from Adam and Eve to the final judgment--a narrative in which the faithful are urged to identify themselves with Christ's cross, because this cross, in its connection with God the Warrior (or more simply, God), is what renders the world intelligible and provides the ground of hope. Menno does not urge his readers to find concepts commensurate with their experience; rather, he clarifies for them that their experience *is* the experience of the cross of Christ. Significantly for us, it is only after Menno has rehearsed the biblical narrative in light of the cross, and understood the cross of Christ (and hence the world) on the basis of this narrative, that he urges his readers: "Therefore, have your feet shod with the Gospel of peace."

Menno's peace theology is a theology of the Gospel, an evangelical theology grounded in the "revealed grace of God" and God's "glorious and truthful Word." The followers of Jesus are to "verify" (he actually uses that term!) the truth of the Gospel "in power and in deed." The faithful know this Gospel and the Christ it attests through the texts of Scripture, by which they identify and understand themselves and the world that rejects them. Theology, for Menno, is an exercise in hermeneutics--not in bridging a gap between Scripture and what we know on other grounds to be true, not in casting about for concepts by which to construct an image of God that enshrines the values we cherish, and not in giving specific expression to a common religious experience, but in having sufficient mastery of the biblical concepts (including the concept of God the Warrior) that we can use them in the practice of giving intelligible expression to that faith whose actions verify the religious claims we make. It is because the real agent in these narratives is God the Creator and Warrior King that, for Menno, both suffering and peacemaking can and must be cruciform.

Menno's theology is intratextual. That term, like many of those I have used in the above paragraphs to describe Menno's theology, is taken from George Lindbeck.[35] Lindbeck proposes that an "intratextual theology" is the one most appropriate for a "post-liberal" Christianity. Menno is certainly not post-liberal, but works with an understanding of the texts more or less common to him and other "pre-liberals," From Luther to Bullinger.[36] They disagreed radically and impolitely on central theological issues, but shared assumptions about the formal way in which text and theology cohere. While we can hardly ignore or even regret the changes that have occurred since the Enlightenment, including their effect on how we read texts, I would suggest with Lindbeck that this intratextual approach provides the most appropriate way to proceed--at least for biblical theology--after the Enlightenment dogmas have themselves been subjected to historical criticism. This suggestion is based, for my part, on (1) observation of how the texts work, exercising their *de facto* authority in the church; (2) the ability of what Lindbeck, perhaps inadvisedly, calls "intratextualism" to account for this *de facto* authority theologically; (3) the increasingly extensive critique of various forms of philosophical foundationalism by literary critics, philosophers and physical and social scientists.[37]

Although I have already illustrated Lindbeck's approach and used his terminology in talking about Menno, it may be useful to contrast this with at least one contemporary proposal, that of Gordon Kaufman. Kaufman begins by agreeing with Wittgenstein (as does Lindbeck) that theology is a kind of grammar that describes how a language works, and that a particular language "provides a principal foundation for our religious experience."[38] Then, however, Kaufman does exactly what Wittgenstein devoted his later years to showing will not work: he seeks to provide foundations for theological language in a common culture and its scientific vocabulary. Thus, he suggests that talk of "sin and salvation, sacraments and faith, Christ and the church" have faded from relevance because they don't square with our experience. This theological vocabulary "can be used only as it does justice to and makes theologically intelligible our experience, as actually grasped and interpreted by us in the language of modern psychology, physics, art and ordinary

life." But these disciplines (I don't know what "ordinary
life" is doing here) do not provide foundations; they are
merely alternative and often contradictory ways of mapping
our vocabulary onto the world, and hence making different
kinds of experience possible. They are not foundational;
they are merely what Wittgenstein called "objects of comparison:" different vocabularies that help us cope with
reality in different ways.[39]

Kaufman's inability to make the traditional theological
vocabulary work is rooted in the opposition between his
proposal and that of Lindbeck. Kaufman is an example of
what Lindbeck calls the "liberal tendency to redescribe religion in extrascriptural frameworks" (124), whether these be
the frameworks provided by historical-critical reconstruction, a culture's self-understanding, or some passing
philosophical fancy (phenomenology, Marxism, process
philosophy).[40] One of these is first regarded to offer the
vocabulary most adequately reflective of reality itself, or
our experience of it, and then biblical or theological concepts must be translated into that vocabulary. As Lindbeck
puts it, "Liberals start with experience, with an account of
the present, and then adjust their vision of the kingdom of
God accordingly, while postliberals are in principle committed to doing the reverse. The first procedure makes it
easier to accommodate to present trends, whether from the
right or the left: Christian fellow travelers of both Nazism
and Stalinism generally used liberal methodology to justify
their positions. When, in contrast to this, one looks at the
present in the light of an intratextually derived eschatology, one gets a different view of which contemporary developments are likely to be ultimately significant" (125-26).[41]

Lindbeck admits that the spirit of the age militates
against this intratextual procedure in theology. It seems
quaint to insist that theology should explicate for the prac-
titioners of a religion the grammar of their language, and
that an interatextual reading of their canonical texts, in
such a way that the world is absorbed into them (rather than
vice-versa), is most appropriate to both such practice and
its explication. And Lindbeck acknowledges that such a
proposal will likely gain acceptance in the church only after
"dechristianization reduces Christians to a small minority...that strive without traditionalist rigidity to cultivate
their native tongue and learn to act accordingly" (133-34).
In this context, when those with wisdom and skill in the
practice of Christianity and the practical use of its concepts displace those who consider "translation a tempting

alternative," it will again become possible to "experience the whole of life in religious terms" (p. 133).

It may well be, as Lindbeck suggests, that the spirit of the age militates against such an approach, and against the use of biblical concepts that I have suggested.[42] It may even be that the biblical images of God are now deemed too offensive to contemporary piety to be theologically useful. Theologians, and peace theologians, can decide that issue. But so long as there are churches in which the Bible is read there will remain a theological responsibility to address the question of how its reading bears on the faithfulness of believers, and on the faithfulness of their talk of God-- including God the Warrior. That issue theologians and peace theologians are not free to decide, even if it entails that they be militantly against the spirit of the age.

How to think and speak of the concept "God the Warrior" remains a genuine problem, and this essay is intended as a modest suggestion of how it can be a theological problem, and thus the subject of and for theological inquiry.

Notes

1. This essay is a revision of a paper originally prepared for a Peace Theology Colloquium sponsored by the Mennonite Central Committee Peace Section and the Institute of Mennonite Studies, at the Associated Mennonite Biblical Seminaries, Elkhart, Indiana, 24-26 June 1985. The title was assigned for that occasion and the essay should be understood as an experimental attempt to deal with the problem of God the Warrior as a concept. I will not argue that this is the only way to deal with that problem. The original version of the essay was later discussed at a meeting of Mennonite biblical scholars at the AAR/SBL annual meeting in Anaheim, California, 23 November 1985. I gratefully acknowledge the helpful comments of those who discussed the essay in these two forums, and apologize for not incorporating the objections raised against it.

2. In Numbers 21:21-25, Israel is simply depicted as engaging and defeating the army of Sihon, an Amorite king. In Deuteronomy 2, the whole episode is elaborately portrayed as Yahweh's victory on Israel's behalf. See Fritz Stolz, *Yahwes und Israels Kriege* (ATANT, 60; Zürich: Theologischer Verlag, 1972) 73-74.

3. See also Psalm 77:16-20; Isaiah 27:1; 51:9-11. These matters have been explored most thoroughly by Frank Moore Cross, *Canaanite Myth and Hebrew Epic* (Cambridge: Harvard, 1973) and Patrick D. Miller, *The Divine Warrior in Early Israel* (HSM, 5; Cambridge: Harvard, 1975). See also Millard Lind, *Yahweh is a Warrior* (Scottdale: Herald, 1980) and Ben C. Ollenburger, *Zion, the City of the Great King* (JSOTSS, 41; Sheffield Academic Press, 1987).

4. On the understanding of symbols presupposed in this paragraph, see the first chapter of Ollenburger, *Zion, the City of the Great King*. A symbol can be broken down into its constitutive motifs, but the way in which motifs are combined within a symbolic construction, and the way symbols are related to each other, ought to guide interpretation.

5. For some examples of "thickly philosophical" talk of symbols see Gibson Winter, *Liberating Creation* (New York: Crossroad, 1981); Mark Kline Taylor, *Beyond Explanation* (Macon: Mercer, 1985). Both Winter and Taylor rely heavily on Paul Ricoeur, Winter to explain what social ethicists do and Taylor to explain what anthropologists do. Taylor has carried this further to explain what theologians ought to do (in "In Praise of Shaky Ground," *Theology Today* 43 [1986], 36-

51), which turns out to be very much like what anthropologists do.

6. Motifs are, on this understanding, general and interchangeable among religions. Symbols are determinate and specific to a religion.

7. Here, of course, I do not mean one particular kind of exegesis, but only the skilled and interested reading of texts. With practice, anyone can do this.

8. It is not necessary to treat metaphors in this way; unfortunately, theologians frequently do. Two very perceptive critiques of this way of thinking are offered by Susan Handelman (*The Slayers of Moses* [Albany: State University of New York, 1982]) and Hans Frei ("The 'Literal Reading' of Biblical Narrative in the Christian Tradition: Does it Stretch or Will it Break?" in *The Bible and the Narrative Tradition* [Frank McConnell, ed; New York: Oxford, 1986] 36–77). Handelman deals with literary criticism, Frei with theology. Both of them draw on Jacques Derrida to make their respective points.

9. As one example, in 11:17–18, the elders speak first of God's reign and the declare that God's wrath has come for "destroying those who destroyed the earth."

10. Rolf Knierim, "The Task of Old Testament Theology," *Horizons in Biblical Theology* 6 (1984) 44.

11. *Interpretation Theory* (Forth Worth: TCU, 1984) 25–28.

12. Ludwig Wittgenstein, *Philosophical Investigations* (New York: Macmillan, 1953) #569, #570.

13. Both quotations are from Toulmin, *Human Understanding* (Princeton: Princeton U., 1972), pages 35, 352, respectively.

14. Both of the last two examples are taken from Roger White, "Notes on Analogical Predication and Speaking about God," in *Philosophical Frontiers of Christian Theology* (Cambridge: Cambridge U., 1982) 197–226. The last example, with which White deals extensively, could have been taken from John Howard Yoder's *The Politics of Jesus* (Grand Rapids: Eerdmans, 1972), which White does not mention. White's essay is an illuminating exposition of Karl Barth's use of analogy, which has more to do with what I am here describing as "concept" and Handelman calls "metonymy" (see above, note 8), than with metaphor. Is it accidental that Barth's theology is almost infinitely more dependent on the reading of actual biblical texts than that of his successors?

15. *Philosophical Fragments* (Princeton: Princeton U., 1962) 51. See also Charles M. Wood, *The Formation of*

Christian Understanding (Philadelphia: Westminster, 1981).
    16. J. Denny Weaver urges us to focus on "the story as a whole," rather than on "exegetical detail," in relating the Bible to ethics. ("Mennonites: Theology, Peace and Identity," unpublished paper for the meeting of Mennonites at AAR/SBL Atlanta, November 22, 1986, p. 12). I concur, except that so long as it matters how the story as a whole is told, and so long as there is disagreement on that point--always, in both cases--exegetical detail will continue to be important.
    17. That is at least one reason why exegesis--the practice of applicative reading of the texts--needs to be guided by symbols and concepts embedded in the texts, rather than only by metaphors from one source or another.
    18. Robert A. Oden, "Theoretical Assumptions in the Study of Ugaritic Myths," *Maarau* 2 (1969) 43-63. The general issue is given a fairly typical survey by Ragnar Holte, "Gottessymbol und soziale Struktur," *Religious Symbols and Their Functions* (ed. H. Biezais; Stockholm: Almqvist & Wiksell, 1979) 1-14.
    19. Whitehead, *Adventures of Ideas* (New York: Macmillan, 1933) 33; Winter, *Liberating Creation*, 118.
    20. These remarks obviously relate to Sallie McFague's *Metaphorical Theology* (Philadelphia: Fortress, 1982), not in order to make simplistic criticisms of her work, but to argue that how we take feminine (or masculine) images of God, or metaphors like "friend," always depends on a larger narrative. Nor is there any need to argue that non-biblical models and mataphors of God, including feminine ones, are automatically illicit. The point is simply that in order to understand biblical images such as "The kingdom of God," as used in the parables, one needs to read more than the parables (42-54).
    21. In speaking about God the Warrior here and elsewhere in this essay I mean the literary--i.e., biblical or even textual, if you will--phenomenon as described in part I, above. Obviously, on this understanding if the biblical texts are not crucial and central to a definition of God the Warrior, then it cannot pose a theological problem; nor can it if we proceed metaphorically, merely ascribing to God the "associative commonplaces" derived from our experience of the term "warrior." See Carol Newsome, "A Maker of Metaphors--Ezekiel's Oracles Against Tyre," *Interpretation* 38 (1984) 152.
    22. It will be understood, at least by those who know me, that the range of theological proposals I am capable of considering is extremely limited.
    23. Kaufman, *The Theological Imagination* (Philadelphia:

Westminster, 1981); Tracy, *The Analogical Imagination* (New York: Crossroad, 1981); Farley, *Ecclesial Reflection* (Philadelphia: Fortress, 1982). See also Francis Schüssler Fiorenza's important book, *Foundational Theology* (New York: Crossroad, 1984), and the previously mentioned work of Sallie McFague.

24. Kaufman, *An Essay on Theological Method* (Missoula: Scholars Press, 1975) 6.

25. *Theological Imagination*, 184–200. Peace theology will, of course, also have to consider the larger question of the Bible's role and place in the Christian community. Kaufman's earlier work could give place to God the Warrior as the kind of imagery Christian piety should now avoid, but even that possibility is now foreclosed.

26. *Analogical Imagination*, 265–66. He proposes that the apocalyptic genre plays a critical role in relation to confessional narratives and doctrinal formulations in the NT and, by analogy, in contemporary theology.

27. See Frei's critique of Tracy in the article referred to above. The kinds of hermeneutical issues Frei raises will have to be decided one way or the other before the matter can be more fully assessed.

28. *Ecclesial Reflection*, 281–91. For Farley, just as ecclesiality is an "ideal-actual entity" that displaces "church" (p. 277),

29. *Ecclesial Reflection*, 286. This is a sophisticated restatement in phenomenological vocabulary of the traditional kernel-husk argument.

30. This criticism of Farley may be too harsh. He does recognize that the nationalistic, militaristic, and patriarchal traditions of the OT are susceptible of critique (290). However, Farley's eagerness to avoid the concreteness of the OT (and much else) in favor of its "ideality" substitutes the Bible's own implicit and dialectical critique for one supplied by a phenomenology of an ideal ecclesial existence. In this way biblical terms can be occasionally retained, but their content is supplied from other sources. As a result, the Bible can be the object of theological criticism but not the context of critical reflection on the church's and theology's own practice. See my essay, "Biblical Theology: Situating the Discipline," in *Understanding the Word* (Butler, Conrad and Ollenburger, eds.: JSOTSS 37: Sheffield: JSOT, 1985), 37–62.

31. Clarence Bauman, *Gewaltlosigkeit im Täufertum* (Leiden: Brill, 1968), 156.

32. The two texts of Menno from which I will quote

extensively are pages 63–86 and 579–622 of *The Complete
Works of Menno Simons* (Scottdale: Mennonite Publishing
House, 1956).   In order not to burden the text, I will quote
Menno without citing specific page numbers.   This may have
the added benefit of leading the readers of this essay to
read Menno instead.

33.   Unlike some other theological practice, Menno does
not here attempt to wrest the concepts from their textual
embeddedness in order to consider them abstractly or to
supply their content from other, non-biblical sources.   When
he does make this kind of foundationalist move, as in his
effort to ground his account of the incarnation in the concepts of biology and agriculture, the results are lamentable
(*see Complete Writings*, pp. 427–40).   The point is not that
non-biblical concepts are illicit, but that they are not foundational.

34.   In this way Menno avoids the kind of contrast Farley
must draw between the universal modality of God's presence
in Christ and the nationalistic particularism of the faith of
Israel (see above, notes 28 and 30).   Menno is able to
understand the OT stories, by referring them to the cross and
vice-versa, as the particular and concrete way in which God's
presence is properly universal.   In this way universality is
not purchased at the cost of an abstraction.

35.   George A. Lindbeck, *The Nature of Doctrine*
(Philadelphia: Westminster, 1984).   Page numbers in the text
refer to this book.   J. Denny Weaver now draws on Lindbeck
as well ("Mennonites: Theology and Identity").   This attention
from Mennonites would probably worry Lindbeck, or at least
confuse him, since he regards the radical reformers as
having made the Bible captive to alien, anti-establishment
frameworks ("Barth and Textuality," *Theology Today* 43 [1986]
364–65).   As evidence, he cites Luther's comments on the
Schwärmer. Apparently, one holds the Bible captive when con-
demning the prince but avoids doing so when encouraging him
in his bigamy.

36.   On Luther see Hans W. Frei, *The Eclipse of Biblical
Narrative* (New Haven: Yale, 1974).   My understanding of Bul-
linger's hermeneutics is drawn from an unpublished paper by
Edward A. Downey, "Covenant and History in the Thought of
Heinrich Bullinger."

37.   On the Bible's authority in theology see David H.
Kelsey, "The Bible and Christian Theology, *JAAR* 48 (1980) 385–
402.   On the move away from "foundationalism" see, for example, Richard Bernstein, *Beyond Objectivism and Relativism*
(Philadelphia: U. of Pennsylvania, 1983).   In my view, the

decision to treat biblical concepts is logically independent
of decisions whether (1) the Bible's authority is a function
of the role played by the Bible in the church, or (2) the
Bible is authoritative because of some intrinsic properties
of the text. These are also independent of the questions
whether the Bible's concepts are religiously or historically
unique, and whether concepts constitute technical terms that
exhibit a systematic inter-relationship with the canon.

38. The quotes in this paragraph are from *Theological
Method,* 6, 58. For a similar critique see Ronald F. Thiemann,
"Revelation and Imaginative Construction," *Journal of Religion*
61 (1981) 242-63.

39. *Philosophical Investigations,* #130.

40. Process philosophy seems currently to fascinate Mennonites, for reasons that escape me. See Carl Keener, "The
Darwinian Revolution and its Implications for a Modern
Anabaptist Theology," *Conrad Grebel Review* 1 (1983) 13-22. J.
Denny Weaver, in an earlier article, suggests that we do
theology on the basis of the presuppositions inherent in "the
Mennonite agenda," rather than adopting a "christendom"
starting-point. He then proposes a radically historicist
revision of biblical authority, a Hegelian vision of God's
immanence in history, and a turn to process theology ("Perspectives on a Mennonite Theology," *Explorations of
Systematic Theology: From Mennonite Perspectives* [Willard
Swartley, ed.; Elkhart: IMS, 1984], 17-36). How would this
differ from the worst features of christendom in the last two
centuries? This approach reaches its zenith in Mike Klassen,
"Einstein and Anabaptism," *Direction* 13 (1984) 44-48. Klassen
observes that the Anabaptists used dynamic biblical terms to
speak of God, not static philosophical ones as the Reformed
did. How then do we account for Menno's description of God
as an "eternal, omnipotent, incomprehensible, invisible,
ineffable and indescribable...Being," in a defense of the
Trinity? (*Complete Works,* 491).

41. It would be helpful if at this point Lindbeck would
venture a specific estimate, or prophecy, regarding 'which
contemporary developments are like to be ultimately [or even
penultimately] significant." This would help us, whether on
the right or the left, to know how to judge contemporary
developments without making the Bible captive to alien frameworks.

42. J. Denny Weaver, who commends Lindbeck's proposal,
makes "a peace perspective" foundational to a reading of the
Bible ("Mennonites: Theology, Peace and Identity," 1). While
beginning from a specific, dogmatic a priori poses its own

dangers, it is also the opposite of what Lindbeck proposes.
Further, it begs the question of what a "peace perspective"
ought to consist in and *why* Christians ought to have one.
Peace is not less important or more nearly dispensable
because it is theologically derivative.

PEACE THEOLOGY AND THE JUSTICE
OF GOD IN THE BOOK OF REVELATION

Ted Grimsrud

I. Introduction

Why Revelation?

For the person seeking to gain a Christian theological perspective on justice, it is likely not self-evident that the book of Revelation would be a crucial source. For example, Jose Miranda's well-known study, *Marx and the Bible*, only tangentially refers to Revelation, and the biblical chapter in the American Catholic bishops' pastoral on the United States ecomomy does not refer even once to Revelation.

We can paraphrase Tertullian's famous question: What has Patmos to do with Rome? What do these obscure and seemingly fanciful visions have to do with justice in the real world?

Of course, I would not be writing this paper if I did not think that the book of Revelation had definite relevance to a Christian theological perspective on justice. One of my purposes is to show what some of that relevance is.

My initial interest in Revelation stemmed from a justice-related concern. Does Revelation picture God and God's justice in such a way as to make it illegitimate to apply Jesus' teaching about God being the model of Christians loving their enemies to a rejection of Christian involvement in warfare? Is the justice of God in Revelation punitive, angry and vengeful in such a way that it becomes a warrant for acts of human "justice" such as just wars, capital punishment, a harsh and strictly punitive prison system, and a "big stick" foreign policy which seeks to punish "ungodly" and "unjust" enemies?

Many of my friends at the time asserted that yes, indeed, Revelation supports such a view of God's justice (and, implicitly, of human justice). Later on, I made some other friends whose tendency was to think of Revelation less in terms of supporting establishment "just wars" and more in terms of supporting "just" revolutions. These views still left me uncomfortable, but they seemed closer to the spirit of the book itself. It seemed doubtful that one who pictured Rome as in some way characterized as the Great Harlot would support an interpretation that assumed God's justice was primarily on the side of modern-day imperial America.

Ultimately, however, this latter perspective seems to me to differ from the former not in its understanding of what "justice" is, but only in its understanding of who the "unjust" are--God still is angry with them and punishes them; and human beings are still implicitly given the warrant, in the name of "justice," to also be angry with the "unjust," to depersonalize them, and, when appropriate, to destroy them.

The question is, is this really the view of God's justice presented in Revelation? My thesis is that it is not, that just as Jesus and Paul give us a picture of God's justice that is different from the justice of "the nations," so too does John.

Some important themes in Revelation.

The book of Revelation is unique in the New Testament and for that reason alone has the potential to make a con-tribution to a perspective on justice. It is the only piece of apocalyptic literature to enter the New Testament canon. As such, it places a special emphasis on eschatology and the idea of the last judgment. Very definitely God's justice here has to do with a view of the ultimate fate of humanity. God's justice is integrally tied up with the direction and final resolution of human history.

A related theme which is often seen to have apocalyptic overtones, which has significance for a view of God's jus-tice, and which receives special attention in Revelation is that of "wrath." One indication that wrath is a special theme in Revelation is that of the two Greek words translated by "wrath" in the New Testament. One (*thymos*) is used ten times in Revelation and never more than once in any other book, and the other (*orge*) is used twice as often in Revelation than in any other New Testament book except Romans.

The predominance of these themes of eschatology, judg-ment and wrath indicate that Revelation contains much material that has to do with a view of God and ultimate reality. There can be little doubt that one's view of God and ultimate reality greatly impinges upon one's view of a socio-political concept like "justice." And Revelation makes the connection explicit when it refers to God and God's actions as "just."

It is also relevant to note that, more so than any other book in the New Testament, Revelation alludes to the situa-tion of the Christians vis-a-vis Rome. As I will discuss at more length shortly, Revelation appears to have emerged out of a situation of perceived powerlessness toward and intense dissatisfaction with the present socio-political status-quo.

The book provides a picture of how the weak in society viewed the strong, or (perhaps) of how the oppressed viewed the oppressors. Such a picture has relevance. On the one hand, how those on the outside view those on the inside greatly affects what the outsiders do should they themselves somehow become insiders. On the other hand (and much more significant to John), the attitudes of the weak toward the strong greatly impinge upon the status of their souls. By hating those who hate us, do we not end up becoming just like them? What kind of justice do the disenfranchised seek? Is it an eye-for-an-eye justice which only maintains the cycle of violence or is it something different? Before seeking to support my thesis that Revelation gives a picture of a diffrent kind of justice, I need to spend a little time discussing the social setting of the book and the significance of its apocalypticism.

<u>The Social Setting</u>.
     The majority of modern scholars, conservative and liberal, agree that Revelation was written sometime in the 90s, somewhere in Asia Minor, and by some man—otherwise unknown—named John.
     It is clear from the book itself that it was John's perception that the churches of Asia Minor were in a crisis situation and that the depth of the their commitment was soon to be put to the test.
     In a recent book, *Crisis and Catharsis: The Power of the Apocalypse*, Adela Yarbro Collins has done some helpful reconstructing of what it was that might have contributed to John's perceptions. She points to four particular areas of conflict:
     (1) *Conflict with Jews.* The split between Christians and Jews with the resultant exclusion of Christians from the synagogue and all that went with that was a relatively recent event (86). It seems obvious that John still thought of things in Jewish terms, since the split had not yet led to a "Gentilization" of Christianity. The wounds were still fresh and tensions still alive. These tensions were particularly reflected in the letters to the seven churches, particularly the letter to Smyrna (2:8-11), which seems to be alluding to some Jews colluding with the government in persecuting the Christians. Overall, Revelation is definitely not an anti-Jewish tract and this conflict is secondary to the others. In fact, in these other areas, the Christians were clearly reflecting traditional Jewish tensions with the non-Jewish world.

(2) *Mutual antipathy toward neighboring Gentiles.* The
Gentiles did not particularly like the Christians, and vice
versa. This was also reflected in the seven letters. Greco-
Roman society tended to be suspicious of the church, not
least due to the early church's rejection of much of what it
saw as idolatrous and/or inhumane in current social practices. This suspicion easily translated into antagonism and
made things unsettled for most Christians. In the face of
this, those who John railed against in various of the letters
(i.e., the so-called Nicolaitans, so-called "Balaam," and so-
called "Jezebel") apparently called for accommodation. This
view was rejected by the Christ of the letters (88).

(3) *Conflict over wealth.* Tensions existed between the
rich and the poor. During the decades prior to the writing
of Revelation, brilliant economic progress had been made in
Asia Minor. But the rewards went totally to the wealthy.
The rich got richer and the poor stayed poor. The result
was widespread social unrest due to growing awareness of
this maldistribution (94). While not a revolutionary zealot,
John saw total discontinuity between the present situation of
great econmomic inequality and the promise of the kingdom of
God's justice.

(4) *Precarious relations with Rome.* It does not seem
likely that during the time John wrote Revelation Christians
were undergoing intense persecution. There is little solid
evidence of persecution of Christians during the reign of the
emperor Domician, which is when Revelation was likely written (69). But in no way was Rome friendly toward Christians.
For one thing, the cult of the emperor was growing and this
was an anathema to monotheistic Christians, a reality which
certainly led to local persecutions and repression. Also,
Roman magistrates were the "enforcers" of many grievances
which non-Christian Gentiles and, to some degree, Jews had
against Christians. Thirdly, in general in the society of
Asia Minor, if the poor made noises of resistance versus the
wealthy, they were reminded of the high priority that Rome
placed on social order (98). John's banishment to Patmos,
likely a kind of "penal colony" for political prisoners, reinforced the basic polarization between the church and Rome
and the precarious legal position of Christians (104).

The reality that stood in contrast with these various
tensions and which heightened them into crisis proportions
was the early Christian experience of the reality of the
kingdom of God. A new set of expectations had arisen as a
result of faith in Jesus as the Messiah and of the belief
that the Kingdom had been established, at least in part. It

was the tension between John's vision of the Kingdom and his environment that moved him to write Revelation (106), and no doubt led him to experience and communicate it as an apocalypse, i.e., a direct revelation from God.

Revelation as apocalyptic literature.

The very first word in Revelation identifies the book as an *apokalypsis* (=revelation). So it is clear that this book is in some sense apocalyptic literature. It would be a mistake, however, to assume that John is using the word *apokalypsis* to self-consciously place his work in a clearly demarcated category of literature with well-established rules of composition and a unified theological perspective. "Apocalyptic" is a term used by later readers to categorize a fluid, diverse group of works written by Jews and Christians mostly between 200 BCE and 200 CE and united primarily by certain broad similarities in style.

The term comes from the book of Revelation itself and is then applied to earlier works. What Revelation and the other apocalypses have in common are: (1) a narrative framework, (2) a direct revelation which comes to a human recipient and discloses a transcendent reality, (3) the promise of eschatological salvation, and (4) the promise of a new or transformed world (John J. Collins, *The Apocalyptic Imagination*, 4).

A dynamic, mythological orientation characterizes apocalyptic literature much more than strict analytic logic (Collins, 13). Apocalypses emerged out of settings of perceived crisis and had as their goal either strengthening the hearers' and readers' resolve to remain faithful to the truth in the face of conflicts or moving the hearers and readers to act to change the situation.

The power of apocalyptic was the power of the human imagination. It contained a challenge to view the world in a way that was radically different from the common perception. Such a perspective could serve to foster dissatisfaction with peoples' present and to generate visions of what might be (Collins, 215). It could buttress the claim that Christians' true identity was to be derived not from the structures and institutions of the wider society, but from a vision of what God was doing on the cosmic level to effect deliverance and salvation (Paul D. Hanson, "Apocalypticism," 39).

Revelation emerged as the creative response to an experience of severe distress—both for John personally in his banishment to Patmos and for the church in Asia Minor in general in the face of ever more powerful calls to depart from the ways of its Lord.

To quote Ernst Kaesemann:

Patmos is the place for exiled rebels deprived of
their major activity, and with every idly spent hour
burning into their marrow. For over there on the
mainline world history is moving, and the churches are
spent and either do not see it or try to come to terms
with it. They praise Christ as the Lord of heaven, and
do not hear him saying to them: 'the world and all
that is in it is mine.' They know the first commandment, and they think it is enough if they keep themselves unspotted from the world, although the
Antichrist has to be faced squarely if one is to keep
alive. They take comfort from the resurrection and do
not know that it begins here and now with the
sovereignty of Jesus in the midst of his enemies and
with the glorious freedom of God's children who, being
ostracized, despise the mark of the beast under the
Pax Romana. They suffer as though that were not
exactly what they are called to do. They ought to
make common cause with all those who are oppressed,
insulted, and appealing in vain to tyrants. They await
him who tramples underfoot the arrogant and the
unjust, who writes on the wall of Belshazzar's palace
while the great feast is at its merriest, and has long
since sent out his apocalyptic horsemen. Visions tor-
ment the man who can now do nothing but cry out to
awaken those who are asleep, to arouse those who are
idle, to strengthen those who are exhausted, and to
confront with the judgment those who are secure (Jesus
Means Freedom, 139-140).

II. The "Just" God of Revelation

It is within the context of his intense desire that
things be set right that John wrote about these visions of
God doing just that. I want to focus now on John's description of this work of God's which is envisioned in Revelation
as a reflection of God's "justice." I will do this by first
looking at the four texts which specifically refer to God's
justice and then by looking more broadly at the book and
discussing why these actions are called "just."

God's justice and the song of the Lamb: 15:1-8.
This passage serves as a sort of preface to the series
of seven bowl-plagues that formally make up chapter 16. The

bowl-plagues are the third and last series of seven-fold plagues. The first two are the seal-plagues in chapter 6 and the trumpet-plagues in chapter 8. 15:1 refers to the bowl plagues as the final, ultimate pouring out of God's wrath.

A careful look at these three plague-series and a deciphering of the imagery indicates that what is being pictured is a vision of human reality as it has always been-- wars, famine, rebellion, disease, tremendous social upheaval and the like are characteristic of all eras of human history.

A key thing to notice here (and, really, throughout the book) is the juxtaposition of plague language with worship language, victory language, and salvation language (even, at times, universal salvation language). John sees the plagues coming; he also sees the worship of the "conquerors" who sing the song of Moses and of the Lamb, and who affirm that God's deeds are great and wonderful, just (dikaiai) and true; and that all nations will come and worship God because God's just deeds (dikaiomata sou) have been revealed.

A clear allusion is made here to Exodus 15 (the account of the crossing of the Red Sea). Those who have "conquered" the beast are direct heirs of the children of Israel in that their faith enabled them to be liberated from the dominance of their contemporary powers of evil. The fact that they are singing the "song of the Lamb" indicates that their triumph was won by no other weapons than the cross of Christ and the faithful testimony of his followers to that way (G. B. Caird, A Commentary on the Revelation of St. John the Divine, 198).

The "song" in verses 3 and 4 contains phrases from various Old Testament passages (Dt 32:2; Pss 86:8f., 111:2; Jer 10:6f. 16:19) which taken together have the effect of emphasizing God's greatness as breaking through heathen blindness and "all nations" coming to God's worship--because God's "just deeds have been revealed" (J. P. M. Sweet, Revelation, 240). The promised result of God's just deeds here is that "all nations shall come and worship before God" (v. 4). These are the same "nations" said to be ruled by the "beast" in 13:7 and raging at God's judgments in 11:18. The effect of God's justice is not to destroy them but to convert them.

The smoke that fills the temple in verses 5-8 through eight both reveals and hides the glory, the awe, and the mystery that surround God (cf. Ex 19:16-18; 40:34-38; 1 Kg 8:11; Isa 6:4). Only when the seven plagues had been poured out was it possible again to enter the temple. God's judgments remain a mystery until they have been executed (Harry Boer, Revelation, 106). The implication seems to be that to a certain extent the ways in which the plagues serve God's

ultimate salvific purposes seem to be unfathomable for human
beings.

Nevertheless, the clear implication of this passage in
its context next to chapter 16 seems to be that the plagues
and out-pouring of God's wrath are somehow part of God's
justice. The references to the song of Moses and the Lamb
serve to tie the plagues in with the Exodus and the Christ-
event. What this means is that the ultimate effect and central manifestation of God's "just deeds" are salvific; i.e.,
the celebration of the "conquerors" and the worship of the
nations. The "conquerors" celebrate because they have, by
their conquering of the Beast, contributed to the nations'
coming to worship God, not the nations being destroyed.

Giving the oppressors their due: 16:4-7.

This passage is the third of the seven terrible bowl-
plagues. God is called "just" twice here, first by the "angel
of the waters," the one pouring out the bowl which turns the
rivers and springs of water into blood; and then by the
"altar," which apparently is a reference back to 6:9-11, where
John saw under the altar the souls of the martyrs who are
crying out for God to avenge their blood.

The specific reference to "justice" here has to do with
God's judgment on those who "have shed the blood of God's
saints and prophets" (v. 6). This judgment is said to take
the form of God giving the blood-shedders blood to drink
thorugh the agency of the angel who turned drinking water
into blood. This seems like a clear case of simple eye-for-
an-eye retributive justice. But I would argue that there is
more to it than that.

The plagues are clearly stated to be instruments of
God's "wrath" (cf. 16:1). The "wrath" in Revelation, while
attributed to God, is seen to be the impersonal working out,
within history, of the process of evil being allowed to
destroy itself. God's wrath here means that people reap what
they sow, that evil rebounds on itself and is self-
destructive. This process is seen to serve God's purposes in
two ways, first by moving some people, at least, to repentance
due to their experience of the destructive consequences of
their rejection of God, and second--according to John's
visions--by ultimately culminating in the destruction of the
evil powers and the establishment of the New Jerusalem on
earth (cf. A. T. Hanson, *The Wrath of the Lamb*, especially
159-201).

The theme of these first four bowls is that of God's
creation itself taking vengeance on those that do harm; the

land, the sea, the fresh water, and the sun all play a part.
The principle seems to be that "whereby a person sins,
thereby he or she is punished" (Sweet: 243).

For example, the "mark of the beast" in verse 2 becomes
ugly and painful sores, the symbol of its punishment. And in
verses 4-7, the ocean of "blood" which the worshipers of the
Beast have shed contaminates their own water supply. This
image is picked up in chapter 17, where we see the harlot
Babylon staggering to her appointed doom, drunk with the
"blood of saints and prophets" (Caird: 202-203).

The images in chapter 16 bear a striking resemblance to
the plagues of the Exodus. All seven judgments here repeat
in varied ways the plagues of Egypt. 15:1-4 indicates that
these plagues conclude in a redemption greater even than
that from Egypt (George R. Beasley-Murray, *The Book of
Revelation*, 232). This promised redemption is the subject of
a full-fledged vision in chapters 21 and 22.

In the context of the whole book, it would seem that
there are four major purposes for the plague visions. One is
to serve as a serious warning to Christians not to conform
to the surrounding culture, not to accept the mark of the
beast. A second is to promise that the evil events of history are not ultimately independent from God's purposes but
in a mysterious way actually serve them. Third, in the context of the plagues, John emphasizes that God is continually
hoping for and seeking repentance on the part of those who
dwell on the earth. And, a fourth purpose is to show that
God's wrath, in hating and destroying evil, serves the purpose of cleansing creation so that in the new creation things
will be whole.

This passage emphasizes that the outworking of "wrath"
is part of God's justice. The implication is that evil has
consequences, that it is self-destructive. The reality of
God's wrath is necessary for evil to be destroyed, which is
the only way creation can ultimately be liberated. Thus
God's wrath serves God's redemptive purposes.

The wedding supper of the Lamb: 19:1-10.
    Following the account of the destruction of Babylon in
chapter 18, John reports a vision of a scene of great
celebration. God's judgments are said here to be "true and
just," for God "has condemned the great harlot who corrupted
the earth by her adulteries. God has avenged on her the
blood of God's servants" (v. 2).

    The "true and just judgments" lead directly to the wed-
ding of the Lamb in verse 7, which is the real focus of the

celebration. This wedding marks the reign of the Lord God
Almighty (v. 6). The "Bride," which symbolizes the followers
of the Lamb, is said to have made herself ready by putting on
the fine linen given to her to wear. The linen "stands for
the just acts of the saints" (v. 8).

Salvation is being celebrated in this passage. Negatively, this means that all that has stood in the way of
God's rule has been removed (cf. the account in chapters 17-
18 and the ultimate effect of the plague series, along with
the visions in 19:11-21 and chapter 20). Positively, it means
the New Jerusalem can now come down.

The affirmation that God's sentences of judgment are
"true and just" alludes back to the altar in 16:7, to the song
of Moses and the Lamb in 15:3, and to the announcement of
judgment in 11:18. Salvation, glory, and power belong to God.
These are political terms and gain significance when seen in
the political context of John's day. Augustus had been
called "savior of the Greeks and of the whole inhabited
world," "savior and benefactor," "savior and founder," and
"savior and god," whose birthday was called the beginning of
"good tidings" (gospel). He was known as the "just and gen-
erous lord" whose reign promised peace and happiness, i.e.,
salvation. The heavenly choir John saw was therefore asserting that it is not Caesar's but God's power and salvation
that is revealed in the justice given out to Babylon/Rome and
its cohorts (Elisabeth Schüssler Fiorenza, *Invitation to the
Book of Revelation*, 177).

The real celebration here is not for the destruction of
Babylon per se but only of that as one element of the coming
of God's reign and the "marriage of the Lamb" (Beasley-
Murray, 274). The key aspects of the references to "justice"
here are: (1) the tying together of God's justice, the
destruction of the evil powers, and ultimate salvation, and
(2) the emphasis on the importance of the Lamb's followers
doing deeds of justice.

The warrior for justice: 19:11-21.

This passage is particularly interesting because it is
the only reference to Jesus' justice in Revelation. It is a
complicated section which has been explained in various ways.

The reference to the rider as "Faithful and True" (v. 11),
"the Word of God" (v. 13), and "King of kings and Lord of
lords" (v. 16) make it clear that this is indeed Jesus, of
whom verse 11 states: "in justice he judges."

The white horse he is riding (v. 11) symbolizes victory.
He comes as the one who has conquered sin, death, and evil

through his death and resurrection. As the following verses make clear, he comes to this apparent battle with the forces of the Antichrist (a "battle" foreseen in 16:14: "The three evil spirits that looked like frogs...go out to the kings of the whole earth to gather them for the battle on the great day of God Almighty") *already* the victor (Matthias Rissi, *The Future of the World,* 26-27). The outcome of the "battle" is not in question.

The rider is called "Faithful and True"; that is, "the faithful and true witness" of 1:5 and 3:14. He is the one who remained faithful and true to God even when it meant a martyr's death. That is how he gained the white horse.

Verse 13 contains a key image: the rider approaches the battle "dressed in a robe dipped in blood." The blood has already been shed *before* the battle begins. This would seem to be an allusion to Jesus' blood shed in his death and the reason why no real battle takes place here (Vernard Eller, *The Most Revealing Book in the Bible,* 177). He can already ride the white horse because the real battle is over and he won it on the basis of his death and resurrection.

The "armies of heaven" (v. 14) would seem to be the saints wearing their bridal linen (vv. 7-8). They carry no weapons; they too are already victorious. The only weapon mentioned at all is the sword that comes out of Jesus' mouth--his word, the gospel (cf. Hebrews 4:12; Ephesians 6:17). This is what eventually brings the nations to their knees (Caird, 245).

The "winepress of the fury of God's wrath" (v. 15) could well be a reference to the means by which the wine which brought down Babylon is prepared. These means are the martyrdom of Jesus and the saints (Caird, 246). The meaning here could be that God is causing the wine to take effect.

I would understand the "great supper of God" (vv. 17-18) to be the same as the "wedding supper of the Lamb" (v. 9). It is the time of judgment. For those who belong, it is a time of great rejoicing: for those who do not, it is a time of condemnation (cf. Jesus' parable of the supper in Matthew 22. The one without the wedding clothes on is booted out.). I would see the picture of the birds eating the flesh of all people (v. 18) as one of judgment. This judgment reveals the true status of people--either they are with God or against God.

The Beast and the kings and armies are all ready for battle (v. 19). They truly are deceived to think that there will even be a battle. The battle is long past (Eller: p. 178). Jesus simply captures the Beast and false prophet and throws them into the fiery lake (v. 20). "The rest of them" (v. 21), those who were deceived by the false prophet, are not judged by the word of Jesus. The birds ate their flesh. Perhaps that also was a reference to their being judged for where their ultimate trust really resides. With the deceiver gone, maybe they have some hope of seeing the light. 21:24 indicates that the kings of the earth bring their splendor into the New Jerusalem.

John is convinced that Jesus, in his death and resurrection, won the only battle necessary to defeat evil. To picture him in another battle would be to imply that his first victory was not good enough. The picture of Christ's victory in this passage is simply the revelation of the one sufficient victory he has already won (Rissi, 29-30).

Jesus' "war" for justice (v. 11) is a war to set things right, a war to fully establish God's Kingdom. It is a war fought with the weapons of the cross and resurrection; i.e., total, all-powerful love.

III. Why God is Seen as "Just" in Revelation

"Just" is a key term used in Revelation to evaluate what God is envisioned doing. Why is God "just" in Revelation?

The ultimate result of God's work is the new Jerusalem.

It is John's intention to show that all that happens in human history is somehow used by God for the purpose of establishing the new Jerusalem. All of God's "just deeds" are ultimately redemptive--for creation, for the faithful witnesses, and ultimately for the "nations" and the "kings of the earth" (cf. 21:24).

It is Jacques Ellul's conclusion in *Apocalypse* that justice in Revelation is consistent with:

the evangelical image of the justice of God which is the parables of the worker at the eleventh hour, and the lost sheep, and the pearl of great price, and the prodigal son, and the unfaithful steward--such is the justice of God. Neither retributive nor distributive. It is the justice of love itself, who cannot see the one he judges except thorugh his love, and who is always able to find in that fallen miserable being the last tiny particle, invisible to any other than his love, and which he is going to gather up and save (212-213).

There are indeed visions of destruction in Revelation (chapters 6-20), but they are bracketed by the overarching vision of God as creator and redeemer (chapters 4 and 5), the one who makes all things new (chapters 21-22). Thus the carnage and chaos are seen to be within God's plan and to lead through into the fulfillment of human destiny in final union with God (Sweet: 47).

This final redemptive product of God's just deeds is not just a collection of individuals. John believed in a purpose for collective human history as well as for individual souls. Into the new Jerusalem are brought not only the souls of the faithful but the wealth and glory of the nations; and down the middle of the city's streets are avenues of the trees of life, whose leaves provide healing for the nations. Any achievement of people in the older order, however imperfect, provided it has value in the sight of God, will find its place in the healed and transfigured life of the new Jerusalem (Caird, 300).

As in the Exodus, so also in Revelation, the crucial event is not the plagues. Those do not exemplify God's justice but only serve the true end of God's justice: the redemption that leads to the new world.

The controlling metaphor in the book is the slain Lamb.

The fulcrum of Revelation is not Jesus' return and the descent of the city of God, described in its closing visions. Rather it is the vision of God and the Lamb in chapters 4 and 5. The slain and risen Lamb pictured there has accomplished redemption, has risen to the throne of God, and has begun his reign with God. The turn of the ages lies in the past (Beasley-Murray, 25). John is saying that if one wants to see the clearest and decisive expresison of God's justice, just look at the Christ-event.

The Lamb in chapter five is also identified as the ruling Lion of the tribe of Judah. The Lamb that is slain is at the same time the bearer of seven horns (the symbol of complete power) and the seven spirits of God (the symbol of the fullness of the Holy Spirit). Revelation proclaims again and again the paradox that the suffering and dying Christ is the victor (Matthias Rissi, *Time and History*, 38-39).

John sees Jesus Christ as both the redeemer and the judge. Not one after the other, but one because of the other. In two passages (14:14-20; 19:11-16) there is indeed a picture of judgment, but it is the judgment of the cross. It is not intended to tell us that Christ and the saints will some time in the future conquer and judge their enemies, but to tell us that by the virtue of the victory won once for all on the cross, Jesus and his faithful followers "are more than con-

querors," and that this applies to all post-incarnational history (A. T. Hanson: 176-177).

That Christ's past historical death and resurrection are
central is seen in the fact that the visions of Revelation
never show him engaged in direct battle with the dragon.
Nowhere does John mention such a battle, not even in the
portrayal of Christ's coming in 19:11ff. It is only as the
Lamb who dies for the world that Christ has won his battle
(5:5,9; 3:21). Therefore, according to the interpretive hymn of
12:10-12, humankind's possibility of victory over the dragon
is found only "by the blood of the Lamb," that is, in the
death of Jesus for them and therefore only "by the word of
their testimony," whose content is the victory promised them
by the Lamb's death (Rissi: *Time*, 55).

This centrality of the Lamb in Revelation leads to a
reversal of conventional wisdom regarding power and justice.
The power of love is true justice. If the Lamb reigns over
history, it is not as a crowned king like Caesar but as the
incarnation of love itself, the love which goes so far as to
give itself, to abandon itself; and his power is no other
power that that of this kind of love (Ellul: 120-121).

Punishment is of evil powers, not people per se.
The book of Revelation affirms that God's just deeds
accomplish the destruction of the evil powers which imprision
humankind. John clearly differentiates between these powers,
who are God's real enemies, and human beings, for whose sake
these powers must be destroyed.

A power of evil beyond the sinful wills of individuals
(personified in Revelation by entities such as the Beast, the
Dragon, the False Prophet, and the Harlot) is seen to be at
work in the processes of history. Its effect is destructive
of all that is good in this world, and it exceeds the wit or
strength of humankind to overcome it. Just as Christ, by his
redemptive deeds, delivers from sin and brings the powers of
the age to come into this world, so too Christ alone can
bring to its final resolution the struggle between the powers
of good and evil for ultimate sovereignty over creation.

It is perhaps here that John's apocalyptic imagination is
the most creative and profound. His visions show a proces-
sion of plagues (most if not all of which reflect natural and
social catastrophes endemic in all eras of human history).
Even after the worst of these plagues, human beings remain
on the scene (cf. 16:21; 18:9-19). The culmination of the
plagues is the destruction of Babylon (chapter 18) and the
casting of the Dragon, Beast, and False Prophet into the lake

of fire (20:10). After this, John reports a vision of the new
Jerusalem, whereby the light of the glory of God "the nations
walk; and the kings of the earth shall bring their glory into
it" (21:24).

The goal of the "just deeds" of God, according to the
overall message of Revelation, is not the punishment and
destruction of people but rather the destruction of the
destroyers of people.

The Lamb's people are called to follow him.

We saw earlier in looking at the marriage supper of the
Lamb (19:1-10) that what makes the Lamb's bride ready for the
marriage feast is the fine white linen which it is given--
linen which was earned by the "just deeds" of the saints.
Discipleship is not a theme elaborated on in much detail in
Revelation, but it is neverthelss an important concern of
John.

A central aspect of this concern is the repeated
exhortation to Christians to remain "pure," not to conform to
the society around them. Revelation speaks not only to judgment against the dehumanizing anti-God powers but also warns
Christians not to give in to these powers' very concrete
pressures. The book therefore begins with the seven letters,
which form a section of censure and challenge to faithfulness. The injunctions, beatitudes, warnings, and promises
which run through the book continue this function (Schuessler
Fiorenza, 30-31).

The only way that the followers of the Lamb participate
in the battle versus the evil powers is to remain faithful
throughout their lives. In that way they will conquer. This
stands in contrast to the concept of the messianic war which
is present in some other apocalypses in which the high point
of the struggle between good and evil is depicted as an
eschatological messianic war (William Klassen, "Vengeance in
the Apocalypse of John," 305).

This participation that Christians are called to in
Revelation is, however, seen to be quite important. The
church has been appointed by Christ to be a "kingdom of
priests" (1:6; 5:10) to mediate his royal and priestly authority to the whole world. Through the church, as pictured in
Revelation, the Lamb is to exercise his authority over the
nations (1:5; 2:26f; 11:15ff; 12:5; 15:3-4; 17:14; 19:11ff).
Through the church he is to mediate God's forgiveness and
lead the world to repentance (3:7-9; 11:13; 14:6-7; 20:1-6).
And all this Christians may achieve only by following the
Lamb wherever he goes (14:4; Caird: 297).

This means that the separation of the church from the
world is thought of more in moral than in physical terms.
Christians are called upon to refrain from moral and
spiritual impurity while acting as agents of God's justice,
maintaining "the testimony of Jesus" and validating it with
their lives in "the street of the great city" (12:13-17; Sweet:
34). It is by their own "just deeds" (dikaiomata, 19:8) that
Christians bear witness to God's "just deeds" (dikaiomata,
15:4).

IV. Toward a Christian Perspective
on Justice

I do not intend to make too many claims regarding the
present-day relevance of this study (I hope!). Even if my
interpretation is largely correct, it remains true that
Revelation is only one part of the Christian Bible and the
Bible is only one element in the mix of present-day Christian
moral discernment. It is my conclusion, nevertheless, that
Revelation is, or should be, an important part of this mix.
In this concluding section I will touch on a few of the ways
that I think taking the message of Revelation seriously can
help our thinking about justice.

"Corrective justice."
The essential thrust of the message of Revelation
regarding justice is that "justice" has much more, ultimately,
to do with concepts like correction, reconciliation, and the
restoration of relationships than with concepts like retribu-
tion and an-eye-for-an-eye. Like most of the rest of the
Bible, Revelation strongly challenges any tendency to separate God's love from God's justice. God's "just deeds" in
Revelation serve God's loving intention of making the New
Jerusalem a reality and, by doing so, decisively bringing
about the healing of the nations (cf. 22:2).

It would seem to me to follow from this that a Christian
concern for justice should always take a redemptive slant.
Certainly injustice must be opposed, but never in a way that
contradicts the dictates of love and reconciliation. It seems
clear in Revelation 21 and 22, that the only way that the
kings of the earth could make it into the New Jerusalem was
to be converted (cf. 21:27); they did not make it as oppressors and worshipers of the Beast. But the hope is that even
they can be converted. They are not objectified as "enemies"
and then disposed of.

A difference in attitude and goals.

In the perspective I am presenting, "justice" is redefined to a certain extent. It is not redefined in the sense that it is now concerned with different kinds of things, but rather in the sense that it is considered with a different attitude and different goals.

Justice, as I am conceiving of it in the light of the message of Revelation, is still concerned with brokenness in the world, scarcity, violation of moral norms, distribution of goods and services, and the like. But the attitude and goals are not so much concerned with how I or someone else can get my or his or her due, how our self-interests can be balanced, how we can maintain a moral equilibrium in the world, how the punishment can fit the crime, etc.

The attitudes and goals take the shape more of how the values of God's Kingdom can be incarnated in the human order, how social brokenness can be corrected for the good of all concerned, how enemies can be reconciled, how victim and offender can experience healing; recognizing that there is something missing from the new Jerusalem if it is not also accessible to the kings of the earth should they somehow be freed from the snares of the Beast.

Faithfulness to the Lamb is crucial.

Revelation asserts that the short-term result of the saints' "just deeds" would be their suffering. Jesus' just deeds resulted in his death. The implication of this is that a Christian perspective on justice cannot expect to be rationally acceptable to evryone in the world (a criteria which seems axiomatic for modern-day philosophical ethics). The message of Revelation points toward a perspective on justice which challenges Christians to embrace the particular insights that they have, based on the Christ-event, concerning justice as care for the outcasts and other needy people, love for enemies, and self-sacrifice to the point of martyrdom.

Such a perspective places a premium on one's faith-commitment and thus immediately parts company with natural law, rational liberalism, and other philosophical approaches. It is not that all of these viewpoints would disagree on all specifics, but the ultimate commitments are totally different. The point of John's apocalyptic exhortation was to call Christians to "follow the Lamb wherever he goes," even when that seems, in many ways, to be "irrational."

The "narrow" way.

As I understand it, the theology of Revelation includes the affirmation that what is best for human society, and indeed for all of creation, is the way of the Lamb and his faithful followers. The book includes an implicit criticism of the worship of coercive power as being ultimately satanic and idolatrous and thus totally self-defeating.

If this theology is at all true (and I am merely raising this as a possibility and not asserting that it necessarily is), then it would seem to follow that the most socially "responsible" things Christians can do is practice the Lamb's justice in every way possible. Revelation promises that such practices will likely lead Christians to share in Jesus' fate. It is not reading too much into history to assert that that promise has often been fulfilled and continues to be, daily, in our time.

Such a stance is, according to social theorists like Ernst Troeltsch (cf. his *The Social Teaching of the Christian Churches*), inevitably "sectarian" and by definition therefore marginal and of little long-term social relevance. Perhaps the term "sectarian" is irredeemable. Many who have been labeled such no doubt have been escapist and selfish and thereby "irresponsible." But Revelation asserts that the real hope for the world and its legitimate structures lies in the perfect obedience of the Lamb and the faithfulness of his followers. I am not so sure that it is total idealism and naïveté to think that maybe John was on to something.

Bibliography

George R. Beasley-Murray. *The Book of Revelation.* Eerdmans, 1974.

Harry Boer. *Revelation.* Eerdmans, 1979.

G. B. Caird. *A Commentary of the Revelation of St. John the Divine.* Harper & Row, 1966.

John J. Collins. *The Apocalyptic Imagination: An Introduction to the Jewish Matrix of Christianity.* Crossroad, 1984.

Vernard Eller. *The Most Revealing Book of the Bible.* Eerdmans, 1974.

Jacques Ellul. *Apocalypse.* Seabury, 1977.

Anthony T. Hanson. *The Wrath of the Lamb.* Seabury, 1957.

Paul D. Hanson. "Apocalypticism." *Interpreter's Dictionary of the Bible,* supp. 28-34. Keith Crim, ed. Abingdon, 1976

Ernst Käsemann. *Jesus Means Freedom.* Fortress, 1969.

William Klassen. "Vengeance in the Apocalypse of John."
Catholic Biblical Quarterly 28 (1966) 300–311.

Matthias Rissi. *The Future of the World.* Allenson, 1972.

—————. *Time and History.* John Knox, 1966.

Elisabeth Schüssler Fiorenza. *Invitation to the Book of
Revelation.* Doubleday, 1981.

J. P. M. Sweet. *Revelation.* Westminster, 1979.

Adela Yarbro Collins. *Crisis and Catharsis: The Power of
the Apocalypse.* Westminster, 1984.

THE TRAJECTORY OF FEMINIST CONVICTION*

Gayle Gerber Koontz

Feminist conviction meets the patriarchal character of much of the biblical material with painfully explosive force. At stake is the authority and role of the Bible and/or the authority and role of feminist consciousness and commitment in Christian theological reflection. This essay values both biblical tradition and feminist conviction and explores some possible ways to respect the authority both of Scripture and of feminist experience in Christian life and thought.

Feminist Conviction

The term "feminist conviction" requires definition. Historically feminism, since its self-conscious emergence in the 19th century, has triggered volatile responses from many in the Christian church and broader society. For some the term "feminist" has meant "a person preoccupied with political rights for women" or "an angry woman," "a bra burner," "a man hater" or "probably a lesbian." Perhaps one of the most unfortunate aspects of current church debates about the relation of "feminism" to the Bible or to Christian faith is the failure to recognize that just as there are varieties of Christians, there are varieties of feminists. Feminism cannot be defined with sole reference to women who are convinced that living separately from men is the only way toward healing for women, for example, any more than Christianity can be defined with sole reference to the Old Order Amish. I have special interest in helping to develop a variety of Christian feminism which attempts to listen to a range of feminist voices but which also pays particular attention to the experiences and perspectives of those who stand in the Anabaptist Mennonite tradition.

For me feminist conviction implies both consciousness and commitment. It is a particular way of seeing or interpreting reality and responding to it which involves 1) the naming and rejection of sexism against women and 2) the affirmation of and action promoting the fundamental equality of men and women, equitable sharing, and mutuality between women and men.[1] While all feminists are one in rejecting sexism, there is divergence among feminists on the second set of commitments and how they are to be reached.

*This essay also appeared in *Conrad Grebel Review* 5 (Fall 1987) 201-220.

If one adopts the above definition, a "feminist" point of view cannot be equated flatly with a "woman's" view. We women--just because we are women--do not necessarily see eye to eye. Women's experience and convictions, especially when one considers women of various races, classes and cultures, are highly diverse. While feminists are interested in paying attention to distinctive women's experience and psychology resulting from biological differences (menstruation, child-bearing, nursing, menopause) and at the experiences women along with other devalued persons have had when they have been socially marginalized, feminist consciousness is centrally concerned with how we as men and women perceive and attach significance to our biological differences in specific social and cultural worlds.

A further implication of this definition is that men as well as women can be feminist or sexist or somewhere in between, that is, not wanting to be sexist but not being sure how to be feminist.

Naming and Rejecting Sexism

Sexism is evidenced when one sex is conceptually and behaviorally favored over the other.[2] In the context of a social order which exhibits sexism against women (in which, for example, what is male is assumed to be normative), females and things associated with females tend to be considered inferior, derivative, marginal, or complementary to men. Viewpoints, judgements and needs of women and other marginalized persons are frequently ignored or trivialized because such persons are assumed to be less intelligent, less valuable, uninformed, and lacking in authority.[3]

Sexism against women is a basic feature of North American society internalized to some degree by all of us-- both women and men. We recognize this well enough to chuckle at the cartoon of a Stone Age woman chipping away at a rock to make a wheel while two men walk by shaking their heads saying, "Women invent the craziest things." Perhaps one of the most destructive aspects of sexism is that we women ourselves grow up with low self-esteem, frequently disliking what we see as female characteristics. As my own feminist consciousness began to emerge I was startled to recognize that almost all of the interesting people I wanted to be like in my adolescent years were men. It took me some time to recognize and respect strength in women.

Equality of Men and Women

Feminists are indebted to the Western liberal egalitarian

tradition.   But they are aware of the fact that the formal
principle of equality does not by itself determine who the
"equals" are; feminists recognize that "equal protection under
the law" does not necessarily include women or slaves.
Affirmation of the equality of women and men is a call to
appropriate individual autonomy and free choice for women as
well as for men. Women must be respected as "ends" and their
interests and aims respected no less than men's.   Equality
language affirms women's intelligence, strength, self-worth,
value.

Equitable Sharing
     This notion recognizes concern for the common good of
all.   It represents universalization of the principle of
equality that includes a claim by all to equitable share in
the goods and services necessary to human life. While simple
equality emphasizes the self-protective right of each to
freedom, equitable sharing presses the need for self-yielding
within the social community as a whole.   Included within this
community are men and women of all social and economic
groups and races.   Consistent feminists are also committed to
working toward racial, economic and social justice in the
human community.

Mutuality
     The language of mutuality implies criticism of much of
the Western liberal philosophical tradition.   When individual
autonomy is the sole basis of human dignity and the single
principle for social arrangements, individuals are atomized.
The primary mode of relating tends to become one of opposition and competition between the self and others. Most feminists join those who have noted this limitation of liberal
philosophy and who have emphasized that humans are relational, a characteristic which, if one also assumes and values
equality of being, points toward mutuality as a primary goal
for adult human relationships.

Patriarchal Order

     Feminist consciousness and conviction, while it may
appear somewhat bloodless in bare definition above, flies in
the face of some of the foundational assumptions characteristic of patriarchal societies.   Patriarchal social order is
the context for most of the biblical writings, has marked
Western history, and has profoundly shaped contemporary
Euro-Canadian-American cultural attitudes and practices.

Like feminism, "patriarchy" is often carelessly used in current conversations about women and Christianity. It refers to a "social organization marked by the supremacy of the father in the clan or family, the legal dependence of wives and children and the reckoning of descent and inheritance in the male line."[4] Feminists have noted that in this social context, humans have tended to assume that reality is hierarchical, that difference in being is not only real but can be ranked in order (God-man-woman-child-animal-nature). Usually it is assumed that it is appropriate for those higher in rank of being to be dominant in some measure over those below. The world as a whole tends to be interpreted as one in which competing factors, people, and groups must strive for dominance. Not equality and mutuality but competition and control characterize the relationships of men to men, men to women, humans to nonhuman creation, spirit to matter, reason to intuition.[5]

Both Christian and postChristian feminists have struggled with the "patriarchal" assumptions which infuse various biblical texts, particularly those involving women. I have not yet encountered anyone, however, who in their biblical interpretation has attempted to distinguish varieties of patriarchal order. In spite of the numerous limitations of typologies (pure types rarely exist) and though my descriptions are fledgling and relatively untested, I have found it helpful to distinguish two sub-types of patriarchal organization--violent or despotic patriarchy and benevolent patriarchy. Each has a somewhat different ethos, that is, distinguishing character, sentiment, moral nature, or guiding beliefs. Each has a somewhat different pattern of interaction--particularly in how powerful "fathers" in each system respond to threats to their authority.

Violent Patriarchy

In the context of violent patriarchy, "fathers" respond to threats to their authority, judgment, wealth, and welfare with strong, often violent reassertions of dominance. Fathers discipline children and wives, accepting the appropriateness of beating "for their own good." Fathers punish quickly and certainly for lack of submission to decisions or accepted mores; wives may be divorced, subordinates may even be killed. Violent means are predominant in settling scores and disputes over property. In such a context it is important for men to develop warlike behavior and attitudes which can establish and maintain dominance in relationships, especially with other men. Rape also expresses dominance. Prison

society and military society exhibit many of these characteristics in sharp relief. Within a violent patriarchal order
most women and others identified as "weak" internalize hatred
of self, do not realize or do not know what to do with their
own anger, live with fear. Women close to powerful men may
exercise violent control over both male and female subordinates.

Benevolent Patriarchy

Benevolent patriarchy has the same hierarchical, legal
and inheritance arrangements as violent patriarchy, but has a
different ethos. Notably, fathers exhibit or are expected to
exhibit firm but genuinely caring concern for dependents--
children, wives and servants. Compassion and mercy is valued
in fathers as well as strength, leadership and protection.
Fathers tend to settle disputes through diplomacy or negotiation when possible; some bending or giving in is acceptable.
Fathers do not have unlimited authority; they must be just
and merciful before God (or fair in relation to commonly
accepted moral principles). Sometimes fathers are recognized
to be wrong in relation to God's will (or moral right) and on
occasion may even be seen to be less perceptive of divine
will than a woman. In this context fathers express control
in paternalistic actions toward rather than violence against
adult subordinates. Women frequently exercise a great deal
of covert influence through the men to whom they are close.

I want to reiterate that I do not think these exist as
pure "types," but that they represent two ends of a continuum
along which individual families and larger social groups
structured along patriarchal lines might be placed.

Feminist Conviction and Biblical Interpretation

In order for me to clearly address the question of the
authority of the Bible and feminist conviction, it is important for you to know not only what I mean by feminist conviction but also to know something of what I have seen and
heard in encountering Scripture with respect to God's intentions for women and men. And that requires a brief
reference to developments in Christian feminist biblical
hermeneutics.

Theologian Letty Russell in her introduction to the collection of essays, *Feminist Interpretation of the Bible*, suggests that what all good exegesis and theology seeks to do
is to liberate the Bible. Phyllis Trible, whose work has
focused on interpreting the Old Testament, adds that lovers

of Scripture have always
    released it from the prison of the past to speak to
    the living.... Theologians of ancient Israel and the
    early church reinterpreted texts in light of sub-
    sequent events...church fathers used allegorical
    exegesis to save scripture from obscurantism....
    Reformers...delivered the Bible from ecclesiastical
    control.   On the current scene, the hermeneutic
    operates among scholars who...liberate the Bible from
    incompleteness and provincialism.   Other commentators
    save it from scholarly captivity to nourish the poor,
    the outcast, and the oppressed.[6]
    Such liberation of Scripture marks *all* interpretation.
By using this principle, Trible reminds us, feminists stand
within a long history; applying it to the patriarchal ethos of
biblical texts and contexts is what is new.

The recent work of Christian feminists who have sought
to struggle critically with the biblical text, to understand
its message in relation to the contemporary situation and
specifically to feminist conviction, is characterized by three
concerns: interpretive humility; interpretive suspicion; and
interpretive reconstruction.

1. Interpretive humility.   Humility in interpretation
grows out of the recognition that what each of us sees is
standpoint dependent.   A particular feminist's perspective is
a unique but also a limited window on reality.   Our knowing,
perceptions, and feelings are fragmentary and significantly
marked by personal capabilities, sex, class, and economic
resources.   As humans our views are also distorted to
greater and lesser degree by ignorance and sin.   Therefore
feminist interpretation of the Bible must always recognize
that what is seen is always subject to correction.

2. Interpretive suspicion.   When others tell us what
they see in the Bible, we need to know where they are standing.[7]   Looking at the biblical tradition in light of women's
experience, as Elizabeth Cady Stanton and others did in the
Woman's Bible in 1895 and as Phyllis Trible has more recently
done with the creation material in *God and the Rhetoric of
Sexuality*, dramatically illustrates how classical theology
has been "shaped by male experience rather than by human
experience."[8]

Interpretive suspicion is based on the recognition that
while much of the Bible is written from the perspective of
the powerless, it has often been interpreted by the powerful.
Interpretive suspicion is a reminder that "in current biblical
study it is almost as important to examine the contemporary

situation of the reader as it is to know the particular
milieu that produced a text many centuries earlier."[9]

In its more radical extension, feminist interpretive
suspicion suggests that not only historical interpretations
of the Bible, but biblical texts themselves are androcentric,
that is, written from a male-centered perspective.

3. Interpretive Reconstruction. This phrase embraces a
concern to move beyond criticism to a "hermeneutics of
remembrance," as NT scholar Elizabeth Fiorenza puts it. The
intention is to move beyond androcentric interpretations and
texts to recover the hidden history of women in biblical
religion. A commitment to creative reconstruction involves
articulating models of historical interpretation which can
place women not on the periphery, but at the center of biblical community and history. It is a creative project because
it involves entering the biblical story with the help of historical imagination and artistic recreation. It means retell-
ing biblical stories from a feminist perspective, doing creative revisioning.[10]

Katherine Sakenfeld suggests that there have been at
least three different options for approaching the Bible which
feminists concerned about reconstructing the meaning of the
biblical story for women have adopted. These include looking
more carefully at texts about women to counteract interpretations "against" women, looking to the Bible generally for a
liberation perspective and, looking to texts about women to
learn from the intersection of the stories of ancient women
and of modern women both living in cultures which exhibit
sexism against women.[11]

My own current work is similar in form to the second
approach. That is, rather than concentrating on interpretation of one or more specific texts or on one of the
theologies present in the biblical material as a whole, I
have wondered about the relationship of various biblical
views to one another, to what extent there might be movement
or direction or a trajectory within Scripture which would be
consistent with or supportive of feminist conviction and
which we might receive as divine intention. However, unlike
some of the feminist liberation theologians who have
developed this second approach, my primary conversation partners have been members of Anabaptist Mennonite communities
rather than Latin American, Asian or Afro-American liberation
theologians.

A Feminist Trajectory in Mennonite Perspective

I would like to invite conversation about the following set of proposals, some of them having to do with biblical interpretation in social/historical perspective, some with the ethical implications of certain convictions about God, some with the meaning of various texts in contemporary U.S. and Canadian settings. I offer them to be tested and refined by others who also care about the meaning of the biblical story for our contemporary relationships to God and creation.

From Violent Toward Radically Benevolent Patriarchy.

The entire biblical story assumes a primary patriarchal framework and ethos. One can distinguish some texts whose social-historical setting might be characterized as violent patriarchy and others which might be characterized as benevolent patriarchy. The biblical trajectory in Christian perspective involves movement from violent patriarchy towards benevolent patriarchy towards radically benevolent patriarchy. I am thinking here in terms of theological-ethical movement (in some measure "live" or available and not necessarily dominant options) rather than in terms of large-scale historical/linear development.

This trajectory includes movement from viewing women simply as property toward consideration of the perspective and judgments of women in the decisions of the fathers, most radically developed in the New Testament in an ethic of mutual submission between Christian husbands and wives. The call for mutual submission challenges some patriarchal assumptions about the roles of the powerful and the weak, but does not in itself challenge the fundamental structure of male-female relationships. Women remain largely dependent on men economically, legally, and perhaps emotionally and psychologically.

The biblical trajectory also involves movement from violent destruction of enemies (at God's or humans' hands) to just treatment of enemies (an eye for an eye) to active, "non-resistant" love--returning good for evil in relation to enemies within a patriarchal social context.

The Trajectory Set By Jesus.

The biblical memories of the historical Jesus picture him redefining male and female identity within a patriarchal context in some fundamental ways.

Jesus' own relationships with and words to women challenged some basic patriarchal definitions of the identity and

worth of women. In his relationships to women Jesus indicates over and over again that the standard for goodness,
beauty and holiness in God's eyes is not that of patriarchal
Judaism--a righteous, healthy Hebrew male--but rather
responsiveness to God's jubilee reign, accepting God's forgiveness for human faithlessness and in turn bearing the
fruits of repentance. Some heard that the self-worth of
women was not primarily dependent on their relationships to
husbands and sons, not primarily on their ability to conform
to the standards for women set by a benevolent patriarchal
order. To Martha serving in the kitchen: he said, "Mary has
chosen the better part." To the one who called out, "Blessed
is the womb that bore you and the breasts that you sucked!"
he responded, "Blessed rather are those who hear the Word of
God and keep it!" To the unclean woman with the flow of
blood who dared to touch a rabbi and to the sinner from the
city whom he permitted to wash his feet with her tears and
dry them with her hair, he said, "Your faith has saved you.
Go in peace."

Such redefinition of identity encouraged Christian
women in the early church to dissent from certain patriarchal
definitions of the worth and appropriate behavior of women
and prepared the soil for the emergence of feminist consciousness in later centuries of Christian history.

Jesus' and the early Christian redefinition of God's
power as integrally connected to self-giving love, even in
relation to enemies, and Jesus' emphasis on servanthood as
the appropriate posture for all of his disciples, challenges
in some fundamental ways patriarchal definitions of the
identity and actions of men. Such redefinition of identity
challenged Christian men in the early church to dissent from
some patterns of masculine attitudes and behavior common
within either a violent or a benevolent patriarchal ethos.[12]

While patriarchal definitions of male-female identity
can provide stable and secure identity for those who "fit"
the standard definitions and related roles, they bind both
men and women who do not fit, for example, those who are not
able to attract men or women because of their appearance or
biological or social circumstance; those who are different--
women who are intellectually gifted or independent in spirit,
and men who are not or who do not choose to be highly competitive and dominant in relation to others.[13] Jesus can be
interpreted as good news for such men and women within
patriarchal culture. On the other hand, Jesus may represent
"hard news" for those women and men threatened by possible
change in habits of male-female interaction.

The Gospel and Social Order.
    The biblical gospel is a message of God's redemptive,
sacrificial care for humankind and a call for our relationships to one another to reflect that holy, redemptive love in
mutual submission and nonviolent love. John Howard Yoder
has suggested over the years that this gospel ethic can be
lived within any social structure. No social structure (neither benevolent patriarchy nor social eqalitarianism) *is
itself the rule of God* Nor is any social structure (not
even violent patriarchy) so far from God's rule that there is
no possibility for humans to experience God's liberation and
redemptive love.
    I agree with Yoder that in correlating gospel perspec-
tives of life in Christ with prevailing social structures,
Christ and not the structures themselves, is the source of
authority of conduct. The spirit and practice of Christian
love (for Yoder that is mutual submission within the
Christian community and active nonresistant love in relation
to those outside the community) are important signs of the
presence of God's spirit in human community. The weight of
the NT witness is that it is such Christian love which is a
central mark of the rule of God. If this is the way we read
the Bible, then it is such Christian love and not the patriarchal social order *within* which NT Christians happened to be
called to follow Christ, which is the primary factor in
identifying the presence of God among and the intention of
God for us as women and men.

Mutual Submission as Good News Within Patriarchal Order.
    Acceptance of an ethic of mutual submission between
Christian men and women within a patriarchal social context
can be good news for the weak. It is good news for the weak
because the powerful are called to learn the meaning of submission. This ethic calls the powerful to be radically
responsible to the weak, begins to challenge their
categorization of others as marginal and inferior, and calls
the identified "powerful" to serve. In a patriarchal context
men must learn to let go of some of their relative power and
social status in relation to women and subordinate men.
Mutual submission means letting go of the desire to sit at
the right hand of Jesus, and in turn adopting postures of
service and self-sacrificial love toward other men and toward
women as demonstrated by Jesus. Men, practiced in seeking
and gaining self-worth, and giving respect in terms either of
successful competitive power exchanges or of patriarchal

standards of righteousness, must learn to love the weak--
women--as themselves.

Mutual submission can also be good news for the weak
in patriarchal contexts because the weak are called to learn
the meaning of mutuality. Mutuality in relationship requires
love of self as well as of neighbor. Women, used to yielding
to men and to patriarchal definitions of female identity, used
to mistrusting their bodies, judgments, and sense of God's
call, are newly empowered through Jesus life, death and
resurrection, by a profound sense of God's love and respect.
Mutual submission between Christian women and men calls
women within a patriarchal social order to claim the desire
and power to act on their convictions, to risk speaking the
truth in love to those Christian men on whom they remain
economically, and perhaps in numerous other ways, dependent.

Missionary Love in Patriarchal Societies.

Christian women and men in patriarchal social contexts
can testify to the gospel in the broader culture through a
missionary posture or presence, exhibiting the reality of
mutual submission within the Christian community itself and
dissenting from expected patterns of male-female behavior in
the larger society where appropriate. Men would presumably
obey "God" rather than other powerful men when interpretations of God's will in Christ conflict with patriarchal
expectations of appropriate action including warlike behavior
for men or when women's views are not considered or
respected in decision making. Such men would thus risk
being categorized as "weak" or "subversive of authority."

Women, in relation to violent or paternalistic behavior
(including that of non-Christian husbands), could, insofar as
they felt they could take risks, challenge patriarchal attitudes and actions toward them and engage in forms of nonviolent resistance which testify to new self-identity in
Christ. Nonviolent love of those who exhibit sexism against
women does not mean repression of righteous anger or submit-
ting to physical abuse. It rather means directing energy
into missionary activity which seeks to keep open the possible conversion and redemption of those who have harmed
women/the weak rather than assuming the need for the physical destruction of such persons. In a patriarchal social
order the "dependent," the relatively powerless ones, the dis-
senters, have some room for action. They are not only "victims" in relation to the powerful, but "agents" of God's
redemptive power. But such commitment is also likely to be
costly. Women of this faith must be prepared to accept the

cost of claiming the power to act on the basis of a new Christian identity in a cultural world which is not practiced in expecting or rewarding it in women.

A Gospel Ethic for Egalitarian Societies.

Just because one believes that the accent of the gospel on mutual submission, repentance, and servanthood love, can be practiced by Christians in any social context—violent patriarchy, benevolent patriarchy, or a modern society which is relatively more eqalitarian—does not mean that there are no reasons to *prefer* one social context over another.

As John Yoder notes in "The Christian Case for Democracy," Christians can welcome changes in political and social orders which give more room to live out one's faith—for example, greater religious freedom.[14] In just such a way I welcome changes in our cultural and political system which provide more autonomy for women and which exhibit less sexism against women.

I am grateful for greater social equality between men and women because a more egalitarian social organization and ethos permits change in men/women relations in the body of Christ. Economic, social and psychological dependence of women on men makes mutual exchange exceedingly difficult. The "dependent" in relationships to the "powerful" tend to be conciliatory rather than to disagree, to frequently withhold what they really think or feel. A more egalitarian social context makes friendship between women and men more likely, increases the chances of women and men speaking the truth to each other in love, and makes possible delight in deeper communion.[15]

I also value movement toward more equality in women-men relations because it makes *reciprocal servanthood* possible. In more egalitarian settings where women and men relate as relatively independent equals, the gospel ethic of mutual submission among Christians takes on a new cast which I think is helpfully distinguished by the phrase "reciprocal servanthood." Letty Russell points out that the context of service is partnership, for true service can only be done in relationship of mutual love and respect not where one is subordinate to the other.[16] A relatively egalitarian social context means that women can *freely* be servants of men, can meaningfully yield in conflict situations. Vincent Harding once spoke about the situation of being a black pacifist in the late sixties. If you don't have the option of violence, he pointed out, pacifist action is a less significant moral action than if you do have the choice of violent response.[17]

If women's *normal role* is to be a servant, it is more difficult for the Christian community or the culture at large to
appreciate the significance of the action than if women were
not expected as a matter of course to be servants and freely
chose that role. It makes a difference if I as academic dean
offer to bring one of my colleagues a cup of coffee or if I
as the only woman (perhaps the secretary) on an otherwise
male committee am expected to bring coffee for the others
because I am a woman.

Not only does increased equality between men and women
provide the possibility for more meaningful moral action for
Christian women, but the change in social context radically
changes the internal emotional dynamic for women who choose
to be servants. Rather than fighting guilt for not being
able to be more "Christlike" and let go of the internal anger
which tends to build up when one always has to follow the
judgments and meet the needs of men, a more egalitarian context frees women to serve men joyfully rather than out of
duty, in a spirit of love rather than with resentment.

A gospel ethic of reciprocal servanthood can also
appear as good news within a relatively eqalitarian social
context. Mutual care, voluntary self-giving love, in a social
context where competitive struggles for power and resources
frequently take place between relative equals, have the
potential to transform situations and relationships between
women and men, men and men, women and women. Commitment to
reciprocal servanthood and nonviolent love offers a critical
perspective on individualistic, predominantly rights-oriented
ethics, and of violent or more coercive means of achieving
fuller justice in relation to women.

Feminist Conviction and the Authority of Scripture

Within the broad circle of scholarly biblical interpretation, feminist reconstructive interpretation has drawn attention to the diversity of biblical testimony concerning women,
finding forgotten positive texts and traditions. It has
listened anew to and pondered the silences of the biblical
story regarding women. But among scholars and teachers of
the church there continues to be a lack of interpretive con-
sensus about the extent to which certain passages do or do
not exhibit sexism and to what extent they are normative for
contemporary theology and ethics. Some texts seem clearly
to reflect sexist views and do not appear to be candidates
for reinterpretation. What is the status of such texts? Are
some parts of the Bible more trustworthy than others? Is the

New Testament more authoritative than the Old? Are texts which give us a glimpse of Jesus' attitudes toward women more definitive than those which reflect Paul's views? These questions spark others. Is movement towards greater equality between men or women really there in the Bible--or is it being read into the Bible by Christian feminists because we want to see it there, because it's too threatening *not* to see it there? Does the Bible rather suggest that benevolent patriarchy (headship) is God's intention for humankind? After all, what we see depends on where we are standing, as Christian feminists themselves point out. Explicit appeals to "the experience of women's oppression and power" as the authority for feminist conviction, especially when feminists suggest at the same time that there is reason to be suspicious of Scripture, has thrown further sticks on a biblical authority bonfire.[18] In what sense is the Bible God's authoritative word for us?

Those who see some form of benevolent patriarchy as God's intention for human order are quick to point out just what happens when human experience (authority of feminist conviction) and not the word of God (the Bible) is the bottom line. For example, Donald Bloesch in *Is the Bible Sexist?* writes:

> Authority in the feminist perspective is rooted primarily in human experience, particularly feminine experience, not in Scripture. The social sciences are considered to have almost as much authority as the sacred tradition, if not equal or superior authority. It is not uncommon to hear feminists, including evangelical feminists, contend that Paul was "wrong" in his attitude toward women.[19]

Susan Foh, another proponent of a headship interpretation of Scripture, explains the source of her similar concerns in *Women and the Word of God.* The problem with feminism, even biblical feminism, she writes, is that human reason becomes the final arbiter of what is God's pure word and what is man's advice. The possibility of error of cultural conditioning means:

> that all biblical teaching must come under scrutiny. The burden of infallibility then falls on our shoulders (and the shoulders of generations to come).... We become the final authority.... With the biblical feminists' concept of the Bible, there is no end to subjectivity.[20]

Bloesch and Foh as two who affirm headship or benevolent hierarchy, are not alone, however, in the concern that the

Bible be allowed to stand in some measure over against our
individual (or assumed cultural) perspectives, ideologies, and
convictions. A number of my colleagues who would affirm a
model of reciprocity or mutuality rather than hierarchy in
men-women relations share Bloesch's and Foh's concern that
the Bible must retain a certain critical authority. On the
one hand, those who hold this concern value the wisdom
garnered and remembered through history. Convictions
testified to in the Bible, convictions formed through many
years of experience with God by persons in varied political,
economic, religious, cultural and social situations, must be
allowed to criticize convictions based on a rather narrow
slice of personal/contemporary experience.

On the other hand, those who hold this concern may also
be pointing to the extraordinary and mysterious love of God
which the Bible reveals and can mediate, a love to which many
Christians throughout history have responded with joy and
energy, but which others have found "foolish," based on the
apparent realities of their lives. I suspect that the views
of Willard Swartley and John H. Yoder regarding the critical
authority of Scripture, for example, are directly related to
their study of the response of the Christian church over the
years to the ministry and call of Jesus in relation to loving
enemies. If Christians follow too quickly convictions
derived from personal experience, they may decide that it
does not make sense to love enemies, that it is too costly
for oneself or one's neighbors to follow the way of Christian
peace. Christians must remain open to the possibility that
in significant ways God's word to us may very well be a contrary word in relation to the convictions we might form
pragmatically.

Given these concerns and warnings, how might we think
further about the relation of the authority of the personal
convictions based on experience each of us brings to the
Bible to the authority of the Bible itself?

I first want to say that *no one* escapes bringing such
conviction, pre-understanding, ideology--eg., culture, to
Scripture. It is not the case that feminists do so and those
who favor hierarchy do not. What Scripture has to offer the
pre-understanding that we bring to it will vary depending on
what we *do* bring to it. What God has to say to each of us
through the biblical material differs depending on who we
are. The interaction of Scripture and experience is a conversation, a dialogue, a circle, a relationship, the content of
which varies somewhat because of who we are before God.   I
suggest it would be helpful for us *all* to approach further

dialogue with each other about the authority of Scripture by asking ourselves just what our deepest convictions are, those convictions with which we approach Scripture, and how those convictions have been confirmed in our lives through the authority of experience. I would suggest that the question of what the origin of those convictions are--whether they are rooted in Scripture or not, whether the biblical materials support or challenge them--is the second question, not the first.

Two Views of the Authority of Scripture

I do not think it is helpful to characterize the biblical authority debate as a struggle between those who want to uphold the authority of Scripture versus those who want to abandon it. I believe the issue is more fruifully seen, as David Kelsey illustrates in his book *The Uses of Scripture in Recent Theology*, as a struggle between two different understandings of biblical authority. Kelsey outlines the following two basic views.

1. **Authority as an intrinsic property of canonical writings.** The authoritative element in Scripture is its stateable content, either doctrines or concepts; this content falls into a systematic structure which constitutes the unity of Scripture. "...Scripture is authoritative because of some intrinsic *property* of the text." Scripture has this property (inerrancy or special status of the Bible's concepts) because "its important content simply *is* the content of revelation."[21]

Kelsey notes that underlying this view of the authority of Scripture is a particular judgment about the presence of God among humans. God is present in and through the teaching and learning of the doctrine asserted by Scripture. Scripture *itself* is revelation, is God's word. This definition of Scripture is commended by direct appeal to the reader's own religious experiences of the Bible as a holy object (140).

The primary model of the authority of Scripture in this view is one of domination-subordination, i.e. of one's intellect to the biblical word. If Scripture teaches about something, it is to be believed. Even the most paradoxical belief counts as highly probable, provided that it finds support in the Bible. As Jeffrey Stout puts it, "Mystery compels the intellect to bow down in humility."[22]

2. **Biblical authority as functional.** All other options Kelsey describes understand authority functionally, that is, as a function of the role played by biblical writings in the life of the church when it serves as the means by which we

are related to revelation, to God's self-disclosure in our
lives.
  The Bible is authoritative for faith and thought because
it provides our one link with God's historical self-
revelation in past events *or* Scripture is authoritative as it
expresses the occurrence of a revelatory and saving event in
the past *and* occasions its occurrence for someone in the
present.[23]
  I personally find the second type of functional approach
most helpful--the Bible as witnessing to and occasioning
God's self-revelation. Such a perspecive does not require
subordination of self at the *outset* of conversation with the
text in a way that does violence either to one's intellect or
to the current convictions one holds. This view of the
authority of Scripture rather invites one to engagement with
the text--and encourages willingness to see what it might
have to say. It seems to me that functional views which
emphasize the authoritativeness of the Bible because it describes God's self-revelation in the past have a more authoritarian shape than those which also speak of the Bible's role
in occasioning the occurrence or recognition of God's self-
revelation in the present. The former suggests that because
the Bible witnesses to authentic revelation, "you should
believe it." The latter suggests that the Bible is authoritative because it freely evokes consent, offers insight
which can be seen to be "of God." A functional view of
authority asks less for "a submission of will than for an
opening of the imagination, the mind and heart."[24]
  This view of authority better fits with my theological
understanding of the persuasive rather than coercive character and love of God as revealed through Jesus Christ. The
Bible makes a "nonviolent appeal" as Paul Ricoeur puts it,
not an authoritarian appeal.

Deepening the Functional Authority of the Bible
  Given this framework, what does commitment to deepening
the functional authority of the Bible mean for Christian feminists? And if one adopts a functional understanding of
authority, how does one avoid the dangers of the "endless
subjectivity" which Foh refers to? I would like to offer
three suggestions.
  1. **Commitment to serious engagement with the Bible.**
Commitment to the process of dialogue between the Bible and
individual or community experience is itself a step which can
potentially increase the power of the voice of God through
the Bible to shape and interpret experience.[25] One who

gives the Bible little or no functional authority seldom reads or studies it, does not work to understand the ancient writings or appropriate them in worship. For a feminist to accept the Bible as authoritative does not mean foregoing an attitude of interpretive suspicion, (it does not mean blind denial of the experience of pain and suffering of many women and men in sexist and patriarchal societies) but it rather means setting such suspicion in a more foundational context of interpretive hope. Perhaps, just perhaps, the continuing engagement of Scripture and contemporary experience will bring the two together in unforeseen and Spirit-filled ways.

What is the word of God in the text and what is human error? None of us can escape questions of faith. The first view of authority (authority as an intrinsic property of the text) has faith that the text itself is God's word/mode of presence. The second view assumes that God's word/presence is mediated to us through the text. Both are faith statements; both are in that sense "subjective" judgements.

The first locates the step of faith at the moment where one accepts the text as the direct word of God. The second locates the step of faith later--at the point of saying--*this* is what God is like as I see God acting in the biblical story; this is what I believe God wants for men and women based on the movement of the biblical material in the light of Christ. Neither views step outside of "subjectivity" in the sense that there is no human judgment involved that God is present and speaking to us in *this* way rather than *that* say.

2. **Commitment to Test Interpretations With Communities of Believers.** A second aspect of increasing the functional authority of the Bible is to commit oneself to engage with the biblical texts within the context of Christian communities of men and women. Foh is legitimately concerned that we humans tend to see what we're looking for--in the Bible as elsewhere. Trusting in or operating primarily on the basis of our individual judgements and interpretations frequently means that our limited perspectives and sinful tendencies distort what God may be trying to say to us. And there is much historical evidence to buttress Foh's perspective, including the history of men-women relations in the Christian church.

My own response to this problem which I believe Foh correctly identifies is commitment to interpret the Bible within Christian communities which include diversity of participants and perspectives. Responsible and faithful biblical interpretation and theological reflection is not just an

individualistic enterprise. One guard against individual
subjectivity is offering one's interpretations to the congregation of which one is a member, to colleagues, to the
wider church for testing. Further it is important to include
diversity among one's Christian conversation partners to
avoid narrowness of personal experience and prejudice. Subjective distortion can be to some degree compensated for if
one takes special pains to understand the experience of God
and the world which underlie the views of those who differ
from oneself.

Christian feminists can seek out communities of interpretation which include and welcome women and men who hold
feminist convictions as well as those wary of such convictions. It is important to be reading the Bible in the midst
of concrete community life where men and women share the
deepest convictions of their experience with one another,
when we tell each other what the world looks like from where
we stand in tandem with joint efforts at biblical interpretation. There are also strong reasons why such communities of
interpretation should include the voices of people with vary-
ing economic, political and cultural/social status. These
factors not only shape the questions we bring to Scripture
and what we hear in encountering Scripture, but also shapes
the content and focus of feminist conviction.

3. **Openness to God's Transforming Power Through Bible
and Community.** Commitment to increase the functional authority of the Bible in the two ways just noted opens the way to
the experience of God's transforming power through the Bible
and the Christian community. The Holy Spirit can liberate
the Bible's power in many ways, as Willard Swartley notes at
the end of *Slavery, Sabbath, War and Women.* The book of
Ephesians itself suggests twelve ways to Swartley including
enriching prayers and guiding our worship, providing models
for our personal Christian ministries, and offering images
which provide vision and motivation for dealing with evil in
the world. With respect to the relationships between women
and men in our world, the Bible can have functional authority
to facilitate the breaking forth of God's redemptive, transforming power within the Christian community. The Bible can
show us our alienation from one another as women and men,
provide standards of Christian self-identity that may call us
to dissent from gender definitions prevalent in our
cultural/historical context, and give us a glimpse of how
such new life in Christ might be correlated with various
social structures, and finally orienting us beyond such
structures, beyond ourselves, toward one another, toward God.

Functional Authority and Feminist Conviction

How, finally, does a functional understanding of the authority of the Bible relate to the authority of feminist conviction and experience? In the context of an interpretive community, what does it mean for a Christian feminist to respect the word of God which might be mediated through the Bible and allow it to be genuinely *God's* word, that is, allow it to stand in critical tension with deep personal conviction?

Again, I would note suggestions. First, Christian feminists can come to Scripture with the awareness of the human need for self-correction. Such a posture is consistent with feminist awareness of how bias affects interpretation and with the biblical emphasis on the human tendency to sin. As Rosemary Ruether points out, "No liberation movement can speak the universal critical word about injustice and hope for all time; it always does so within the limitations of its social location."[26]

Second, we can respect the integrity of biblical materials by trying to hear what they have to say in their own historical context--neither assuming they are simply "feminist" (overlooking patriarchal and sexist elements) or "hopelessly patriarchal" (overlooking aspects of God's redemptive work, of the possible good news for women in that context).

Third, we can recognize that one need not assume either an immediate antagonism or an immediate compatibility between "feminism" and "biblical faith." Ironically Bloesch and Foh are similar to radical feminists Mary Daly and Naomi Goldenberg in that respect--both argue that feminism and Christian faith are mutually exclusive. The divide between feminism and the Bible is clear and deep; one must reject one or the other--Daly and Goldenberg, Bloesch and Foh have simply chosen to stand on different sides of the gulf.

I find it helpful to reconceive the gulf. Feminism is not a monolithic position; there are varieties of feminism. Neither is Christian faith a monolithic position; there are varieties of Christians. It is more appropriate, I believe, to attempt to discern what is God's word to us through the Bible interpreted in the Christian ' community of men and women and to attempt to discriminate what of *both* "secular" feminism and "sacred" Christianity are consistent with God's intentions and purposes for creation. That means practically that not all forms of Christianity may be compatible with the biblical witness to God; it also means that not all forms of

feminism may be compatible with (or antagonistic to) the biblical witness to God. We can seek to be more discriminating
than the gulf walkers: more open to recognizing the work of
God in "secular feminism" than the Christian hierarchalists
and more open to the work of God in the midst of benevolent
patriarchy than secular feminists.

We can note, for example, that the seeds of feminist
consciousness, which have come to fruition in the 19th and
20th centuries, were present in the biblical story. We do
not need to seek to demonstrate that the biblical materials
exhibit and recommend the kind of equality envisioned by
many modern feminists in order to recognize in the movement
from violent to benevolent patriarchy to the mutual submission of men and women, the emergence of the seeds of feminist consciousness.

We can also note that not every idea or insight or
structure which we consider valuable or even "of God" has its
origins in the Bible. As Willard Swartley points out, the
New Testament is even less critical of the institution of
slavery than it seems to be of benevolent patriarchy. For
Christians an origin of an idea is not the ultimate test of
its harmony with the will of God. That is measured by God's
word to us in Jesus Christ interpreted in the Christian community of women and men through the Holy Spirit.

Further, if as I have suggested earlier, God's word in
Christ calls us to mutual submission which in a relatively
eqalitarian social structure takes the shape of reciprocal
servanthood, not all varieties of feminism or all aspects of
modern feminism are compatible with such commitment. The
word of God through the biblical story stands over against
feminist stances which emphasize the autonomy of women
without a vision for eventual reciprocity of men and women,
that is, those which are intentionally separatist. The biblical gospel also stands in tension with forms of feminism
which do not recognize the need for self-yielding as well as
self-affirmation on the part of women in relation to men and
which do not leave open the possibility for repentance on the
part of women and men whose experience and convictions are
marked by sexism.

At the same time, a follower of Christ can welcome some
of the central expressions of secular feminism--movements
toward equality, equitable sharing and mutuality in legal,
social, economic, and familial spheres which enhance the
potential for reciprocal servanthood--Christian love,
voluntary submission between relative equals, in the
Christian church.

Authority Through Embodiment

If it is the case that the Bible calls men and women to mutual submission in whatever social context, the functional authority of the Bible in relation to this ethic will likely continue to be weak among those feminists (Christians, ex-Christians, uncertain Christians) who feel they have few resources left to love men and women who embody sexist attitudes. What is perhaps most painful to such persons is the fact that the Christian church itself has been the source of much of the practice of and justification for sexism against women. Those of us who do have interpretive hope for the Bible, those of us who do believe that the power of God's transforming word has been and can continue to be mediated through the Bible, those of us who would like to see the functional authority of the Bible increased in the life and work of the church because we have seen and can testify to the power of its message in our own lives bear a special burden in relation to such persons.

It is my conviction that the biblical call to mutual submission will not, perhaps cannot be heard as good news to such persons until genuinely reciprocal servanthood between men and women is embodied in our families, our congregations, and our church institutions. Without models of reciprocal servanthood among us, that is mutual submission between relative equals, it is hard to believe that patterns of domination-subordination can be transcended.

A friend from South Africa recently told a story. After critiquing Marxism from a Christian point of view to a group of young black South African Marxists, he said a student responded, "Sir, if what you say is true, show me a place where this is actually being lived and I will believe you." Others can become more open to the functional authority of the Bible, to the power and presence of God through the biblical story, when it is possible to see a reconciling community of men and women actually being lived.

Although concrete attempts to embody Christian feminist convictions in life together are critical for those who are particularly sensitive to the sins of churches and societies against women, I agree with Letty Russell that Christian feminists have much to learn about the authority of the Bible from the black church who, in spite of the blindness and blatant sins of white Christians, listened to the Bible for "experiences which could inspire, convince and enlighten."[27]

Katie Canon points out that the Bible is the highest source of authority for many Black women. Because of their

respect for the Bible as God's word they have listened and
have learned from its pages "how to refute the stereotypes
that depict Black people as minstrels or vindictive militants,
mere ciphers who react only to omnipresent racial oppression." Through biblical faith Black life has become more
than defensive reactions to anguish and desperation. The
Bible has fed the rich, colorful creativity that emerged and
reemerges in the Black quest for human dignity. "Jesus
provides the necessary soul for liberation," as Paulo Freire
puts it, the incentive to chip away at oppressive structures,
bit by bit. Like the Black church, Christian feminist men
and women can identify with biblical characters who hold on
to life in face of formidable oppression, and can search
Scriptures together "to learn how to dispel the threat of
death" in order to welcome life.[28]

Notes

1. Margaret A. Farley, "Feminist Consciousness and the Interpretation of Scripture," in Letty M. Russell, ed. *Feminist Interpretation of the Bible* (Philadelphia: Westminster, 1985) 44-48, suggests these three principles and defines them as I have below.

2. Dana V. Hiller and Robin Ann Sheets, *Women and Men: The Consequences of Power* (Cincinnati: Office of Women's Studies, University of Cincinnati, 1976), 50.

3. Rosemary Radford Ruether, "Feminist Interpretation: A Method of Correlation," in Russell, ed., *Feminist Interpretation*, 114.

4. *Webster's New Collegiate Dictionary.*

5. See Elizabeth Dodson Gray, *Patriarchy as a Conceptual Trap* (Wellesley, Mass.: Roundtable Press, 1982), chapter 4.

6. Phyllis Trible, "Postscript: Jottings on the Journey," in Russell, *Feminist Interpretation*, 147-48.

7. Robert McAfee Brown, *Theology in a New Key* (Philadelphia: Westminster Press, 1978), 80-85, briefly explains hermeneutical suspicion as it has been identified by Latin American liberation theologians.

8. Ruether in Russell, *Feminist Interpretation*, 113.

9. Barbara Brown Zikmund, "Feminist Consciousness in Historical Perspective," in Russell, *Feminist Interpretation*, 22.

10. See Elizabeth Fiorenza, *In Memory of Her*, chapters 1-3 and Fiorenza's essay in Russell, *Feminist Interpretation*, 133-34.

11. Katherine Doob Sakenfeld, "Feminist Uses of Biblical Materials," in Russell, *Feminist Interpretation*, 56.

12. James B. Nelson in *Embodiment* (Minneapolis: Augsburg, 1978), 66, for example, delineates a constellation of values associated with dominance and control.

13. Definitions of male-female associated with modern benevolent patriarchy also hide a "class" bias and a "married" bias. Poor women, women alone, women who head single parent families do not have the *option* of being dependent, "feminine" in patriarchal terms.

14. *The Journal of Religious Ethics* (Fall 1977), 209-223.

15. Social equality does not imply that everyone must do the same tasks, think and behave alike. Friendship implies mutuality and equality, but friends are not necessarily alike, nor do they contribute to the relationship or to the community in exactly the same way. Careful inclusion in the decision making process of all members who are affected by

the decision and the presence over time of a pattern of reciprocity in yielding when making decisions are central indicators of genuine equality and mutuality in a household, congregation or Christian group.

16. Letty Russell, *The Future of Partnership* (Philadelphia: Westminster, 1979), chapter 3.

17. "The Religion of Black Power," *Religious Situation 1968* (Boston: Beacon Press, 1968), 33.

18. Farley in Russell, *Feminist Interpretation*, 64.

19. Donald Bloesch, *Is The Bible Sexist?* 19.

20. Susan Foh, *Women and the Word of God,* 7. Also see her comment that "A doctrine of Scripture that admits error eventually results in apostasy or heresy," 201.

21. David Kelsey, *The Uses of Scripture in Recent Theology* (Phildadelphia: Fortress Press, 1975), 29.

22. Jeffrey Stout, *The Flight From Authority* (Notre Dame: University of Notre Dame Press, 1981), 9.

23. Kelsey, *The Uses of Scripture*, 50 and 83.

24. Margaret Farley in Russell, *Feminist Interpretation*, 59.

25. Kelsey, *The Uses of Scripture in Recent Theology*, 164-66, deals with the question, why take biblical texts as authority at all? For theology or for the common life of the church? He suggests that no more or less compelling reasons can be given for this than what one gives for being a Christian. One can give an account in terms of the particularities of one's own history, or by wrestling with big questions and addressing the meaningfulness of understanding personal identity in terms of communal self-identity. He concludes that perhaps the most that can be said was said in a general way by Barth, that Scriptures when used in common life of Christian community drive us "out beyond ourselves and invite us, without regard to our worthiness or unworthiness, to reach for the highest answer in which all is said that can be said, although we can hardly understand and only stammeringly express it. And the answer is a new world, the world of God."

26. Rosemary Ruether in Russell, *Feminist Interpretation*, 164.

27. Letty Russell, *Feminist Interpretation*, 17.

28. Katie Canon, "The Emergence of Black Feminist Consciousness" in Russell, *Feminist Interpretation*, 40.

AN ETHIC OF CHARACTER: THE NORMATIVE FORM OF THE CHRISTIAN LIFE ACCORDING TO STANLEY HAUERWAS

Harry Huebner

Introduction

Every theological ethic employs a central metaphor that gives shape to a specific account of moral living. Insofar as an ethic is theological it places moral existence in relation to God's reality. Hauerwas quarrels with what he interprets to be the dominant metaphors of contemporary theological ethics, viz., the command-obedience metaphor of Barth and Bultmann[1] and the decision metaphor of Joseph Fletcher's situation ethics.[2] The latter he argues is but the logical extension of the former. Not wishing to deny their valid insights, he nevertheless replaces them with the language of character which "does not exclude the language of command but only places it in a larger framework of moral experience" (*Character*, 3).

Our task in this study will be threefold: First, to ask why Hauerwas finds it necessary to critique the contemporary models; second, to analyze the nature and implications of his replacement metaphor of character and its concomitant categories of virtue, vision and narrative; and third, to examine the contributions of his approach to ethics, especially in relation to the Mennonite ethical self-understanding.

The Failure of Contemporary Christian Ethics

Hauerwas is critical of the ethical approaches of both classical Protestantism and Catholicism. Both have a tendency to embrace moralities alien to the gospel. Both confuse apologetics with ethics and both tend to reduce ethics to pastoral/psychological concerns (*Vision*, 97). For mainline Protestantism, ethics is an altogether dubious enterprise in any event since it is but a disguised way of substituting works for grace. "Indeed some go as far as to suggest that ethics is sin insofar as it tries to anticipate God's will."[3]

Given the strikingly negative disposition towards ethics within classical Protestantism, one might expect Hauerwas to adopt a more Catholic approach. Insofar as he speaks favorably of such classic Aristotelian notions as character and virtues, this is indeed the case. Nevertheless, rather

than employ the traditional metaphysical philosophy of
essences, he emphasizes the historical. His procedural genre
focuses on story, history and narrative.[4]

It is difficult to fully appreciate Hauerwas' contribution
to ethics without first seeing his critique of the ethic of
modernity, a critique with both philosophical and theological
dimensions. The following are some key problems he
identifies.

1. **A problematic understanding of freedom and the self.**[5]
The combined impact of Protestantism's emphasis on the individual plus the Enlightenment's emphases on rationality and
individual happiness have led to a contemporary conception of
freedom as an end in itself. It is this presumption, according to Hauerwas, that underlies the moral view of America's
political liberalism that "unlike other societies, we are not
creatures of history, but that we have the possibility of a
new beginning. We are thus able to form our government on
the basis of principle rather than the arbitrary elements of
tradition."[6]

Moreover, the modern understanding of freedom is almost
entirely associated with the individual. "We have made
'freedom of the individual' an end in itself and have ignored
that fact that most of us do not have the slightest idea of
what we should do with our freedom" (*Community*, 80). It is
because of freedom that we can fight, and it is freedom that
we fight for. This is true for both the selfish among us and
for the altruists, except that "the idealists among us are
reduced to fighting for the 'freedom' or 'right' of others to
realize their self-interests more fully" (*Community*, 80).

Hauerwas' critical reference to "rights" in connection
with freedom is instructive. He argues that our interpretation of rights in relation to freedom and the individual has
made it an extremely problematic concept. We should pay
more attention to the fact that the notion of rights is itself
an outgrowth of enlightenment thinking where the "autonomous
person" is the moral paradigm. Hauerwas comes very close to
suggesting that what we call a moral right today is but the
moralization of desire. Desire which once was a vice, has now
become a virtue.[7] He emphasizes that rights language, at
least as it is used in North America today, is in tension
with the notion of community. In fact, it is a threat to all
corporate social realities because it perceives the individual and the corporate to be in moral conflict. This is why
the family has always been an anomaly for the liberal
tradition. Only if human beings can be separated in a
substantial degree from kinship can they be free indi-

viduals subject to egalitarian policies. Thus we
assume--and this is an assumption shared by political
conservatives and activists--that it is more important
to be an 'autonomous person' than to be a 'Hauerwas',
or a 'Polaski', or a 'Smith'. For example, the Supreme
Court recently held in Planned Parenthood vs Danforth
that a husband has no rights if his wife wishes an
abortion, because 'abortion is a purely personal right
of the woman, and the status of marriage can place no
limitations on personal rights' (*Community*, 81).

This way of thinking has made modern ethics
unintelligible, according to Hauerwas. We exist first of all
as individuals who are free to have our desires fulfilled.
And all desires are equal before the bar of justice. Hence,
freedom is seen as both the foundation and the goal of
morality.[8] Yet the freer we become, the more desperately we
search for community. Somehow intuitively and existentially
we know that a freedom that has nothing whatsoever to say
about how it ought to be used, cannot be a freedom that lends
truth to our moral experience.

Hauerwas points out several unfortunate implications of
this perspective on ethics. First, it has led us to do ethics
from the standpoint of moral quandaries.[9] Here the central
moral question is 'What would I(you) do in a given situation?"
Second, the ethic of modernity is the ethic of choice. We
are constantly called upon to make decisions[10] and we
believe them to be moral in so far as they are products and
protection of our freedom. Third, ethics has become abstract
and unqualified.[11] The assumption is that we are moral
beings insofar as we are individual human beings. Hence,
moral authority is autonomous. All specific (concrete)
heteronomous authorities, e.g., family, tradition, Christianity,
Judaism, etc., are morally irrelevant.

2. **The limitations of the teleological and deontological
theories of ethics.**[12] Contemporary moral philosophers have
argued that there are two general approaches to ethics:
teleological and deontological.[13] Teleological theorists
claim that moral rightness and wrongness, goodness and bad-
ness, can be determined by the non-moral value such as happiness, pleasure, self-realization, etc., that is brought into
being. Deontological theorists deny this. They argue that
rightness and wrongness are determined on the basis of something inherent in the object of moral judgement. For example, it simply is our duty to tell the truth, even though
telling a lie may produce more happiness (or other non-moral
value) than telling the truth.

Hauerwas rejects this distinction because he argues that the imagination out of which it flows sees rules, obligations and decisions as the paradigmatic components of morality. While rules play a very important role in our society, focusing on them as our moral foundation, as both deontologists and teleologists do, is to misunderstand the complexity of moral life. Both incorrectly assume that the primary element of morality consists in being confronted with a given situation and bein© called upon to make a decision on how to act in relation to that situation. It assumes that the situation as well as the moral notion are givens, when in fact they can only arise out of communal perception and definition.[14]

Furthermore, to see our morality from the standpoint of obligations and rules, "also has the effect of distorting our moral psychology by separating our actions from our agency" (*Peaceable*, 21). It is dangerous to understand our moral selves as an unconnected series of moral actions that do not have continuity and unity. The only way that a connection can be maintained is on the view of a moral self-understanding that arises out of community. "Communities teach us what kind of intentions are appropriate if we are to be the kind of person appropriate to living among these people" (*Peaceable*, 21). Consequently it is much more important that we know what we ought to be so that we may strive to become that, than that we know what we ought to do on the basis of certain "justified" rules and obligations.

The problem here, according to Hauerwas, is not that an "ethic of virtue" comes prior to an "ethic of obligation," but that to focus on the latter does not emphasize sufficiently the importance of community out of which our moral training arises, i.e., out of which comes the appropriation of virtues that are needed in order for us to live by moral rules. This, argues Hauerwas, is what is most needed in our society today, particularly as we face the growing threat of violence. Hence, says he, "...the kind of pacifism I defend does not neatly fit into the current philosophical options for understanding normative ethics. That is, it is neither consequential nor deontological even though it may well involve aspects of both. For the emphasis is not on decision or even a set of decisions and their verification."[15]

The general difficulty which Hauerwas sees with the teleological and deontological models is that their emphasis on rules, laws and ideals cannot deal with the constant temptation to be separated from the moral source that sustains Christian life. For this, ethics must be grounded in a personal relationship with the source. This Barth and Bultmann have attempted to do.

3. **The failures of Barth and Bultmann.**[16] Hauerwas has
an ambivalent relationship to Bultmann and Barth. On the one
hand they both appropriately emphasize the utter sinfulness
of man and our resultant unmitigated dependency on God. It
is this affirmation that guides them to the appropriate
insight that the fundamental paradigm for the Christian life
is that of relationship--as opposed to rules and principles--
between us and God.[17] Yet on the other hand they "refuse to
translate their theological insights into discernible forms
for the moral life" (*Character*, 177). Clearly the reason that
they fail at this point is that their "ethics is associated
primarily with the language of decision--ethics is concerned
with what we do rather than what we are" (177). Hence, "neither Bultmann nor Barth found a completely adequate means to
suggest how the believer's actual moral self is determined in
Christ" (176) Why this failure? Because "they both fail to
exploit the language of growth and character" (177).

Hauerwas evaluates both theologians from the general
standpoint of their failure to appreciate the idea of character. This naturally involves him in the nitty gritty of each
theologian's system of thought.

3.1 Bultmann's denial of ethics is grounded in his view
of the nature of the ethical task. If one means by ethics,
"any intelligible theory valid for all human behavior"
(*Character*, 132) then, Bultmann maintains, Jesus in fact taught
no ethics, because through Christ we have been set free from
the need to justify ourselves. This latter need is what
ethics has traditionally engaged in.

Bultmann's view of self is intimately associated with
history. We cannot understand ourselves apart from our acts
and our decisions. Hauerwas quotes Bultmann as follows:
"what man has *done* and *does*--his decisions--constitute him in
his true nature, that he is essentially a temporal being"
(*Character*, 147). Hence we are always in the process of
choosing who we are. Given this point of departure, the
notion of character becomes a problem. It is in tension with
our freedom to create ourselves, especially since Bultmann
wants to claim that it is precisely the grace of God that
saves us from ourselves in that we are set free from the
past and are opened to the future.

It is this notion of radical freedom in Bultmann's theology that Hauerwas objects to most. He contends that the radical discontinuity of the past as well as the failure to take
account of the social determination of the self, makes freedom impossible. This is the way of allowing oneself to be

determined by the immediate situation. "Rather than an ethic of openness, Bultmann's analysis is a stultifying limitation of man's potentiality to confront his future with the kind of hope and openness that the Gospel claims is possible for us as men" (*Character*, 166).

3.2 Barth's basis for the rejection of ethics is theological rather than ethical. It is because of who God is that we are not able to work out a proper view of Christian ethics. God's demand of grace is such that each action is but a response to God. Ethics is another word for obedience to the command of God. This is not to suggest that the command of God is capricious. In fact God's command is absolutely consistent. Yet since our decision to obey must be constantly repeated, it is the command of God that determines our moral actions and not our character.

For Barth, human agency is at the center of understanding the self. Hauerwas quotes Barth as follows: "the being of a person is a being in act", since "to exist as a man means to act. And action means choosing, deciding. What is the right choice? What ought I to do? What ought we to do? This is the question before which every man is placed."[18]

The major difficulty Hauerwas sees with Barth's ethic is that throughout his discussion on ethics and sanctification, his emphasis is far more of the One in which we are already justified and sanctified than on the believer. God's grace can never be in our possession. It is exactly because of the distance that remains between God's being and ours that it is unclear how the sanctification of God can be embodied in human agency.

Moreover the only continuity of which Barth can speak is the continuity of God's grace. This, according to Hauerwas, makes it extremely difficult to speak about the significance of character for ethics. Hence, Hauerwas concludes "the agonizing thing about Barth's ethics therefore, is not that he failed to appreciate the idea of character, but that he really does not integrate it into the main images he uses to explicate the nature of the Christian life" (*Character*, 176).

In summary, Hauerwas argues that Barth and Bultmann rightly reject the view that the fundamental paradigm of ethics is that of rules and ideals. Nevertheless they fail to establish an adequate metaphor beyond command-obedience which can do justice to our own moral determination in relation to the reality of God. In the final analysis to talk only about the grace of God is insufficient. Eventually Christian ethics must become fundamentally concrete, i.e., we must talk about our being in this world and our moral expe-

rience. Situation ethics is one attempt to concretize the
ethic of Barth and Bultmann.

   4. The limits of Situation Ethics.[19] According to
Hauerwas the basic contribution Fletcher makes in his *Situation Ethics*[20] is that he brings to the attention of the
reader the fundamental concreteness of ethical reflection.
To put it another way, for the ethical enterprize to be
involved purely with the contemplation of the Absolute and
the subsumption of individual situations under its domain, is
inadequate. With this Hauerwas appears to be in agreement.
In fact, it provides for him the excuse for a critical comment on Barth's ethical approach.[21]

   However, Hauerwas is far more critical of Fletcher than
he is positive. Fletcher's error stems from his agreement
with Barth and Bultmann that the primary ethical question is
the question of decision. Fletcher does not seem to realize
that "prior to decision must come the idea of our moral
notions" (*Vision*, 12).

   Hauerwas' basic critique of Fletcher is that he fails to
understand moral notions. Relying on Julius Kovesi[22] for an
explication of moral notions, he argues that "we do not come
to know the world by perceiving it, but we come to know the
world as we learn to use our language" (*Vision*, 17). The
implication of this is that there can be no such things as
uninterpreted facts and raw values. "We never simply know
facts, but we know them for some reason" (16). Hence, a
notion—moral or otherwise—"is like a bag by which we group
together some of the significant and recurring configurations
of relevant facts in our lives" (16). Moral notions, consequently, always contain both valuative and descriptive
aspects. Consequently we have notions only "in so far as we
are rule following rational beings" (17).

   The problem of ethical living is therefore not just a
problem of decision in relation to the factual situation, but
it is as much a problem of vision.[23] To say this in another
way, the moral task is not properly defined as bringing the
situation together with the rule, but rather as the task of
how we create proper moral notions on the experience of the
every day life. Hauerwas argues that Fletcher fails in his
understanding of the phenomenology of moral experience. The
reason that we resort to "It depends" when asked the question
"Is it always wrong to tell a lie?", is not because the moral
notion of lying lacks normativity and hence we substitute in
its stead the situation itself, but because the notion of
lying is not a complete moral notion. It is an open moral
notion. Just because we are not clear on what acts can all

be subsumed under the notion of lying, does not imply the moral irrelevance of the notion.[24]

Hence, Hauerwas concludes that "the problem with our moral notions is not necessarily the role they play in our common sense; it arises when we try to make them do more than their formal element was intended to do" (*Vision*, 22). Fletcher may well have done us a service in identifying for ethical thinking the limitations of the traditional usage of moral notions, nevertheless, he "fails to appreciate the fact that moral notions are not atomistic ideas separated from actual life, but rather gain their position because they play a part in the whole way of life. To deny their significance in the name of the situation in the way that Fletcher does is not only to question them but to deny there can be such a thing as a moral way of life" (23).

Moral notions are in fact not abstractions from our moral experience, but rather they are moral notions precisely to the extent that they help us in the task of sorting out how it is that we ought to live together. On this basis, the Christian moral notion can only derive from the Christian vision itself. "The moral life is therefore not just the life of decision but the life of vision--that is, it involves how we see the world. Such seeing does not come from just perceiving "facts," but rather we must learn how the world is to be properly "seen" or better known" (20). This is the task of the Christian who is called to live the life of one worthy of that name. "To be a Christian in effect is learning to see the world in a certain way and thus become as we see. The task of contemporary theological ethics is to state the language of faith in terms of the Christian responsibility to be formed in the likeness of Christ" (29).

The Nature and Task of Christian Ethics

Hauerwas identifies as significant the fact that the early Christians did not have a Christian ethic. For them it was unnecessary to do ethics as an explicit task. The reason for this is that the early church understood itself as a community whose task it was to live the new reality which was begun by Jesus Christ. Hauerwas' thinks of ethics in the same way.

1. **The Ethic of Character.** Hauerwas has argued persuasively that the modern view of ethics is problematic because it confuses the order of two very important ethical questions: "What ought I to be?" and "What ought I to do?" Most ethicists since Kant argue the priority of the latter

over the former. Hauerwas, however, argues that the question
"What ought I to be?" precedes "What ought I to do?"
(*Peaceable*, 116). To understand ethics on this basis neces-
sitates a fundamental rethinking of the central ethical metaphor, which for Hauerwas is character.

Hauerwas defines character "as the qualification of our
agency."[25] That is to say, character "is the very reality of
who we are as self-determining agents" (*Vision*, 59). We form
or mold our character by appropriating certain intentions,
beliefs and virtues and not others. Hauerwas does not wish
to suggest, however, that we are in an unlimited way our own
self-choosing. To emphasize the self-determining nature of
our character does not negate the fact that much of what we
are happens to us.[26] Nevertheless "our character is our
deliberate disposition to use a certain range of reasons for
our actions rather than others. .. " (*Vision*, 59).

Hauerwas' notion of character is dynamic. "To have
character is necessarily to engage in discovery" (*Vision*, 63).
Character provides for the possibility of connecting our past
to our future.[27] We can never face the future as nobodies.
We therefore do not come to it in an unconditional manner.
Rather we see the future through our character, we act in the
future out of our character so that its impact is always only
in elastic tension with the past out of which it is formed.
Nevertheless, in the final analysis we are responsible for
our character.[28]

1.1 Character and Freedom. As we have seen above,
Hauerwas' major criticism of modernity is that it understands
freedom primarily in relation to choice. "Put simply, we
assume that only if we have a choice are we free" (*Peaceable*,
37). But freedom does not necessarily consist in having a
choice. In fact, taking Hauerwas' notion of character
seriously implies that a well formed character is not free to
make certain choices. For example, a committed pacifist is
not free to make a decision to use violence. In such a case
the behavior that flows from "who we are" excludes certain
actions from the realm of actual choice. In fact, this is what
Hauerwas argues is the true nature of our freedom. "Our
'freedom' in regard to our decision depends exactly on not
having to accept the determinism of those who would encourage us to assume that we have to 'make' a 'decision' because
'this is the way things are'" (125).

Our "freedom" is therefore not properly defined as our
ability to make choices.[29] Nor is it related to our self-
awareness, but rather it depends on the kind of character we
have shaped by the vision which we have embodied and by the

virtues we have appropriated as we have lived out our story
to the present moment. In the end, says Hauerwas, "our freedom is dependent on our having a narrative that gives us
skills of interpretation sufficient to allow us to make our
past our own through incorporation into our ongoing history"
(*Community*, 147). Hence, narrative and not freedom is the
fundamental precondition for Christian ethics.

1.2 **Character and Narrative**. Hauerwas argues that the
quest for objectivity in ethics has led us to view ethics as
a science. Here we have emphasized the importance of logical rules and principles.[30] But such a syllogistic way of
dealing with ethics has severe limitations. In fact, ethics
can be much better understood on the model of rational narrative than on syllogistic logic. "What we demand of a narrative is that it display how occurrences are actions.
Intentional behavior is purposeful but not necessary" (28).
The narrative understanding of events and actions relies on
the contingent connection inherent in such events and
actions. It is devoid of logical necessity. Moreover, narrative understanding is understanding in the temporal mode. It
raises the question of the connection between different
events/actions in time.

Hence Hauerwas contends that the narrative mode of
understanding is appropriate to the understanding of
Christian existence because we must understand ourselves as
contingent beings, and as historical beings, and that it is
within this understanding of ourselves that we can best see
the form of God's salvation. "Christian ethics, therefore, is
not first of all concerned with 'Thou shalt' or 'Thou shalt
not.' Its first task is to help us rightly envision the world.
Christian ethics is specifically formed by a very definite
story with determinative content" (*Peaceable*, 29). Learning
to be disciples is learning to shape our story on the theme
of God's kingdom.

1.3 **Character, Virtues and Vision**. For the Greeks and
the early Christians, virtue or Arete was the key moral concept. When the question was raised about what individuals
should be, the ancients gave the answer in terms of certain
virtues that they should possess. Plato, for example, argues
for the virtues of courage, temperance, wisdom and justice.
Why? Because he had a particular vision for the Republic.
The nature of the Republic, since it was a moral community,
could not materialize unless the functions which these
virtues determined would be realized by its citizens.

Hauerwas argues that there is no one set of natural
virtues which can be shown to be universally applicable.

This is so because there is not one vision which is acceptable to everyone. Nevertheless when we talk about a particular character, e.g., the Christian church, then we can talk about virtues that are appropriate to it. Then it is not only possible but becomes necessary to identify the virtue and the functions which claim to bring about this vision. Moral communities or individuals therefore require training in order to become virtuous. Hauerwas talks of virtues as skills. "To be a person of virtue, therefore, involves acquiring the linguistic, emotional and rational skills that give us the strength to make our decisions in our life our own" (*Community*, 115). Moreover, the "capacity to be virtuous depends on the existence of communities which have been formed by narratives faithful to the character of reality" (116).

As examples, Hauerwas discusses two Christian virtues--hope and patience--which he argues are important for Christians in our society to embody. Because we participate in so many different communities all at the same time each of which constitute its own vision and hence has its own account of what it means to be virtuous, we would despair without hope. And "patience is training in how to wait when there seems no way to resolve our moral conflicts or even when we see no clear way to go on" (127). We must train ourselves to hope even when there is no empirical basis for hope. We must train ourselves to be patient when most of what we see is injustice. This however, "does not mean that we do not plan and/or seek to find the means to promote justice in the world, but that such planning is not done under the illusion of omnipotence. We can take the risk of planning that does not make effectiveness our primary goal, but faithfulness to God's kingdom" (*Peaceable*, 105).

2. The Task of Christian Ethics. For Hauerwas, the task of Christian ethics is identical with the task of being the church. Hence it is not the task of any one ethicist or scholar to present the ethical wisdom sufficient for the new life in the church. Whenever ethics is done as an abstract independent discipline of thought concerned primarily with ideas, it does not have much to do with being Christian.

Moreover Christian ethics also ought not to be seen as a sub-discipline of theology but rather "Christian ethics is theology" (*Peaceable*, 54). Christian ethics is "...at the heart of the theological task. For theology is a practical activity concerned to display how Christian convictions construe the self and the world" (55).

The church is first and foremost to be the people of God

whose purpose it is to allow God to create their community
into a "people capable of witnessing in the world to the
kingdom" (Peaceable, 69). Hence the church, for Hauerwas is a
training base where we are molded into the kind of people
that reflect the true character of God. "The task of
Christian ethics is imaginatively to help us understand the
implications of that kingdom. . . . (it) imaginatively tests
the images most appropriate to orchestrate the Christian life
in accordance with the central conviction that the world has
been redeemed by the work of Jesus Christ" (31).

For Hauerwas the church does not really have a social
ethic at all; rather it is the social ethic. Hence it must
concentrate on keeping itself holy, not in the sense of dis-
associating itself from the world, but in the sense that it
concentrates on molding its being after the being of God.
This it does by "imitating" God.[31] How? Not by mimicking
every action of Jesus, but rather by being like Jesus at the
point of the cross. "Thus to be like Jesus is to join him in
the journey through which we are trained to be a people
capable of claiming citizenship in God's kingdom of nonviolent love--a love that would overcome the powers of this
world, not through coercion and force, but through the power
of this one man's death" (Peaceable, 76).

Character, the Church and Nonviolence

As we have seen, the pacifism of Hauerwas is not based
on assumptions of the goodness of human nature or the possibilities of good within society. Nor is it based upon any
prudential calculations of success in changing violent structures in our society. Rather, for Hauerwas non-violence has
its basis in an understanding of the church.

He defines the character of the church by the event of
Christ. In this sense it sets itself apart from mainline
society. It is a holy nation, a sanctified body. Hauerwas,
relying heavily on J.H. Yoder, argues that this way of defining the church does not mean that he is talking about a
withdrawn church nor a "withdrawal ethic." Rather, it means
that "the first duty of the church for society is to be the
church, i.e., the body of people who insist on the primacy of
faith by refusing to accept obligations that might lead them
to treat in an unbrotherly way an 'enemy' of the state."[32]
In other words, the church is the body of Christ--the
autobasileia.[33] We are the ones to witness to the meaning of
love in social relations. "The crucial question is not whether
the church should or should not be responsible for society,

but rather what that responsibility is . . . . The church cannot attempt to become another power group among others in
society that seek to dominate in the name of the good"
(*Community*, 44).
  The church is both like and unlike any other polity. It
is like any other in that it is based on a political gospel.
"Christians are engaged in politics but it is a politics of
the kingdom that reveals the insufficiency of all politics
based on coercion and falsehood and finds the true source of
power in servanthood rather than dominion" (*Peaceable*, 102).
On the other hand it is "unlike any other insofar as it is
informed by a people who have no reason to fear the truth.
They are able to exist in the world without resorting to
coercion to maintain their presence" (102). Hence the church
can best be understood as "a community which tries to
develop the resources to stand within the world witnessing to
the peaceable kingdom and thus rightly understanding the
world" (102). The church is a "community of character" and a
"community of virtues".
  The church is best characterized, according to Hauerwas,
by three New Testament concepts, viz., forgiveness, the cross
and the resurrection.
  1. **It is possible for the church to live peaceably only
because it is a forgiven people.** In fact, says Hauerwas, "we
must remember that our first task is not to forgive, but to
learn to be forgiven" (*Peaceable*, 89). Why? Because to be a
forgiven people means that we live by trust and not by control. The Christ-like nature of the church teaches us to
learn to trust other people as we have learned to trust God.
It is in this sense that we can become a whole, and indeed a
holy people.[34]
  2. **Peaceable people are people of the cross.** But the
cross is more than a mere symbol of the importance of self-
sacrifice. "The cross is Jesus' ultimate dispossession
through which God has conquered the powers of this world.
The cross is not just a symbol of God's kingdom; it is that
kingdom come" (*Peaceable*, 87). To be a people of the cross
therefore means that we are people in training to become
dispossessed.[35] As people of the cross we commit ourselves
to relinquish all power over the lives of others.
  3. **"Through Jesus' resurrection we see God's peace as
present reality."** (*Peaceable*, 88). To be a church characterized by resurrection is to be one that believes in the transforming power of love. A love which is "the non-violent
apprehension of the other as other. But to see the other as
other is frightening, because to the extent others are other

they challenge my way of being. Only when my self—my
character—has been formed by God's love, do I know I have
no reason to fear the other" (*Peaceable*, 91).
The pacifism of Hauerwas is squarely rooted in his
ecclesiology. To be pacifist is to be the church. "Christian
pacifism is not based on any claims about the proximate or
ultimate success of non-violent strategies, though we
certainly do not try to fail as if failure in and of itself is
an indication of the truthfulness of our position. Faithfulness, rather than effectiveness, is the ultimate test of
Christian pacifism."[36] Nevertheless the pacifist church is
not merely to be passive in the face of injustice. For that
was certainly not the way of Jesus. And "the pacifist is no
less obligated to resist injustice, for not to resist means
we abandon our brother or sister to injustice. Pacifists,
however, contend the crucial question is how we are to
resist" (100). And this "how" can only be given shape by the
true character of the church of Jesus Christ.

Critical Comments

No contemporary non-Mennonite theologian has made a
greater contribution to the understanding of biblical
pacifism, than Stanley Hauerwas. For this we owe him our
deepest gratitude.
This is not the place to give serious attention to his
many contributions to Christian ethics. Nevertheless, we do
want to identify just a few aspects of his approach that aug-
ments our own Mennonite ethical understanding.
First, the single most important contribution Hauerwas
has made to theological ethics is the re-introduction of the
notions of character and virtue. This, as Alasdair MacIntyre
maintains,[37] actually makes it possible for us to speak
intelligibly about ethics once again. It liberates us from
the bondage to the ethics of situation and decision. While
Mennonite ethicists have not used these categories
explicitly, nevertheless, their use holds out considerable
promise in articulating a coherent Christian pacifist ethic.
Second, Hauerwas has introduced a new perspective on how
the church critiques the world. His analysis of liberal
democracy, with its underlying assumptions regarding human
freedom and technological power, and his rejection of modern
ethics based primarily on rules, principles and on the situation, are creative new ways of defining the world which Mennonite theologians have often pointed to in much less elo-
quent fashion. Moreover, his placing the church/world

dichotomy in the framework of a community of character suggests that the key to understanding this separation is moral. This moral dualism does not lead to a "withdrawal ethic," but must be seen as a way of being in the world that enables us to speak truth to the world from the standpoint of the Christian community.

Third, he presents a helpful critique of rights language.[38] Mennonites have recently come to speak the language of "human rights" without careful enquiry into the underlying philosophical and theological assumptions which gives it meaning. On the one hand we have felt compelled not to reject this language since it seems to provide a base from which to speak internationally and inter-religiously about such things as suffering and poverty. On the other hand, we have felt it to be at odds with our tradition since it is the language of demand and we have wanted to see ourselves as people of the cross. Hauerwas has helped us see more clearly the inherent tension between rights language and Christian pacifism.

Fourth, and perhaps most significant of all, in developing the model for relating narrative and ethics, Hauerwas has helped us understand the significance of the relationship between our own tradition and ethic. At this point he is really analyzing what we have been doing in our ethical reflections all along. This "making explicit" our own ethical self-understanding is a service for which we owe him a great debt.

These are some all too brief identifications of Hauerwas' contributions to Christian ethics. Let us also identify some areas where important questions need to be raised.

First, is there not a danger in simply identifying theology with ethics?[39] Are there not important epistemological and even metaphysical considerations to be taken into account for which, at least, a theoretical separation between theology and ethics is important? Our theology will no doubt impact how we live because of the essential practical nature of Christianity, but nevertheless, for proper and clear understanding, they deserve independent attention. And since this is so, does his claim not border on reductionism? For example, a question like "Who is God?" is appropriately seen as a metaphysical question even when it is argued, as I believe Hauerwas would, that the proper way it should be answered is in terms of God's character. And while such questions should never be divorced from how God has acted in history, and therefore how we must live, nevertheless the question itself, as well as notions like "act of God," deserve

careful philosophical scrutiny and conceptual analysis. Analyzing the nature of such issues is important to theology and
should at times be done independently of ethics, albeit never
without the recognition that the God of whom we speak is one
whom we come to know most profoundly in our following and
not in our thinking.[40]

Second, Hauerwas is ambiguous in his use of power language. He makes it clear that the church should not become
another power group seeking to dominate. While this should
not be disputed, one sometimes gets the impression upon reading his view of the church that this means that the church
ought not to exercise any power at all. But if this is
implied, it is really quite problematic. Redemption is itself
powerful, i.e., it effects profound change. And the church is
an agent in this process. Hence, when we hold out the possibility of overcoming the sting of poverty to a family by
assisting in building a house for them, we are incarnating
the transforming power of the love of God. In this sense it
is correct to say that when the church is engaged in being
the body of Christ, it is the transformation of the world.
There is no power greater than this.[41]

Third, I want to pursue somewhat more carefully Hauerwas'
relationship to Barth's ethical paradigm, viz., command-
obedience. From reading through Hauerwas' writings, it would
appear that he is not nearly as critical of Barth, Bultmann,
et.al., who adopt the command-obedience metaphor, in his later
writings, as he suggests in his earlier writing. While in
his early writings his criticism of Barth is focused on
command-obedience, his later critique seems less focused here
and much more on the nature of the command which Barth
ascribes to God.[42] What appears to be wrong with Barth in
the final analysis is that he does not have God command nonviolence. Had Barth said this, I doubt there would be a
criticism of his ethic at all.[43]

Although this is not the place to trace the details of
how Hauerwas moves ever closer to employing command-
obedience as his own moral metaphor, let me nevertheless
briefly give some evidence for this claim. I then want to
show what the weaknesses of this metaphor are, and suggest
an alternative model which I feel can strengthen the case
Hauerwas wants to make. One major reason for my claim is
Hauerwas' apparent acceptance of the effective-
ness/faithfulness dichotomy. He is critical of any ethic that
strives to be effective. This is, of course, a valid
criticism in one sense. It clearly follows from an embrace
of an ethic of the cross and from a rejection of

situationalism, that an effective calculation of personal consequences cannot determine the actions of the faithful.
Nevertheless, to try to articulate a Christian ethic on the
basis of speaking about faithfulness over against effectiveness and vice versa, raises the problem of how to conceive
our role as agents in God's kingdom. How are we to
understand ourselves as both under God and simultaneously
also agents of social change? Or are we in fact not to be
agents of social change (effective) at all?

Hauerwas emphasizes the hard-to-disagree-with point that
the church ought to concentrate on being the church, and that
we should let God be God. This comes out strongly in
several of his later writings but nowhere more clearly than
in his declaration in the *Christian Century*.[44] Here he and
William Willimon viciously attack the presuppositions of
modern liberalism. They argue that they have become "less
sanguine about inherent American goodness or the effectiveness of governmental and legislative attempts to create justice" (100). But what precisely do they mean by this statement? Do they mean that the attempt to create justice really
is not the task of the government [perhaps the government
lacks the insight or the ability or the moral mandate], or do
they mean that justice cannot be created by governments,
period. Perhaps they mean that justice, properly understood,
is a gift, and cannot be strategically acquired. It must be
lived. Whatever their precise meaning, the issue which they
are identifying as crucial has to do with appropriate
Christian moral agency.

Now we add to this their response to Liberation Theology
as unfaithful, particularly that of North American
theologians because they see this as "the last gasp of the
old liberal naivete wedded to newer strategies of
governmental coercion" (100). The problem here is similar.
Human strategies (actions?) cannot bring in the kingdom of
God. Or is it merely human coercive strategies (actions?)?
It is beginning to appear that what is meant by letting God
be God is that God is responsible for bringing in the kingdom and we are not. But this begs the central question of
Christian ethics, viz., how can we be God's moral agents?

It is similar reasoning that makes Hauerwas critical of
Ron Sider's address delivered at the Mennonite World Conference in 1984.[45] In response to Sider's claim that today
Anabaptists have a special "rendezvous with history," and
that they must "profoundly effect the course of world history," Hauerwas says "my problem with this kind of phrasing
is, I fear, that it associates faithfulness with effective-

ness...." and "once you start looking for effectiveness, it may
mean you overlook the necessity of communities learning how
to live peaceably even in a violent world."[46]

This discussion raises for us a very important problem
that stems from interpreting ethics via the dichotomy of
effectiveness and faithfulness which we contend results from
a too heavy reliance on the command-obedience metaphor. All
of the criticism Hauerwas makes of Sider must be made, but to
make them within the context of command-obedience, results in
an inadequate rendering of moral agency. If we follow
Hauerwas' logic a little farther, we get to some very star-
tling notions. Surely he is not suggesting that how the
Christian community lives in this world will in fact make no
empirical difference to this world, or that the difference it
makes is morally irrelevant, even to God! Worse still, that
there is indeed no relationship between God's will for this
earth and the being/action of God's faithful people! And yet
unqualified sentences like "God's purposes are not dependent
upon our survival as a church or a nation"[47] raise this question. Are God's purposes dependent on us at all? Are God's
purposes for this earth and the faithfulness of God's people
related in any way whatsoever? Or is God as commander in
the end really the sole agent of social change?

I know full well that Hauerwas wants to locate Christian
moral agency in the church, and I wholeheartedly applaud
this. But is not one sign of the church's faithfulness its
activity transforming of the world? I am sure that Hauerwas
would agree that it is. But then the relationship between
God's activity and ours must be stated differently.

The argument that one's being/action is or is not effective while quite irrelevant *vis-a-vis* the moral justification
of such being/action, is nevertheless not irrelevant regarding the poor and the oppressed. It is precisely effectiveness that is the most important here. The issue is never
whether some course is or is not merely effective or
immediately effective, but rather whether it is profoundly
effective. To say this another way, the issue is one of
Truth. As Christians we believe that the faithful way *is* the
effective way, even though it may not be immediately
apparent. It is the only way that can deliver what it promises. To turn this around and say that the effective way is
the faithful way is of course not true. But in the final
analysis, unless salvation effects change, it cannot be salvation. And when our salvation does not effect change in the
lives of the "unsaved" we need to take a closer look at how
we are being God's people.

The point is made by Hauerwas, a la Yoder, that the way of the cross demonstrates that even Jesus was not concerned to make history come out right. Although profoundly true at one level, it is quite misleading at another. Is not the way of the cross a demonstration that Jesus knew that any complicity with violence could not move history in God's direction because that was not the way of God? Saying it this way is not merely a matter of semantics, it is theologically and ethically significant. For example, Hauerwas' way of putting the matter leads to a prohibition of non-violent direct action, while the other way, although equally faithful to the call of Christ, wills and plans to effectively redeem the world from sin, albeit via the only "way" radical enough to ensure ultimate victory. This is the way the faithful are invited to travel.

It is unfortunate that Hauerwas gets trapped by a false dichotomy. But it is not surprising, because it follows quite naturally from his reluctant allegiance to the command-obedience metaphor.

What then is the weakness of this metaphor, and what is an appropriate alternative? Its primary weakness lies in the fact that, as one would expect of army language, it asserts disparity between the commander and those subject to his command. The commander has one role, and the subjects have another. In fact, the commander is not beholden to the ethics commanded of the subjects. The character of the commander is often fundamentally at odds with the character which is required of the underlings. The way of the commander is not the way of the subjects. The responsibilities are different. That is why one is the commander and the others are not.

This metaphor begs a very important question regarding the character of the commander-God and the relevance of God's character to our own. The suggestion implicit is that the character of God is not what matters most; rather it is the nature of God's command. But this is extremely problematic since it puts into question the basic tenet of the Christian faith, namely the incarnation. Does not the incarnation symbolize that God's way and character is our way and character? How can we believe that we ought to do what is commanded us when we do not simultaneously believe that the One who so commands embodies the truth and hence would do likewise? In fact, is it not our basic conviction that the way of God is the way of God's people because it is the way of truth?

This metaphor also creates problems for our understanding of human agency. As long as we maintain this breach

between God's being/action and our being/action we will feel
compelled to think of the God/human relationship in terms of
roles, i.e., who is responsible for what. And as long as we
do this, we will trivialize the role of human action and the
church as moral agent.

An alternative metaphor which, I believe, is more consistent with an ethic of character and more accurately
catches the power of the divine/human relationship, is the
metaphor of invitation-participation. God invites us to "put
on the whole armour of God" and to participate in God's
kingdom.

The strengths of this model are many. First, it connotes
community and not disparity. We are asked to join in the one
being/action. The very message of wholeness and reconciliation to which we are invited, is embodied in the symbol that
makes this possible. This is the very thing one would expect
from love's being. Love does not command, it invites. Second, it affirms that there is a way of God to which we are
invited--it is not a way created by us. This was the primary
value of the command-obedience model and that part of it is
retained. The Christian moral paradigm cannot rest on
autonomy. But neither is it simply heteronomous. Here Paul
Tillich is right that a third model, which he called theonomy,
is required. Third, this way has already been disclosed to
us in the life, death and resurrection of Jesus the Christ.
The invitation is to all to become a part of a new people--
people with a vision to become a community through opening
themselves up to radical transformation via the loving
character of God, and who likewise, through their loving
character, will the radical transformation of the world.

The invitation-participation metaphor also overcomes the
effectiveness-faithfulness dichotomy. No longer are there
two ways, God's way and our way, but one way which we are
invited to join. And when that way is perfectly incarnated,
then the questions about whether it was faithful or effective,
and whether it was God's doing or ours, simply disappear.

Allow me an analogy. When student musicians train for
their performance, their success depends on how closely they
can emulate their master. This takes much training. When
the performance takes place, their effectiveness depends on
how faithful they have been. Surely the relationship between
the student and the master is not command-obedience, but
invitation-participation. And would it not be appropriate to
say after the performance that the master has become alive?
It would certainly be folly to argue about who the real agent
was, the master or the student.

Hauerwas has done us a tremendous service in articulating an approach which allows us to speak meaningfully about Christian ethics again. The critical comments made in this paper arise out of a deep commitment to this same approach. It is because of this commitment that the need exists to critique its weaknesses and offer alternatives. I hope our alternative suggestions can point in the direction in which some of the deficiencies can be overcome.

Notes

1. Cf. esp., *Character and the Christian Life: A Study in Theological Ethics* (San Antonio: Trinity University Pess, 1975). Hereafter cited as *Character*.

2. Cf. Stanley Hauerwas, "Situation Ethics, Moral notions, and Moral Theology," in *Vision and Virtue: Essays in Christian Ethical Reflection* (Notre Dame: University of Notre Dame Press, 1974). The latter hereafter cited as *Vision*. Cf. also *Character*, p. 177f.

3. The Peaceable Kingdom: A Primer in Christian Ethics (Notre Dame: University of Notre Dame Press, 1983) Hereafter cited at *Peaceable*, 52. Elsewhere Hauerwas says "Barth, for example, goes as far as to say that any 'general conception of ethics coincides exactly with the conception of sin, since any such conception necessarily replaces God's command with man's." *Character*, 131.

4. "Theology has no essence, but rather is the imaginative endeavour to explicate the stories of God by showing how one claim illuninates another." (*Character*)

5. Cf. *Peaceable*, 37-46.

6. *A Community of Character: Toward a Constructive Christian Social Ethic* (Notre Dame, Ind.: University of Notre Dame Press, 1981), 78. Hereafter cited as *Community*.

7. "The genius of liberalism was to make what had always been considered a vice, namely unlimited desire, a virtue." (*Community*, 72.)

8. "Freedom itself is at once the necessary and sufficent condition of being moral." (*Peaceable*, 8.)

9. Hauerwas makes extensive use of the very interesting article by Edmund Pincoffs, "Quandary Ethics," in *Revisions: Changing Perspectives in Moral Philosophy*, eds. Stanley Hauerwas and Alasdair MacIntyre, (Notre Dame: University of Notre Dame Press, 1983).

10. Cf. *Peaceable*, esp. the section entitled "Decisions, Decisions, Decisions," 121.

11. Cf. esp. *Peaceable*, 17-23.

12. *Peaceable*, 17-24.

13. Cf. e.g., William K. Frankena, *Ethics* (Englewood Cliffs, N.J.: Prentice-Hall, Inc., 1963), 13-16.

14. "No account is given for why and how we have come to describe a certain set of circumstances as abortion, or adultery, or murder, and so on." (*Peaceable*, 21.)

15. "Pacifism: Some Philosophical Considerations," *Faith and Philosophy* (April 1985), 101.

16. Cf. esp., *Character*, 131-178.

17. "In summary, clearly I am in sympathy with Barth and Bultmann's attempt to describe the Christian life in terms of the fundamental relationship of the self to God. They rightly reject as inadequate the attempt to understand the Christian life solely in terms of obedience to laws, rules, ideals, etc. They have both perceived that when Christian ethics is so developed the constant temptation is for it to become separated from the source that sustains it." (*Character*, 176.)

18. *Character*, 151f. Hauerwas also quotes Barth as saying "for it is as he acts that man exists as a person. Therefore the question of the good man, and value and rightness of the genuine continuity of his activity, the ethical question, is no more and no less than the question about the goodmen, value, rightmen, and genuine continuity of his existence of himself" (155n).

19. Cf. esp. "Situation Ethics, Moral Notions, and Moral Theology," in *Vision.* Cf. also *Character*, 177f.

20. Joseph Fletcher, *Situation Ethics*, (Philadelphia: Westminster Press, 1966).

21. "In this context Barth's claim that the ethical good is determined solely from the command of God is simply fantastic. Ethics is fundamentally reflection on our received human experience as to what is good and bad, right and wrong. It cannot escape from that experience to the realm where the good or right can be known with more exactness." (*Vision*, 28.)

22. Cf. *Vision*, 13.

23. "The moral life is therefore not just the life of decision but the life of vision--that is it involves how we see the world. Such "seeing" does not come from just per-ceiving "facts," but rather we must learn how the world is to be properly "seen" or better known. Such learning takes place by learning the language that intends the world and our behavior as it ought to be that the good may be achieved. The moral life is a struggle and training in how to see." (*Vision*, 20.)

24. Hauerwas attempts to make this point clear with the following: "Suppose, however, that instances of intentionally deceiving someone else to save the life of another were so common in our experience that we had a notion for it, for example, "saving deceit." Moreover, this notion was not even associated with lying but instead had an entirely com-mendatory connotation. If this were the case then we might be much more willing to say that lying is always wrong because in such a circumstance the formal element of lying

would be much more complete." (*Vision*, 21).

25. "Toward an Ethic of Character," *Vision*, 61.

26. Cf. esp. *Vision*, 61.

27. "Character is morally significant because, if rightly formed, it provides a proper transition from our past to our future; for the task of this transition is not to accept the future unconditionally, but to respond and remake the future in the right kind of way." (*Vision*, 64).

28. Cf. esp. *Community*, 139. On this point Hauerwas relied heavily on Aristotle and Aquinas who suggest that we have character precisely insofar as we have the ability to make our actions our own. This means that what we do arises out of the virtues we have appropriated.

29. "To use an extreme example, I may be free to choose to die by starvation or torture, but that is hardly to be free." (*Peaceable*, 37.)

30. Cf. "From System to Story: An Alternative Pattern for Rationality in Ethics," *Truthfulness and Tragedy: Further Investigations in Christian Ethics* (Notre Dame: University of Notre Dame Press, 1977).

31. For a helpful discussion on Hauerwas' understanding of the "imitation of God," cf. *Peaceable*, 76-81.

32. "The Non-resistant Church: The Theological Ethics of John Howard Yoder," *Vision*, p. 211.

33. Cf. *Community*, pp. 44ff.

34. "But because we have learned to live as forgiven people, as people no longer in control, we also find we can become a whole people." (*Peaceable*, 89.)

35. "Discipleship is quite simply extended training in being dispossessed." (Ibid., p. 86.)

36. "Pacifism: Some Philosophical Consideration," *Faith and Philosophy*, April 1985, pp. 99f.

37. *After Virtue: A Study in Moral Theory*. (Notre Dame: University of Notre Dame Press, 1981).

38. For a helpful summary of Hauerwas' critique of natural law and human rights language cf. Merold Westphal, "Ethics that Begin with Jesus," *Sojourners*, (November 1984), 33.

39. Cf. esp. *Peaceable*, 54.

40. On this point I prefer the way James Wm. McClendon makes the point in "The God of the Theologians and the God of Jesus Christ," *Is God GOD* ed. Axel D. Steuer & James Wm. McClendon, (Nashville: Abingdon Press, 1981).

41. I agree that it is an important corrective to see the church through symbols other than power, such as character and the embodiment of truth. Yet it is one thing to

choose other categories, and it is quite another to perceive them as the embodiment of powerlessness. Just because truth and power are not to be equated does not imply that truth is powerless.

42. For an interpretation of Hauerwas as basically sympathetic to Barth cf. Robin W. Lovin, *Christian Faith and Public Choices: The Social Ethic of Barth, Brunner and Bonhoeffer* (Philadelphia: Fortress Press, 1984).

43. One may well wonder why this shift in Hauerwas' thought has taken place. There are perhaps several reasons for this, but no doubt a strong influence has been his reliance upon the thinking of John H. Yoder. Yoder tends to adopt the command-obedience model of ethics. Cf. e.g., J. R. Burkholder, "Mennonite Social Ethics and *The Politics of Jesus*," (Unpublished paper presented at the Peace Theology Colloquium, 1976.) Burkholder says, "if one looks for an ethical model (in *The Politics of Jesus*), it seems to be that of divine command or obedience--an obedience, however, not to principles but to the person of Jesus." (p. 13) Just the structure of Yoder's reading of Scripture, e.g., connecting the "be still and wait to see the salvation of Yahweh" (p. 88) motif with the "revolutionary subordination" motif, suggests that our relationship to Yahweh is that of obedience/faithfulness to God's command/voice. Yoder states it clearly when he says, "The relationship between the *obedience* of God's people and the triumph of God's cause is not a relationship of cause and effect but one of cross and resurrection." (*The Politics of Jesus*, p. 238) [Emphasis mine.]

44. "Embarrassed by God," *Christian Century*, (Jan. 30, 1985), 98-100.

45. Reprinted in the *Gospel Herald,* December 25, 1984. I should say that I also have difficulties with Sider's presentation, but they are based upon a different view of the divine/human relationship.

46. Letter to the editor *Gospel Herald,* (December 25, 1984), 903, entitled "The Faithful are not always effective."

47. "Embarrassed," 100.

ON GOD: ETHICS AND THE POWER TO ACT IN HISTORY

Response

Stanley Hauerwas

I am indebted to Professor Huebner for his more than fair analysis of my work. It is refreshing to read a paper about my position that doesn't accuse me of "sectarianism." Because Professor Huebner has avoided those far too easy criticisms generated by mainstream presuppositions, his challenge to me is far more searching than I normally receive. I cannot pretend to deal adequately with the questions he raises, but let me say just a few things that may help indicate how I would go about thinking about these matters.

He raises the issue of whether I indentify theology too closely with ethics. Of course, that depends on what you think ethics is about. The way I prefer to put the matter is whether I am right to insist that all theological discourse is fundamentally practical in nature. I do think the latter is the case, but ethics may be a far too limiting term for how one is to think of the "practical." However, let me try to situate why I want to insist on this point.

It has been my conviction that one of the fundamental mistakes of modern theology was the assumption that some account of theism needed to be given before you could make Christian convictions intelligible. Put in its crudest form, if God does not exist, theologians have thought accounts of Christian convictions would not make sense since the fundamental object of the Christian faith does not exist. This presumption meant that Christian theology was dependent on a prior theoretical account of God's existence *qua* existence. This account of the matter made appeals to past attempts at natural theology which allegedly was about "proving" God's existence apart from revelation of God as trinity. Kant's attack on natural theology, particularly as it took the form of natural theology, made it appear that all that was left to Christian theology was something called "faith," now construed as an epistemological category which was correlated with an equally irrational category called "revelation."

It has been my intention from the beginning of my work to deny this way of thinking about God. Indeed I want to suggest that something has gone fundamentally wrong, both philosophically and theologically, when we assume that we can have knowledge of God's existence and even develop predications, of God abstracted from our knowledge of God which is dependent on our living in faithful continuity with those

204

historic communities we call Israel and the church. By calling this knowledge practical, I have wanted to remind us that
we do not even know what it means to call God good separate
from learning what it means to be a creature and redeemed
through the cross and resurrection of Jesus of Nazareth.
Therefore "practical" names the necessity of transformation
of the self by inclusion in a truthful community so that we
can even gain the skills capable of speaking of God as
trinity.

This does mean that I think that natural theology is an
inherently problematic enterprise.   Indeed I think once one
begins within the rationality of Christian claims about God
as trinity, we can then indicate how the very finite character of existence is a witness to God.   But the witness is not
just to God's existence, but to a very particular kind of God
that we have learned to name through the very means that God
has made available to us--that is, through the ongoing practices of a community who has learned what it means to be a
creature and redeemed.

Having said that, however, I must admit that I think Huebner has really put his finger on a weakness that has been
present in my work.   That weakness is, quite frankly, that I
have not shown how central God is in all that I say.   Thus
when people read me they cannot help but see how much I talk
about Jesus and the church, but I do not relate those fundamental realities decisively enough to God.   In that sense I
have not been consistently enough a Barthian.   I need to show
how the very reality of Jesus and the church are reminders
that the God we worship is always the God that also calls
into question our presumption of knowledge of God.   I think
that the latter conviction is so strong in me that I have
always been hesitant to try to speak in my work too directly
about God.   Hopefully this is more a matter of the
appropriate humility we should all feel in the presence of
God than it is a sign that I may in fact have written into my
own work the unbelief which constitutes most of our lives
most of the time.

Professor Huebner suggests that I should be more willing
to analyze notions like "act of God."   That is certainly the
case, but again I have long suspected those theologies that
thought the primary thing that Christians and Jews want to
affirm about God is that God acts in history.   This way of
talking about God is often supported by making specious com-
parisons between Greek ways of thinking about God and more
dynamic Hebrew ways of thinking about God.   Again I think it
is simply unintelligible to try to talk about God acting, as

if that is an intelligible notion in and of itself. In this respect I think that MacIntyre is right that we must remember the primitive notion is not action but intelligible action. I note in my new introduction to *Character and the Christian Life* (San Antonio: Trinity University Press, 1985) that I made the mistake of assuming in that book that human action is a basic notion.   As a result, I continued to underwrite certain presumptions about agency as if we could be guaranteed agency *qua* agency separate from any ongoing narrative tradition.   Just as human action in and of itself is not intelligible, neither is it coherent to say God acts, as if that is a primary characteristic of God.   We simply cannot say what it means for God to act separate from what it means for God to be the creator of all that is, for God to be the one who calls Israel, and for God to be the one who has redeemed time through the cross and resurrection of Jesus of Nazareth.   So any attempt to give an account of God acting separate from coherence of those narratives seems to me to be a fundamental mistake.   (For a more definitive analysis of these issues see Thomas Tracy's fine book *God, Action and Embodiment,* Eerdmans, 1984.)

Which brings me back to my original point of why it is I want to emphasize the importance of the relation between theology and ethics as a way to emphasize that our language about God works best as practical discourse.   For by practical I mean to contrast that with the theoretical mode of knowledge of God that was sponsored fundamentally by the theistic and deistic presumptions of the Enlightenment.   By emphasizing the practical, I want to remind us that there is no way any of us can ever be known by God and thus claim to know God separate from the necessity of having our lives transformed by God's power.

So Professor Huebner is quite right to see these issues related to the question of how power is to be understood.   I certainly agree with him that there is no way we can or that we should want to avoid the language of power.   The problem as I see it is that almost all accounts of power sponsored by modernity are coercive in form.   In contrast, I want to say any account of power, which is inherently political, requires a sense of how community is necessary to enable us to cooperate in a manner that increases our power exactly because we have learned to cooperate.   So rather than power being those forms of life that make it possible for some to make others to what they do not wish to do, I want to understand power as those forms of life which enable us to do what we would otherwise not be able to do.   So I want to

accept Professor Huebner's fundamental suggestion that there
is no greater power in the world than the transforming power
of love insofar as that literally creates possibility through
human cooperation that otherwise could not exist. Indeed it
is not just human cooperation but rather how God's coming
among us through prayer creates a reality that is beyond our
human capacities but is no less powerful for that.

   Put in that context, I think he is exactly right to challenge the distinction between effectiveness and faithfulness.
In the same way I think we are right to heed Paul Ramsey's
call that those of us who are pacifists cease suggesting that
the difference between pacifists and just war theorists is
that the latter wants to control history while the former
does not. (For Ramsey's discussion of this issue see his
*Speak Up For Just War and Pacifism: A Critique of the United
Methodist Bishops Pastoral Letter "In Defence of Creation"*,
University Park, PA: Pennsylvania State University Press,
1988, with an epilogue by Stanley Hauerwas.) Ramsey is quite
right to remind us that those advocates of just war are
finally not assured that history will come out right. Rather
they are taking the risk that justice will be done even
though the heavens fall. So it is not, at least in principle,
that there is a fundamental difference between pacifists and
just war advocates in terms of the question of effectiveness.
Of course, those of us committed to nonviolence want to be
effective as we want to live in societies in a way that our
nonviolence makes it possible for all people, Christian and
nonChristian, to live as nonviolently as possible. What we
must see is that we simply cannot think about effectiveness--
faithfulness, control, and lack of control--in the abstract.

   However, having said that, I think that an issue still
remains. I think the issues are put squarely by Yoder in *The
Politics of Jesus* (Eerdmans, 1972) where he says:
   No mystical or existentialist or spiritualistic
   depreciation of preoccupation with the course of
   events is justified for the Christian. But the answer
   given to the question by the series of visions and
   their hymns is not the standard answer. "The Lamb
   that was slain is worthy to receive power!" John is
   here saying, not as an inscrutable paradox but as a
   meaningful affirmation, that the cross and not the
   sword, suffering and not brute power determines the
   meaning of history. The key to the obedience of God's
   people is not their effectiveness but their patience
   (13:10). The triumph of the right is assured not by
   the might that comes to the aid of the right, which is

of course the justification of the use of violence and the other kinds of power in every human conflict; the triumph of the right, although it is assured, is sure because the power of the resurrection and not because of any calculation of causes and effects, nor because of the inherently greater strength of the good guys. The relationship between the obedience of God's people and the triumph of God's cause is not a relationship of cause and effect but one of cross and resurrection." (238)

That quote nicely puts what I take to be the fundamental issue, namely whether history is to be read eschatologically or whether we are to see eschatology as the more fundamental reality than history. I am quite well aware that that way of putting the matter may appear but a linguistic quibble, but the former always invites progressivist notions of history that want to underwrite causal patterns that ultimately seduce Christians into violence. Yoder's way of putting it in terms of how the cross and resurrection must be more determinative for our explication of history than cause and effect really is the basic issue. The problem is we have so little way of knowing how to read history in terms of cross and resurrection. I take it to be one of the continuing issues before us--how this might be done in a way that is compelling for Christian and non-Christian alike. It obviously also has to do with how our account of the power that is enabling through the participation in God's kingdom has real empirical hold for Christian and non-Christian alike. At the very least we can start by reminding ourselves that the very existence of the church, in all of its unfaithfulness, nonetheless remains the great miracle of the Holy Spirit and remind ourselves that there is no more fundamental fact than that.

Finally I have little to say about Professor Huebner's interesting suggestions concerning the metaphor of invitation/participation being a more adequate way to talk about our relation to God than the command obedience metaphor. Again, as I noted in the new Introduction to the new edition of *Character and the Christian Life*, I made a fundamental mistake in that book when I tried to juxtapose the metaphor of command and obedience to that of virtue. Obviously virtue is not a metaphor. In several places now I have tried to suggest that a much more fundamental way of thinking of the Christian life and that juxtaposition is to see us fundamentally as a people on a journey. That allows for an appropriate account of development both as a community and appropriate account of development both as a community and as individuals that will indicate the nature of the Christian life as one that involves the necessity of constant transformation since the One who makes that life possible is inexhaustible. It may well be that that invitation/participation metaphor can better do that than journey, but I am a bit worried about the language of participation as it always invites a certain kind of mystical and individualistic excesses that I think is better to avoid. Which is but to remind us that any metaphor must be controlled by the ongoing narrative we find about God and God's willingness to share God's life with us. Again I am in Professor Huebner's debt for making me reconsider these matters, for in doing so he again reminds me how much we depend on one another.

ISSUES AND QUESTIONS RAISED
DURING THE IMS-MCC PEACE COLLOQUIUM
AMBS, June 1985
from assigned listeners,
Gayle Gerber Koontz and Perry Yoder

To J. Lawrence Burkholder's Paper

1. Why does one do a peace theology? For/with whom and for what purpose or goal? Is systematic theology a valid way for a peace theology to be done?

2. *How* we do theology is important, not only the *content* of theology. Both the process and method are affected by peace commitments.

3. Is treating the traditional theological *loci* the best way to do a peace theology? What is the relationship of structure to content?

To Ted Koontz' and John Redekop's Paper

1. What is the basis of the Christian witness to the state and society; from where do the middle axioms come?

2. What ought to be the central function of the state? What is the primary calling of the Christian and what does this have to do with Christian action in relation to the task of the state?--it was noted that the ethical question cannot be formulated as a simple "we-they" problem. This was particularly clear in relationship to the Canadian context where many church members hold state supported jobs.

3. What is the function of the state in a fallen world vis-a-vis the church--what can the church expect from the state? There was a call for more work on the biblical basis for the view that it is acceptable for the state to use violence even though it may not be acceptable for Christians to use violence. Are there any "norms" assumed concerning the state in the Bible?

4. A major theological understanding of church-state relations hinges on eschatology. There were differing judgments as to what extent the kingdom is already/is likely to be a present reality. What kind of eschatology takes the resurrection seriously? How does one envision the kingdom coming? How do we frame positively a two kingdom viewpoint in which Christians speak to and participate in the state? Is it still helpful to cast our conversation in dualistic terms--church/X? Why not a positive theology of order/justice, etc.?

5. What is the role of ecclesiology in peace theology? Is our ecclesiology ecumenical enough? A community base is important in the process of doing peace theology. How might our reflection on our peace actions in the world be enriched/enabled by a more diverse membership at the colloquium?

6. Are there certain content areas that a peace theology "ethics" should address in order to be more inclusive (Redekop)? The ethics of labor relations is one needy area.

7. Where does one appropriately put the weight in a Christian peace theological system: on suffering love, governmental restraint, fallenness, restoration, etc.?

To Duane Friesen's and Ron Sider's Papers

1. Methodological issue: what is the relationship of the authority of the biblical story, of tradition, to the authority of contemporary culture, specifically sociological analysis, in theological work? This question affects definition of terms: "power," "politics," "coercion," "church." It was recognized that political and economic analysis is an important area that has not been fully recognized as critical for ethics and which needs furthr work.

2. There seemed to be agreement that power is a central unavoidable moral issue. Continuing discussion needs to focus on what is a "Christian" use of power within the church as well as outside the church. As Perry put it, Shalom involves changing structures, which means being political. Christians can't avoid questions of power and politics.

3. Discussion continued to focus on priorities as related to peacemaking action in the church, in one's own country, in other national settings. What is the integrity of foreign peace action if the theology which supports such action is not related to the reality of "peace" at home or in the church? Is it important to work at peace at home first, or can peacemaking work be done with integrity on all fronts at once?

To Ben Ollenburger's and Gerber-Koontz' Papers

1. The New Testament itself does speak to people engaged with/in social structures. Perhaps the papers too quickly assumed that the NT is not directly relevant for dealing with structures.

2. Does the Bible picture God as doing things people should not do? Yes, Romans 12. What is the implication of this? Does God work differently through God's people than through others?

3. What is the nature of canon and authority as it relates to our enterprise today? How do we talk about historical movement and make judgments about this movement today?

4. Christology—the example of Jesus: how normative, where and in what ways? What do we do when it does not measure up to our vision and hopes? What are the relevant hermeneutical factors for us? Both communty and tradition are relevant and important.

To Harry Huebner's paper

1. How can a peace theology adequately combine an emphasis on the power and love of God, the judgment and the "pacifism" of God? What is the relationship of our understanding of God to our understanding of our own actions—is all that is true or permissible for God's actions also true or permissible for human actions?

2. Granted the criticism of a too heavy reliance on the command-obedience metaphor in theology generally. But focusing on more pluriform models rather than selecting one alternative model (e.g., invitation-participation) is a more creative direction. Traditional models with biblical roots might include meditation-imitation and obedience-reward; power-empowerment is another option.

3. What is the relationship of ethics to theology—is ethics the way Hauerwas does it the way to do theology or should theological procedure determine how ethics fits in?

4. What is the relationship of peace theology and peace action? Do we get our story straight first, then act to change the world or does our story grow out of our interaction with the world? Or do we always proceed with a mix of these two?

5. What priorities are central for Christians committed to peace and what implications do they have for peace theology? Should emphasis be placed on worship, character building, "getting one's house in order," on intellectual activity, on peacemaking action?

CONTRIBUTORS

J. Lawrence Burkholder, former President of Goshen College and Professor at Harvard Divinity School, teaches part-time at Goshen College.

Duane Friesen is Professor of Bible and Religion and chair of the department at Bethel College, Newton, Kansas.

Ted Grimsrud, completing a dissertation at Berkeley in Social Ethics, is pastor of the Eugene Mennonite Church in Oregon.

Stanley Hauerwas, well-known for his many writings in Ethics, is Professor of Ethics at Duke University, North Carolina.

Harry Huebner is Associate Professor of Philosophy and Theology at Canadian Mennonite Bible College, Winnipeg, Manitoba.

Gayle Gerber Koontz is Associate Professor of Theology at the Associated Mennonite Biblical Seminaries.

Ted Koontz is Associate Professor of Ethics and Director of Peace Studies at the Associated Mennonite Biblical Seminaries.

Edgar Metzler is Associate Secretary for Peace and Social Concerns of the Mennonite Board of Congregational Ministries (MC) in Elkhart, Indiana and is National Coordinator for New Call to Peacemaking.

Ben C. Ollenburger is Associate Professor of Old Testament at the Associated Mennonite Biblical Seminaries.

John H. Redekop is Professor of Political Science at Wilfrid Laurier University, Waterloo, Ontario.

Ron Sider is Professor of Theology at Eastern Baptist Theological Seminary, Philadelphia, Pennsylvania .